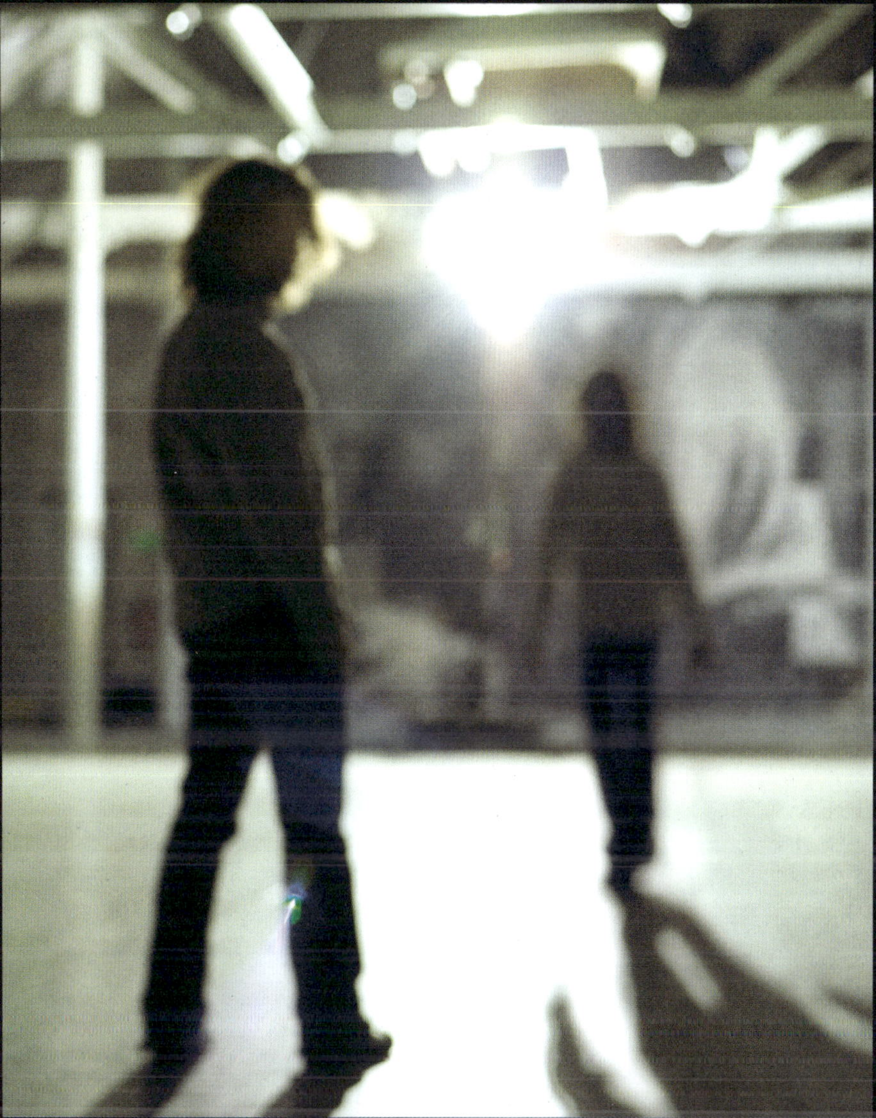

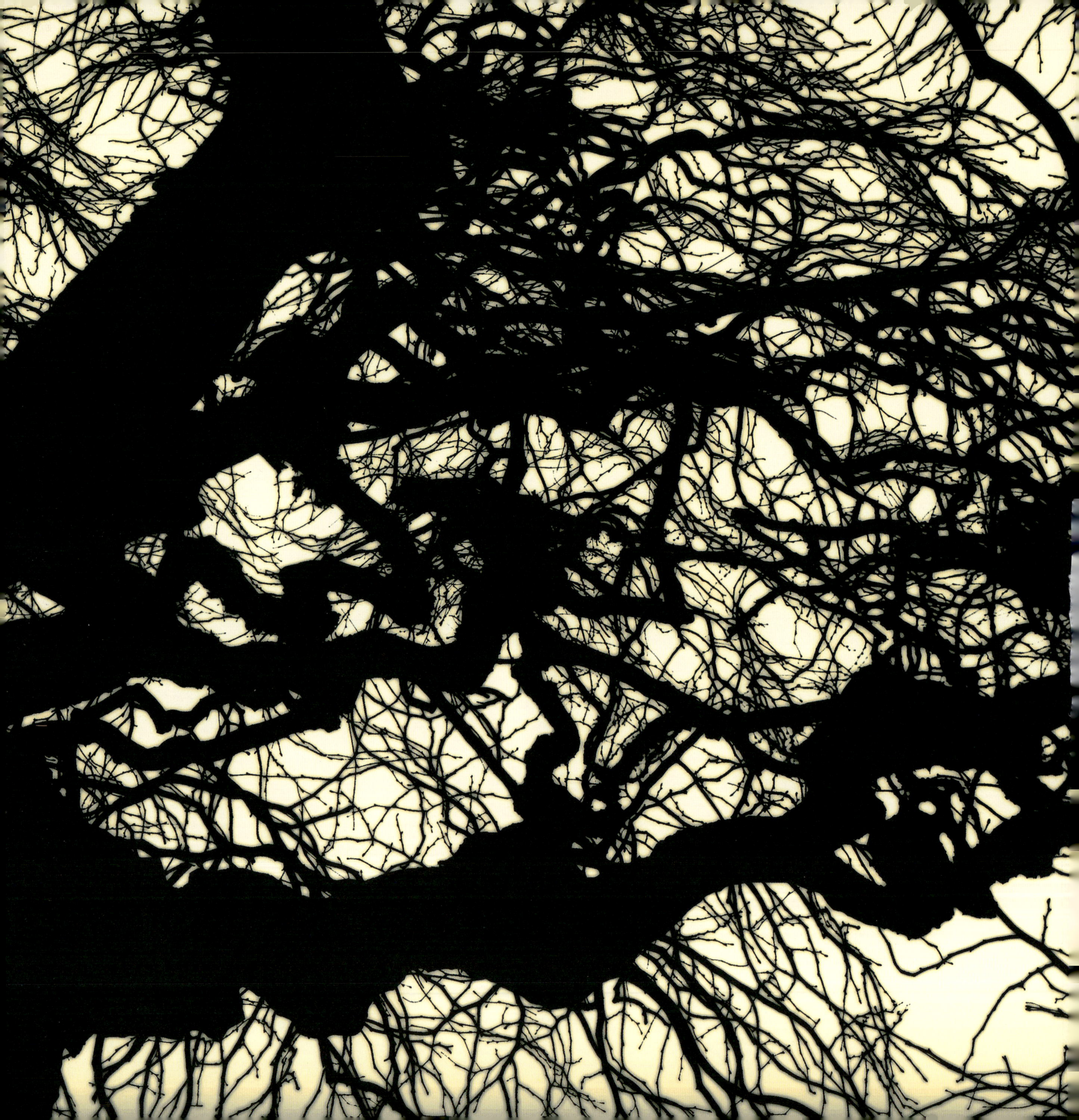

GRAVITY OF LIGHT

SKIRA RIZZOLI
NEW YORK

DOUG + MIKE STARN

GRAVITY OF LIGHT

EDITED BY JAMES CRUMP
WITH AN ESSAY BY JAN ÅMAN

CONTENTS

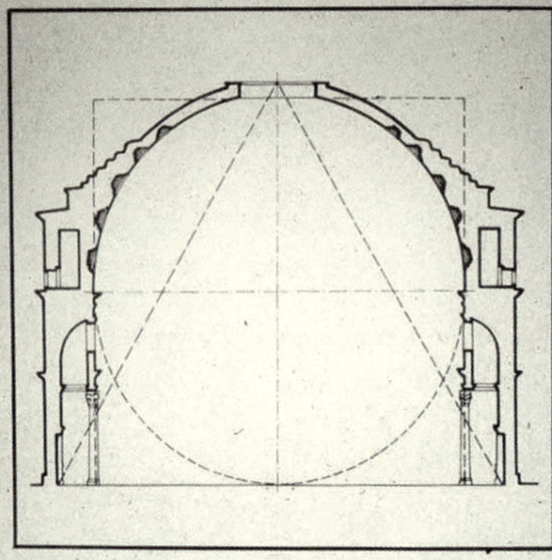

Schéma du Panthéon montrant les tracés géométriques régissant la composition: le

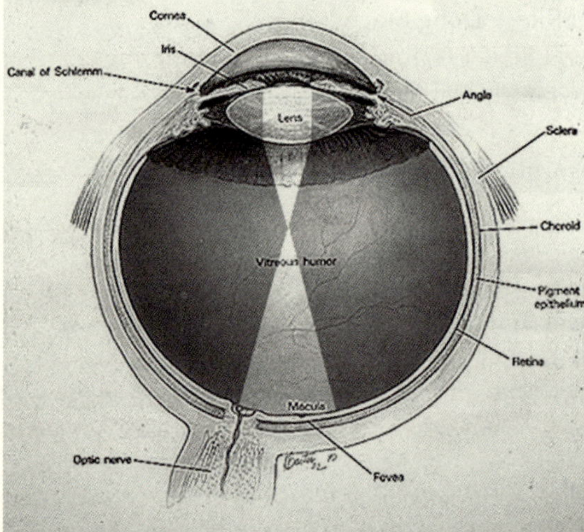

JAMES CRUMP

The universe seen from within is light; seen from without, by spiritual perception, it is thought.
—RUDOLPH STEINER

DEEDS & SUFFER-INGS OF LIGHT & DARKNESS

Officiating at the ceremony of the consecration of the Great Buddha in Nara, Japan in 743, the Indian monk Bodhisena wrote "In order to make clear the meritorious service of this monk, there is nothing equal to the construction of a portrait and transmitting it to later generations." "Although his wisdom died with him," Bodhisena continued, "his merits will continue to exist along with his portrait."[1] The monumental image of the ancient Buddhist monk Ganjin (688–763) that anchors Doug and Mike Starn's *Gravity of Light* is likewise a transmission—one in a series—that utilizes photography as a metaphor for vision itself, of matter and decomposition and the essence of eternal time.[2] [Fig. 1] Widely considered by scholars as the first and most important example of Japanese portrait sculpture, Ganjin was a worthy subject; he spent eleven years trying to reach Japan from his native China, encountering many hardships along the way and in the process losing his eyesight. Although blind, Ganjin's gently closed eyes signify the great Buddhist teacher's inner vision of light and knowledge, features that clearly resonated for the Starns. "When we photographed this, we didn't realize all the connections between our personal philosophies and those of Buddha," they said in 2008. "Ganjin was blind . . . living in blackness, but he was *shotogaku*, which means enlightened—he saw the light within the black."[3] Light, of course, is the basic element of photography, but for the Starns, "Light is [also] thought. Light has gravity, light is what attracts us . . . But black is not only the lack of light, black is the complete absorption of light . . . We are what controls us, because what controls us defines us. The light is us."[4] Emblematic of lightness and dark, of reflectivity and absorption, of life and death, and of reality, perception, and representation, Ganjin embodies the core themes of *Gravity of Light*.[5] Part scientific laboratory, part art exhibition, *Gravity of Light* is also a chamber for immersion, experience, and contemplation that links the total output of these two artists, from the mid-1980s forward.

For Mike and Doug Starn, light is not simply about enlightenment, but rather the enormity of all of our past experiences, combining with all that is our present and our future, "the conscious and unconscious, external and internal factors that drive our lives."[6] Their concept of nonlinear time and of conscious and unconscious experience calls to mind the work of French philosopher Henri Bergson who also believed that time is a range of seeming intervals that unite the past with an

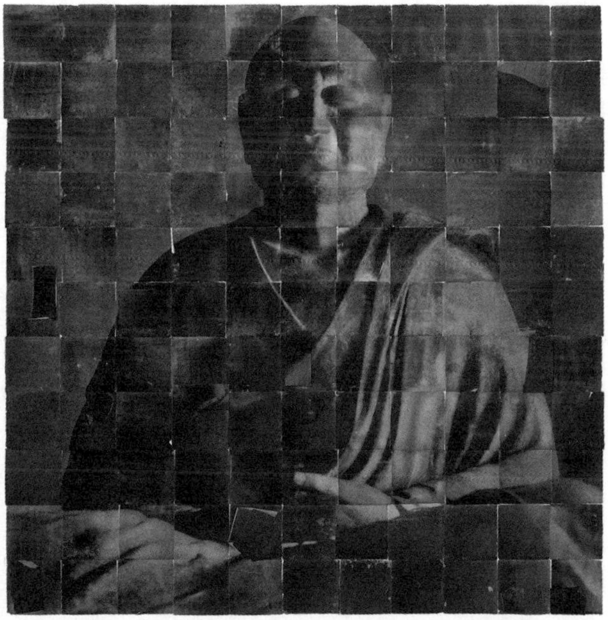

[Fig. 1]
Ganjin, 2000–03, Sulfur-toned hand-coated silver emulsion on tea-stained Thai mulberry paper, 252 x 252 in.

ever-changing present. In *Creative Evolution*, Bergson wrote that "in reality, the past is preserved by itself automatically. In its entirety, probably, it follows us at every instant; all that we have felt, thought, and willed from our earliest infancy is there, leaning over the present which is about to join it, pressing against the portals of consciousness that would fain leave it outside."[7] "Time," for Bergson, "is invention, or it is nothing at all."[8] Bergson's notion of time is not a linear sequence aiming at some fated end, but rather nonlinear and constantly evolving, apt phrases for describing the Starns' career and their working methods. This Bergsonian notion of time, consciousness, and constant change combines in *Gravity of Light* with the concepts of intuition, order and chaos, growth and decay, interdependence and interconnectedness.[9] Composed of the series Structure of Thought, Attracted to Light, and Black Pulse, *Gravity of Light* illustrates these overarching themes. The installation also forms a veritable link between the Starns' work of the 1980s and 1990s and the conceptual principles of their more recent and widely known *Big Bambú: You Can't, You Don't, and You Won't Stop*, mounted on the rooftop of the Metropolitan Museum of Art in New York in 2010 [Fig. 2] and, later, adjacent to the Peggy Guggenheim Museum at the Venice Biennale in 2011.

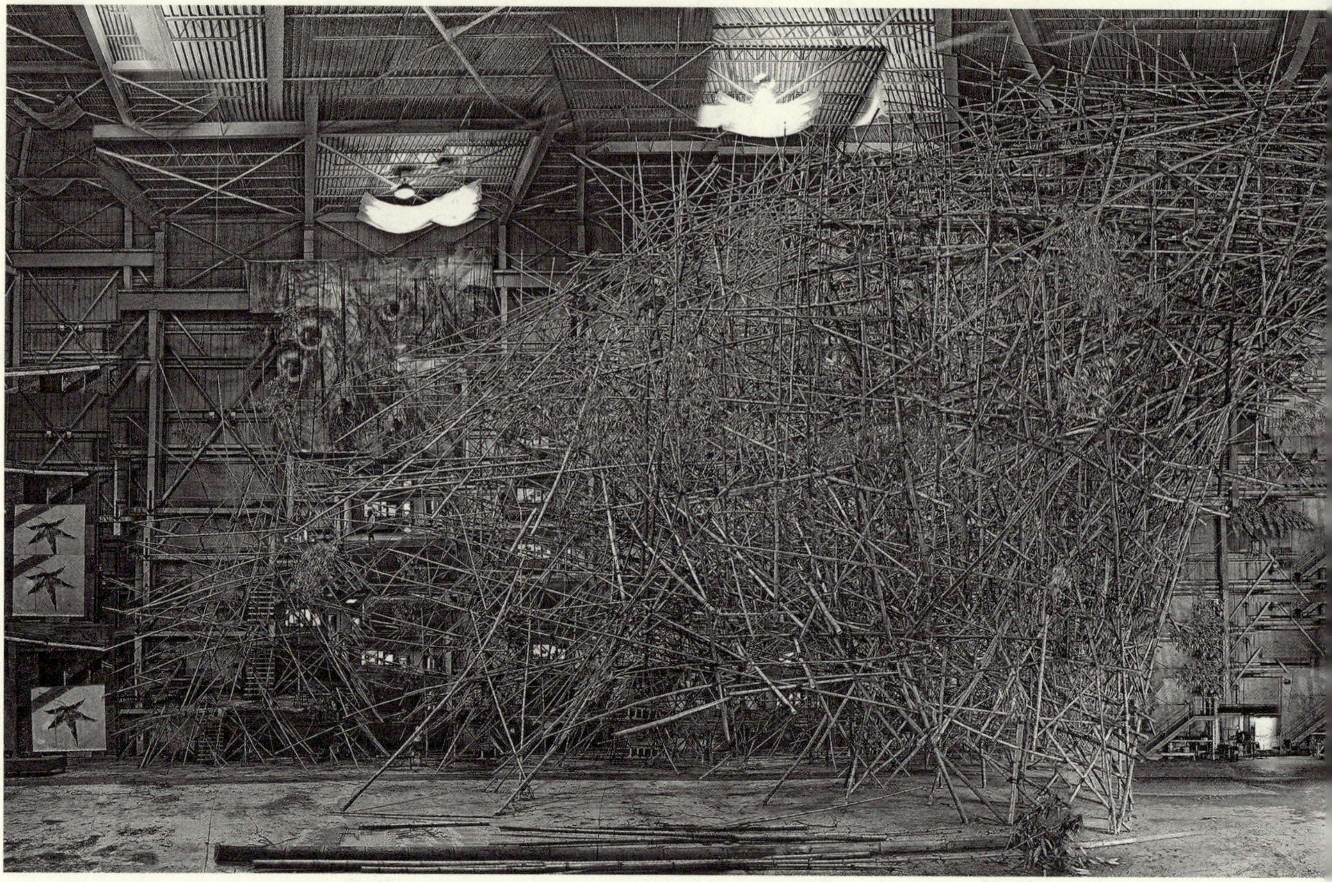

[Fig. 2]
Big Bambú, studio view, August 13th, 2009, Digital file, Beacon, New York

Illuminated by only one source of nearly blinding white light, the monumental pictures in *Gravity of Light* instill physical sensations of the infinite void of space and the human scale in relationship to a greater whole. The Starns have described even their earliest works as having to be seen as both a macrocosm and a microcosm. "Each piece is complete in itself but it is also part of something much larger. To really understand our work one must view many pieces, finding threads that connect them all."[10] The idea of scale has recently been cited as a core concern of their sculptural installation *Big Bambú*, but scale also foregrounds *Gravity of Light*. Here the viewer is reminded of his relative smallness in relation to the colossal photographs, some measuring twenty-two feet in height.[11] Scale and, through juxtaposition, the relationship between the microcosm of humanity and the cosmos were also principal features of the Renaissance-era cabinets of curiosity, whose function it was to reveal the veiled networks between *naturalia* (nature or that created by God) and *artificialia* (the man-made).[12] *Gravity of Light*, too, is a kind of *Wunderkammer* itself where, as in Ganjin, human ingenuity in the form of a true likeness of a once-living individual is positioned opposite the immense image of an eighteenth-century cadaver specimen the artists systematically photographed in Naples. Taking its title from a William Burroughs song for the play *Black Rider* directed by Robert Wilson, the image entitled *Take Off Your Skin, It Ain't No Sin* conjures medieval representations of death and *vanités*, often made of ivory or boxwood and traditionally viewed in cabinets of curiosity. *Take Off Your Skin, It Ain't No Sin* also points to the narrow line separating beauty found in nature, and the transcendent work of artists that ennoble it. The Starns make this evident in *Gravity of Light*, particularly with their images of leaves in decay in the Black Pulse pictures, their images of trees in Structure of Thought, and in Attracted to Light, pictures of moths that allude to the brittleness of their very existence.

Desiccated leaves, redolent of autumn and the seasonal transition of winter, are the subjects of the

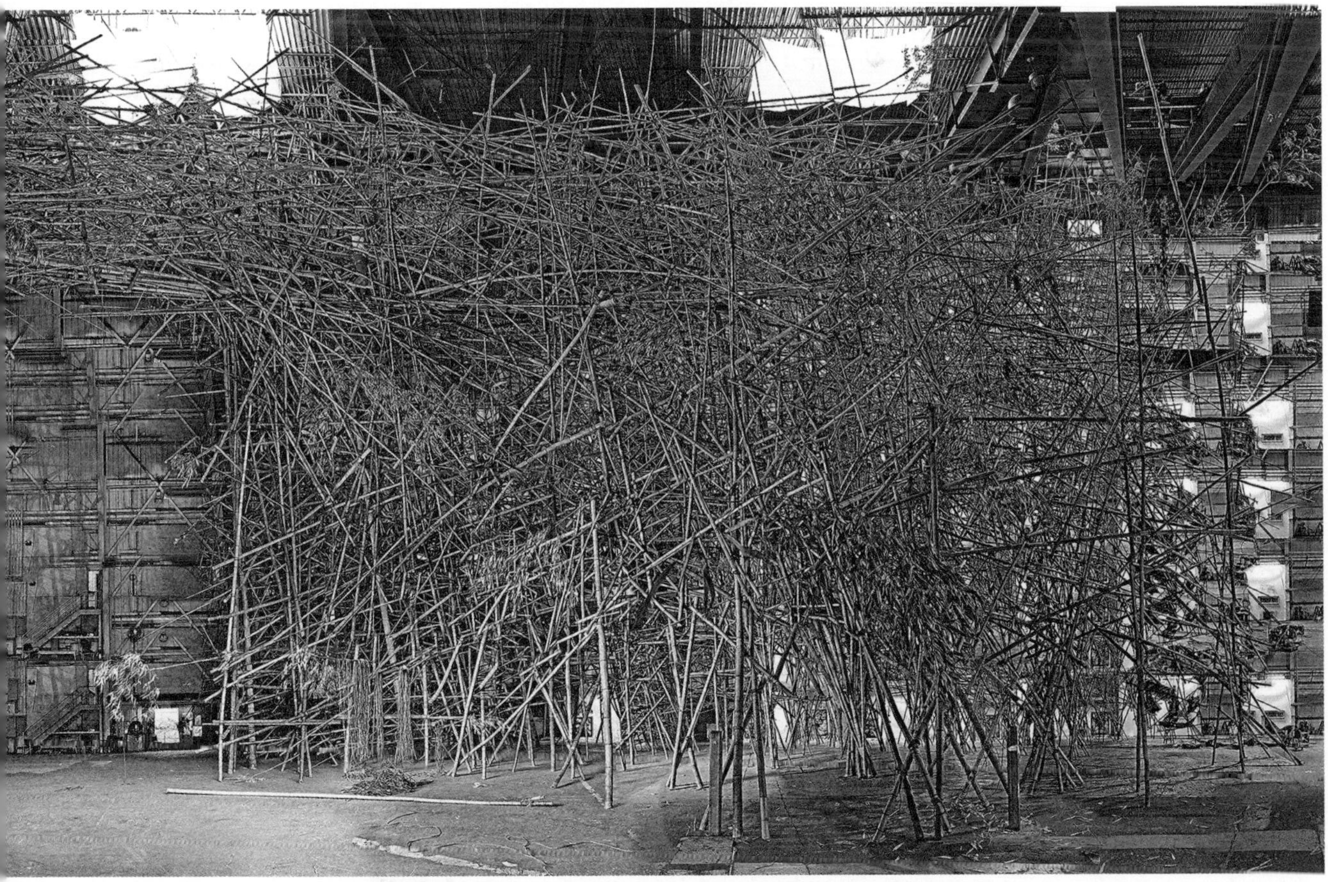

Black Pulse pictures. The broken veins and decomposing cells of each leaf's surface seem to reinforce the menacing processes of aging, degeneration, and disease; the inevitability of life coming to an end, or regenerating anew, ashes to ashes, dust to dust. The Starns have noted their interest in life after death or reincarnation, and the images from Black Pulse seem to express this notion most forcefully, in starkly beautiful and oversized compositions that feature each leaf on a bright white ground, chromatic investigations that appear almost forensic in their minimalism and focused detail. The veins of the Black Pulse pictures also share a relationship with the hundreds of bamboo poles that make up *Big Bambú*. Indeed, the pictures from Black Pulse and *Big Bambú* all represent a kind of network built from chaos, though an intuitive, intentional chaos; the photographic prints of the former begin as high resolution scans of actual leaves that the Starns flay in the computer and which are then modeled using Maya 3D imaging software, while the latter is the result of open-ended construction lasting months.

Nabokov wrote of the "mysteries of mimicry" that held a "special attraction" and inspired his interest in the moth and the butterfly.[13] In the series Attracted to Light, the Starns share an equal interest in mimesis. Initially conceiving this series with traditional, purist, black-and-white gelatin silver prints, the artists were later inspired to replicate the fragile, dusty media—the wings, that is—that facilitate the moth's journey toward light and eventual annihilation. Like the disintegrating veins of the leaves found in Black Pulse, the flaking, destructible moth wings serve as mememto mori, marking the moth's transience between being and extinction; another reminder of our own mortality and the brevity of life. Printed on hand-coated Thai mulberry paper and toned with sulfur, the shivery sheets that contain the moth images of Attracted to Light are strangely moth-like, transparent, and seemingly weightless. "Black is the void and reservoir of what we want and need," the Starns wrote in 2003.[14] In its uncontrollable craving for light, the moth represents a contradiction in terms, signifying both the weight of human yearning and transcendence by passing through light into the great void of infinite darkness.

The series Structure of Thought is loaded with symbolic potential that helps illuminate the mysteries of nature and the design structure of life itself. Here, the Starns employ trees, the trunks and branches of which have been photographed and reproduced in silhouette so as to resemble the dendrites of the human body's neural cell structure—the tree-like branches that supply electrochemical signals to the cell body. This complex of vein-like forms in Structure of Thought as well as those seen in the desiccated leaves of Black Pulse underscore the artists' fascination with interconnectivity—single parts of a whole, the microcosm versus the macrocosm—and the distribution and flow of energy, not unlike the body's vascular system delivering blood to the vital organs or the roots of a tree delivering valuable nutrients to its elemental parts. It is tempting to compare the Starns' curiosity for discovery in nature with the early inventors of photography who likewise married their polymath interests in science to their creative processes. Imaging the interrelationships found in nature—patterns and forms with analogous utility—the Starns, however, unite art and science in ways that suggest less obvious comparison to Johann Wolfgang von Goethe. Goethe's phenomenological study of leaf organs and photosynthesis, published as *Metamorphosis of Plants* in 1790, and his influential *Theory of Colors* (1810) concerning the dichotomies and interplay of light and darkness make him an apt forebear who relied not simply upon technical knowledge for discovery, but equally so upon lived experience. Much like the Starns' combinations of art and technology, Goethe's way of science, according to architectural phenomenologist David Seamon, offers a "rich, intuitive approach to meeting nature and discovering patterns and relationships" that is both intellectually and spiritually gratifying.[15] The Starns recognize the symbolic power of trees as objects of spiritual and intellectual contemplation and their timeless association with sacred knowledge and transcendence. "Trees are transcribed thought," they suggested in 2005.[16] Andrew Solomon has succinctly written about how the tree pictures in Structure of Thought articulate the relationship between light used in photography and the transformative power of light in photosynthesis.[17] The seeming chaos of the Black Pulse pictures was, for Solomon, epitomized by the images from Structure of Thought which, after close scrutiny, finally reveal themselves, addressing the beholder with the true beauty of natural order.[18]

G*ravity of Light* exemplifies the Starns' fascination with combining art and technology in an effort to explore spirituality, or as they declared of their first sun-inspired pictures from the mid 1990s, "bringing something personal to a universal level."[19] The impetus for the installation is a unique light designed by the artists—inspired by the very first electric light invented in 1804 by Sir Humphry Davy—and suggests their

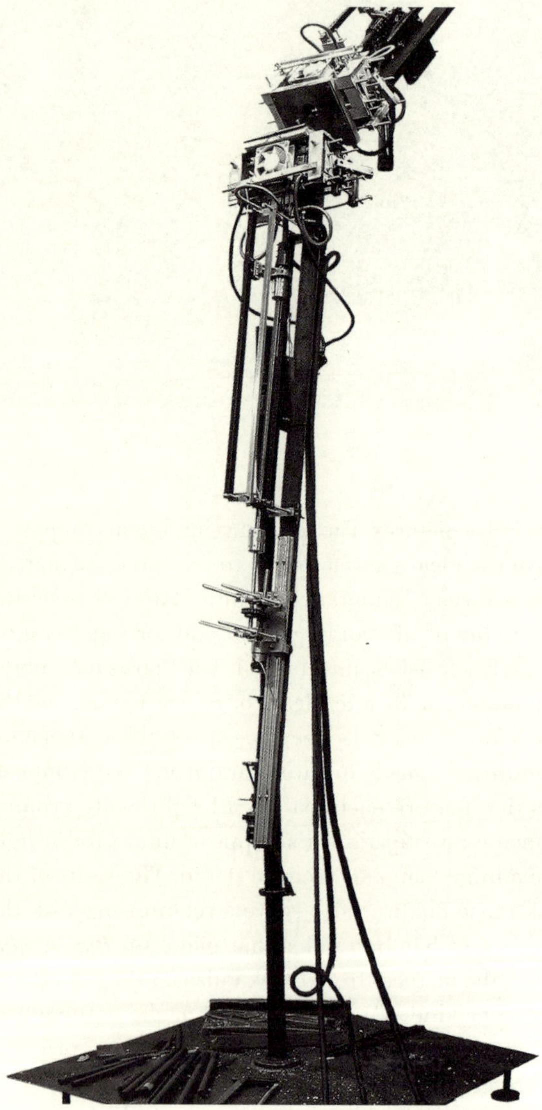

[Fig. 4]
Leonardo's St. John or this is my middle finger, 2004,
Steel, carbon, electronic components, 144 x 48 x 72 in.

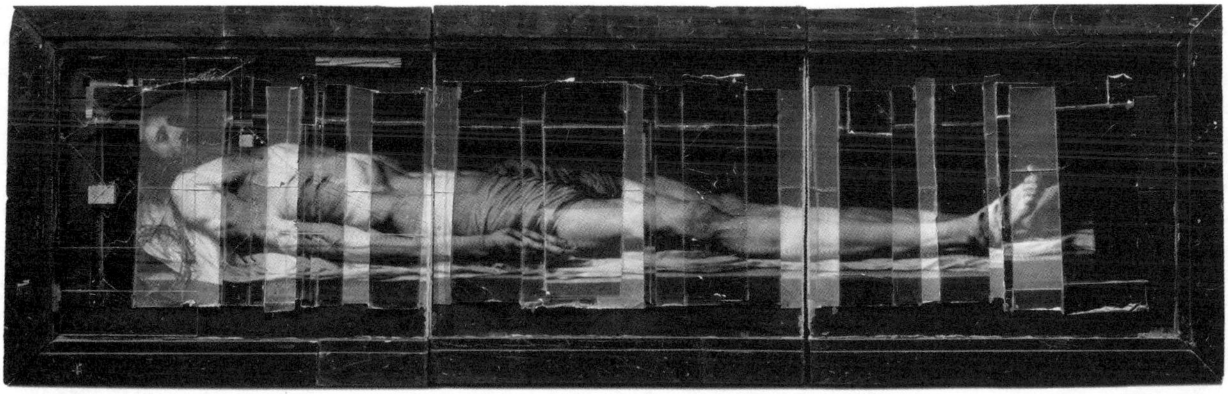

[Fig. 5]
Christ (Stretched), 1985–86, Toned silver print, tape, wood, glass, epoxy, 28 x 142 x 45 in.

obsession with scientific investigation and their personal exploration of the natural world and phenomena. [Fig. 4] The Starns' arc lamp, however, was conceived as an artwork itself and not simply a source for illumination, but the white-hot light emanating from their creation is, more importantly, the catalyst for experiencing the chapel-like spaces formed by the towering photographs in *Gravity of Light*.

Davy, a physicist, described the arc created by two poles of carbon as "producing a most beautiful coruscation of purple light"—near-blinding flashes that produce with them a kind of afterglow effect and color sensation that in *Gravity of Light* filters how one receives the photographs.[20] Viewing *Gravity of Light* is further mediated by the use of goggles that must be worn to protect the naked eye from the otherwise devastating levels of ultra violet light. This element of danger may be an allusion to Ganjin's blindness, but this induced frisson again recalls Goethe, who wrote that "colors are the deeds of light, deeds and sufferings."[21] Physicist and contemplative spiritualist Arthur Zajonc has also described Goethe's "deeds and sufferings of light and darkness"; the conflict of light meeting darkness, as when light in *Gravity of Light* penetrates the absolute black spaces that absorb these artificial rays that are cast onto the surface of the photographs.[22] The deeds and sufferings of light and darkness summon links between Ganjin and the Starns' images of the entombed Christ—light incarnate, or the "light of the world" according to the Gospel of John—and the Mater Dolorosa, or Mary, the mother of Christ who sorrows at the death of her son, among the Starns' earliest series of works.

In early works such as *Christ (Stretched)*, 1985–86, [Fig. 5] created with transparent tape, wood, and fiberglass, the artists interrogated the perceived limitations of the photographic print—tearing, folding, scoring, and otherwise abrading the work in an effort to break free from convention—while distinguishing themselves from the emerging leaders of contemporary photography whose work remained predicated on "straight" camera aesthetics and printing techniques—artists as varied in approach as Philip-Lorca diCorcia, Nan Goldin, and Cindy Sherman, among others. Then as today, the Starns, like F. Holland Day nearly a century before, were exploring sacred subjects with the camera, Ganjin in *Gravity of Light* being the most recent example.[23] Fragmenting, splicing, and cutting the image of Christ, theirs is a reconsecration of this hallowed icon most fitting for a new age; a far cry from the pristine platinum prints that marked Day's work with this subject. In ambitious early works, such as *Sphere of Influence*, 1990–92, [Fig. 6] they endeavored to transpose photography to a realm commensurate with painting and sculpture, merging media and materials much like they do today. Of these earlier bodies of work, the art historian Robert Pincus-Witten posited that the Starns were "inaugurating a new moment of Romantic figuration," in his effort to distinguish their work from conceptual photographers of, or peripherally associated with, the Pictures Generation artists such as Sherman, Sherrie Levine, Barbara Kruger, and Louise Lawler.[24] Other critics pointed to the rehabilitated interest in the mysteries of nature, the life cycles of civilization, and time and experience that firmly place Doug and Mike Starn in an expanding band of Romantic visual

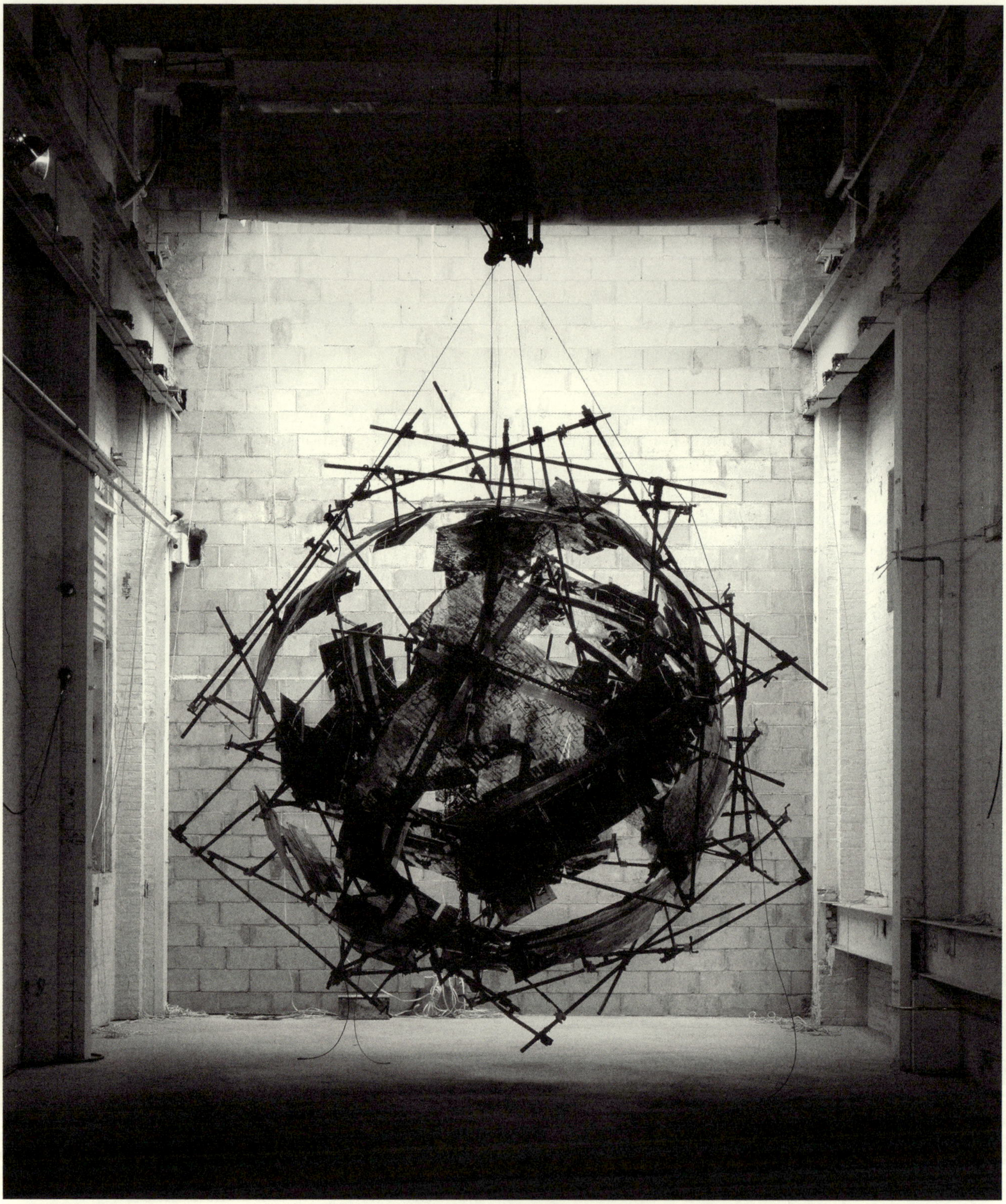

[Fig. 6]
Sphere of Influence, 1990–92, toned ortho film, pipe clamps, wire and motor, 168 in. diameter, Leo Castelli gallery, 1994 Crosby Street installation, New York

expression.[25] Seen alongside the work of Anselm Kiefer, for example, whose epic canvases addressing the darkest periods in German history share certain concerns, the "overtly Romantic drama and passion" found in the Starns' earliest works continue to resonate.[26] The images found in *Gravity of Light* together adumbrate a necessary shift in humankind's relationship to nature, and the futile reliance on technology and science alone to resolve the man-made destruction to the planet and our steady march toward apocalypse.

Just as its constituent parts are capable of standing alone as autonomous works, *Gravity of Light* in its totality represents a remarkable achievement of installation art, and helps reconcile many of the Starns' varied and sometimes seemingly disparate interests and curiosities, between photography and the art of painting and sculpture; between Western and Eastern modes of thinking; and between aesthetics and the technical fields of optics and physics. Goethe and Sir Davy stand in as apposite predecessors. Both men born in the eighteenth century, their work transcends art and science while spanning an era that gave rise to a renewed embrace of man in nature; a reaction, in part, to the pitfalls wrought by the Industrial Revolution. New forms of representation emerged which elevated art to a kind of alternative religion. Infused in much of the Starns' work that both precedes and follows *Gravity of Light* is a neo-Romantic urge that links them to this historic rupture as they themselves examine the relative concerns of the new millennium.

Sir Davy's arc lamp is the obvious keystone in *Gravity of Light*, but its function as an object also serves to unite the artists' interest in the history of Western science to their personal and spiritual philosophies. In this regard, it is interesting to note that certain concerns advanced in *Gravity of Light* and, more recently, *Big Bambú*, are coincidentally shared by the Mind & Body Dialogues, a forum series established in 1987 and hosted by His Holiness the Fourteenth Dalai Lama of Tibet. This series has brought together noteworthy scientists, philosophers, and others interested in uniting scientific excellence with human spirituality to "promote well-being on the planet."[27] From these dialogues sprang the Mind and Life Institute, which in 2003 hosted the first public dialogue that examined the collaborative potential of Buddhism and bio-behavioral science; the nature of reality and the role that real, sensorial human experience can play in contemporary scientific discovery. The Starns are central in this current of contemporary ideas that seek to marry more than 2,500 years of Buddhist practice with more than 400 years of steadfast achievement in Western science. "The more known about the science and physics of our subject matter, the more there is to be seen within the work," the artists stated recently. "Our curiosity informs us as we make our decisions in the studio. We liken that to Nabokov; paraphrasing, he said that the more knowledge of even seemingly trivial aspects of something, the more beauty emerges."[28]

Gravity of Light in its entirety provides a liminal space that pitches the viewer between physical and ethereal realms. [Fig. 7] The combined effects of the darkened interior, the crackling and buzzing sound and the intensity of the living light emitting from the arc lamp, and the strange *chiaroscuro* brought about by the combination of ambient light and razor sharp shadows falling onto the photographs allow for an immersive physical and sensorial experience with the objects populating the installation. We enter the void of blackness that the artists have talked so much about; the architectural volumes and the constancy of light solicit raw, corporeal responses that are both transportive and disorienting. The images in *Gravity of Light* produce a kind of afterglow of competing energies whose interpretation summons the aid of phenomenology; again we return to Bergson, this time his *Matter and Memory*, which engaged the philosophical opposition between matter and the images of things produced in consciousness and the nervous system's role in perception. If we consider the body as merely a center for action, Bergson noted, "we must see what consequences thus result for perception, for memory, and for the relations between body and mind."[29] For Bergson, "matter exists just as it is perceived; and, since it is perceived as an image, the mind would make of it, in itself, an image."[30] Bergson collapses matter and image into one unifying whole. He speaks of images vibrating with sensation onto the sensory nerves, and through perception offering us "things-in-themselves."[31]

The energies suffused in the images of *Gravity of Light* similarly evoke painter Francis Bacon, who subscribed to a process of unbridling rational observation, exposing the physical body and the psyche to the raw and transformative power of images that return one to "life more violently."[32] For Bacon, the act of viewing was capable of "unlocking the areas of sensation" where one

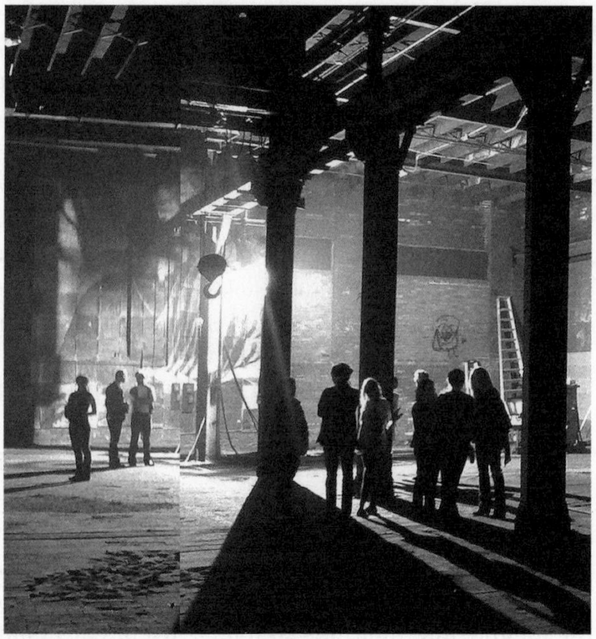

[Fig. 7]
Gravity of Light, 2008, curated by Murray Horne for the Wood Street Galleries, the Pipe Building, Pittsburgh, Pennsylvania

"unlocks the areas of feeling, which lead to a deeper sense of the reality of the image."[33] For Bacon, the power of images "has to do with endurance. I think that you could have a marvelous image made of something which will disappear in a few hours, but I think that the potency of the image is created partly by the possibility of its enduring . . . Images accumulate sensation around themselves the longer they endure."[34]

For more than two decades, the Starns have deftly explored what for many remain ineffable subjects: the divinity of human existence and the phenomenology of light, perception, and enlightenment scratch only the surface of their aesthetic investigations. Their best works are also concerned with earthly realities that suggest the impermanence of beauty. In *Gravity of Light*, the Starns show us the kind of potent images that Bacon sought, with new forms of art that defy the test of time.

ENDNOTES

1 Hisashi Mori, *Japanese Portrait Sculpture*, trans. W. Chiē Ishibaashi (Tokyo, New York and San Francisco: Kodansha International Ltd. and Shiibundo), 97.
2 Manuel Santos, "Tiempos de belleza y decadencia," *Lapiz*, Vol. 12, Issue no. 104 (June 1994), 48–49. Of their earlier works that brought them initial critical acclaim, the Starns described photography as a "process of *transmission*" and a medium "completely dependent upon transparency." Translation from the Spanish language text and italics by the present author.
3 "A Conversation of Art, Science, and Philosophy: Doug and Mike Starn. Interview by Colette Copeland," *Exposure*, Vol. 41, Issue no. 1 (Spring 2008), 11.
4 *Mike & Doug Starn: Attracted to Light* (New York: Powerhouse and Blindspot, 2003), unpaginated introduction.
5 As in the great temple portrait hall, *Toshodai-ji,* in which it continues to reside in Nara, the image of Ganjin presides over all else in the Starns' *Gravity of Light*. A supreme example of the ancient dry-lacquer technique, the sculpture of Ganjin has been described by the artists as a three-dimensional negative, its highlights and shadow areas reversed as a result of its gold leaf finish disintegrating.
6 Demetrio Paparoni, "Tree of Life," in *Mike & Doug Starn: Attracted to Light* (New York: Powerhouse and Blindspot, 2003)
7 Henri Bergson, *Creative Evolution*, trans. Arthur Mitchell (New York: Henry Holt and Co., 1911), 5.
8 ibid., 341.
9 Doug and Mike Starn have used these terms in numerous interviews and in conversation with the author. See, for example, Copeland, op. cit., 6, and Christine Temin, "Doug and Mike Starn: Reveling in Chaos," *Sculpture* (October 2010), 30 and 33. See also, Santos, op. cit., 47.
10 Santos, op. cit, 47. Translation from the Spanish language text by the present author.
11 Ivan Vartanian, "Doug + Mike Starn: Parts of a Whole," Ivan Vartanian, *Art Work: Seeing Inside the Creative Process* (San Francisco: Chronicle Books, 2011), 133.
12 See Virginia Spenlé, "The Wunderkamer Olbricht," in *Mémoires du futur: la collection Olbricht* (Paris: Fage éditions and La Maison Rouge, 2011), 227.
13 Vladimir V. Nabokov, *Speak, Memory: An Autobiography* (New York: Putnam, 1979), 124.
14 Starn, op. cit., unpaginated.
15 David Seamon, "Goethe, Nature, and Phenomenology," *Goethe's Way of Science: A Phenomenology of Nature*, eds. David Seamon and Arthur Zajonc (Albany, NY: University of New York Press, 1998), 10.
16 Doug and Mike Starn, unpublished draft ms. of Andrew Solomon's text cited below in endnote 17.
17 Andrew Solomon, "From Imaging to Image," *Doug & Mike Starn: Absorption + Transmission* (Washington, DC: National Academy of Sciences, 2005), 19.
18 ibid.
19 Diana C. Stoll, "On Location Studio Visit with Doug and Mike Starn," *Aperture* 146 (Winter 1997), 31.
20 Sir Humphrey Davy, quoted in Frederick Kaufman, "Elemental Vision: Matter, Paradox and Other Absorptions of Doug and Mike Starn," *Aperture*, no. 175 (Summer 2004), 53.
21 Lesley Sharpe, *The Cambridge Companion to Goethe* (New York and Cambridge, UK: Cambridge University Press, 2002), 173.
22 Arthur Zajonc, *Capturing the Light: The Entwined History of Light and Mind* (Oxford, UK: Oxford University Press, 1995), 210–11, n. 24.
23 On Day's "sacred subjects" see the author's book, *F. Holland Day: Suffering the Ideal* (Santa Fe: Twin Palms Publishers, 1995).
24 Robert Pincus-Witten, "Being Twins: The Art of Doug and Mike Starn," *Arts Magazine* (October 1988), 72–77.
25 Robert Rosenblum, "A Postscript: Some Recent Neo-Romantic Mutations," *Art Journal* (Summer 1993), 74–84, see esp. 80–81.
26 ibid., 81.
27 See the URL http://www.mindandlife.org/dialogues/.
28 Doug and Mike Starn, correspondence with the author, January 31, 2012.
29 Henri Bergson, *Matter and Memory*, trans. Nancy Margaret Paul and W. Scott Palmer (London and New York: George Allen and Co., Ltd. and Macmillan, 1913), 303.
30 ibid., viii.
31 ibid, 303. In his convincing use of Bergson to explicate the work of artist Doug Aitken, Michael Speaks masterfully summarized this section of *Matter and Memory*. See Michael Speaks, "Temporal Ecology of Images," *Doug Aitken: A–Z Book (Fractals)*, ed. Marion Boulton Stroud (Ostfildern, Germany: Hatje Cantz, 2003), unpaginated.
32 David Sylvester, *Interviews with Francis Bacon*, enlarged edition (London: Thames & Hudson, 1987), 141.
33 ibid., 66.
34 Ibid., 58.

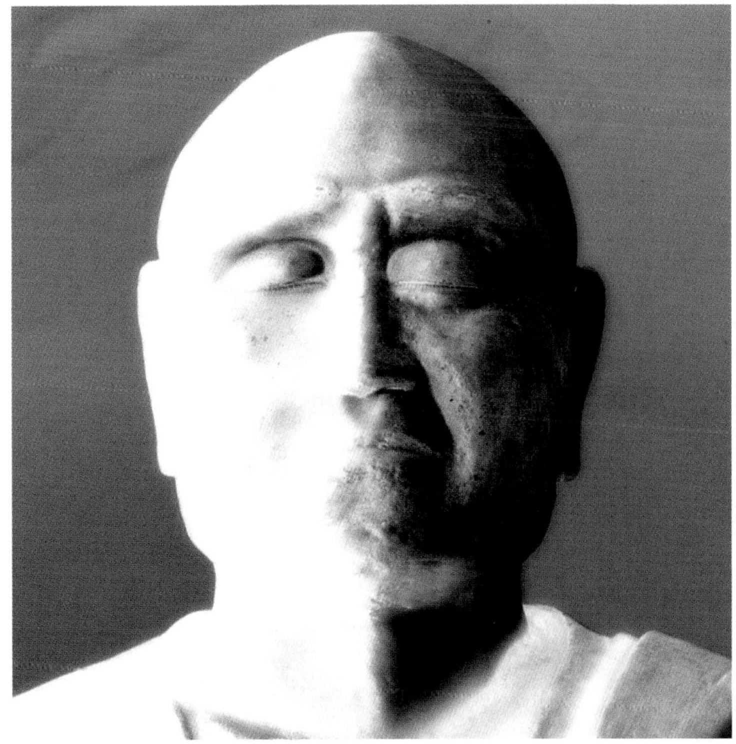

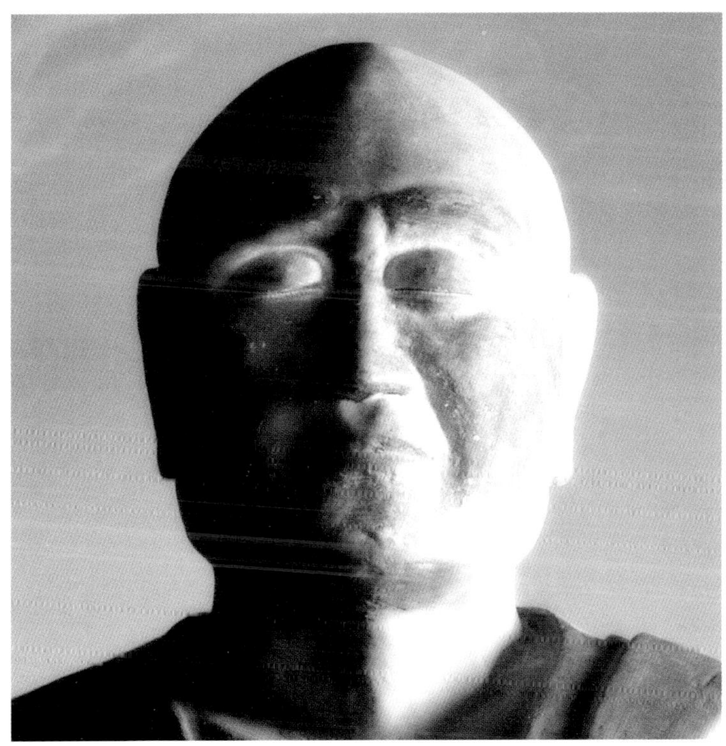

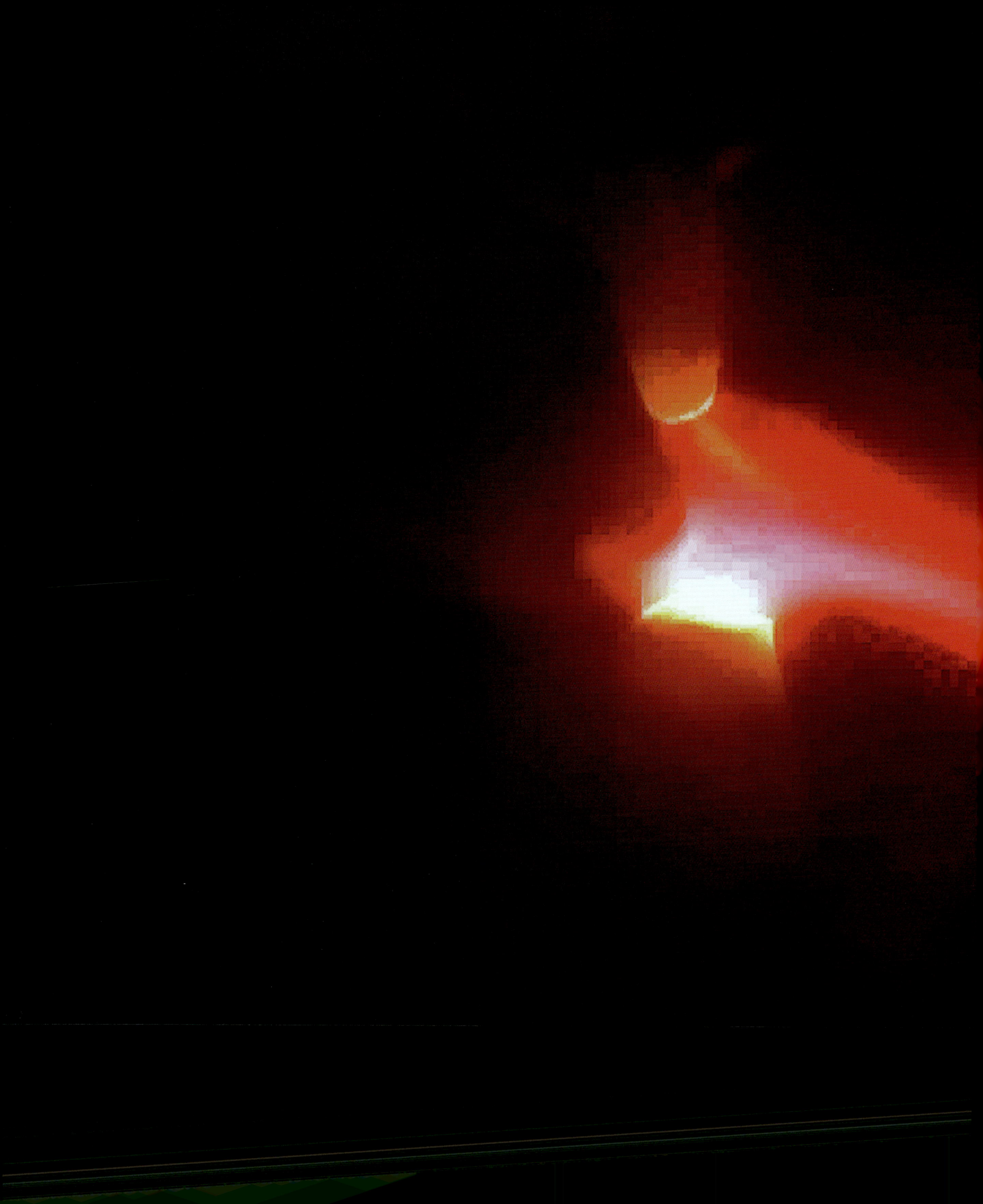

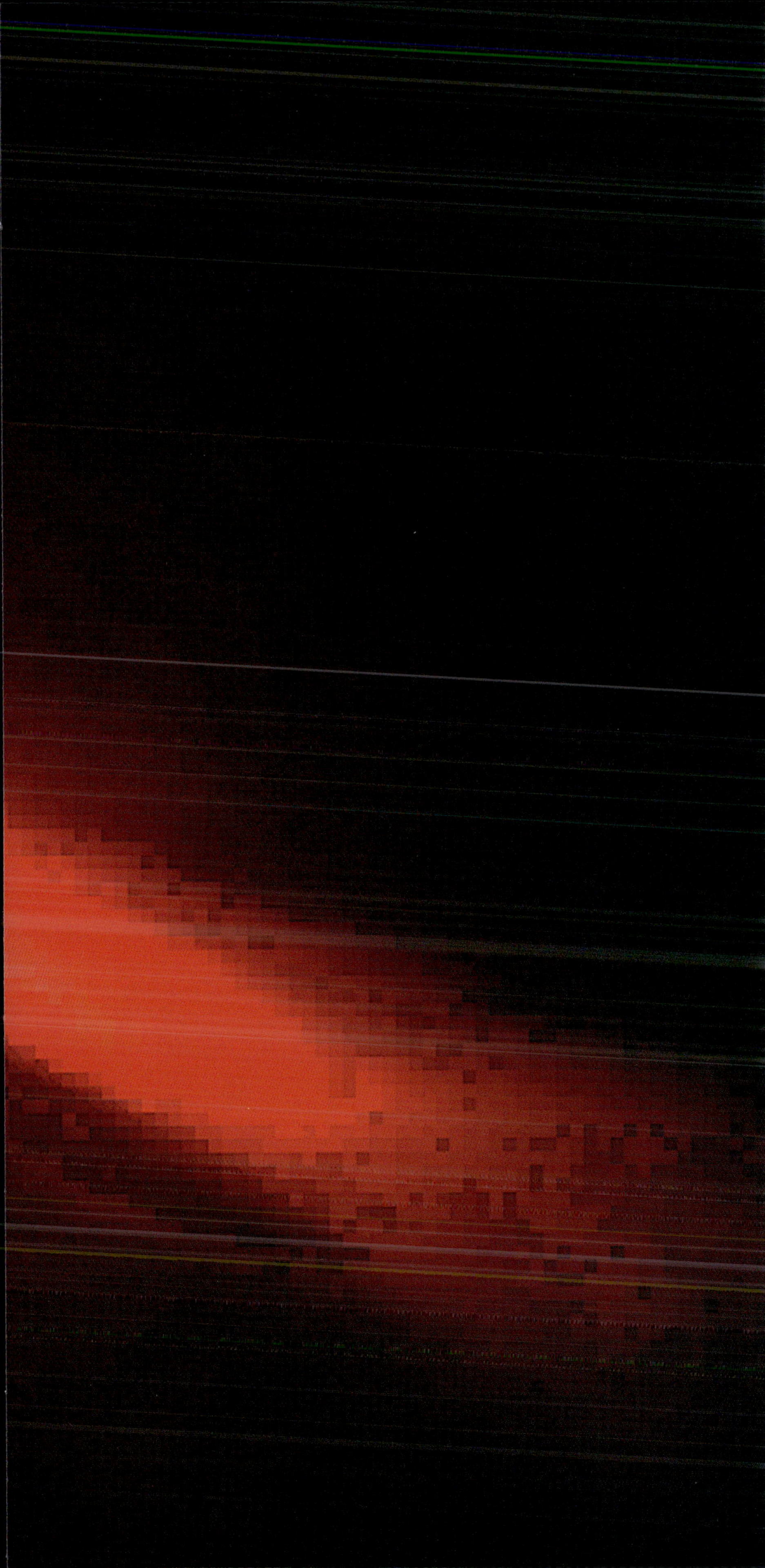

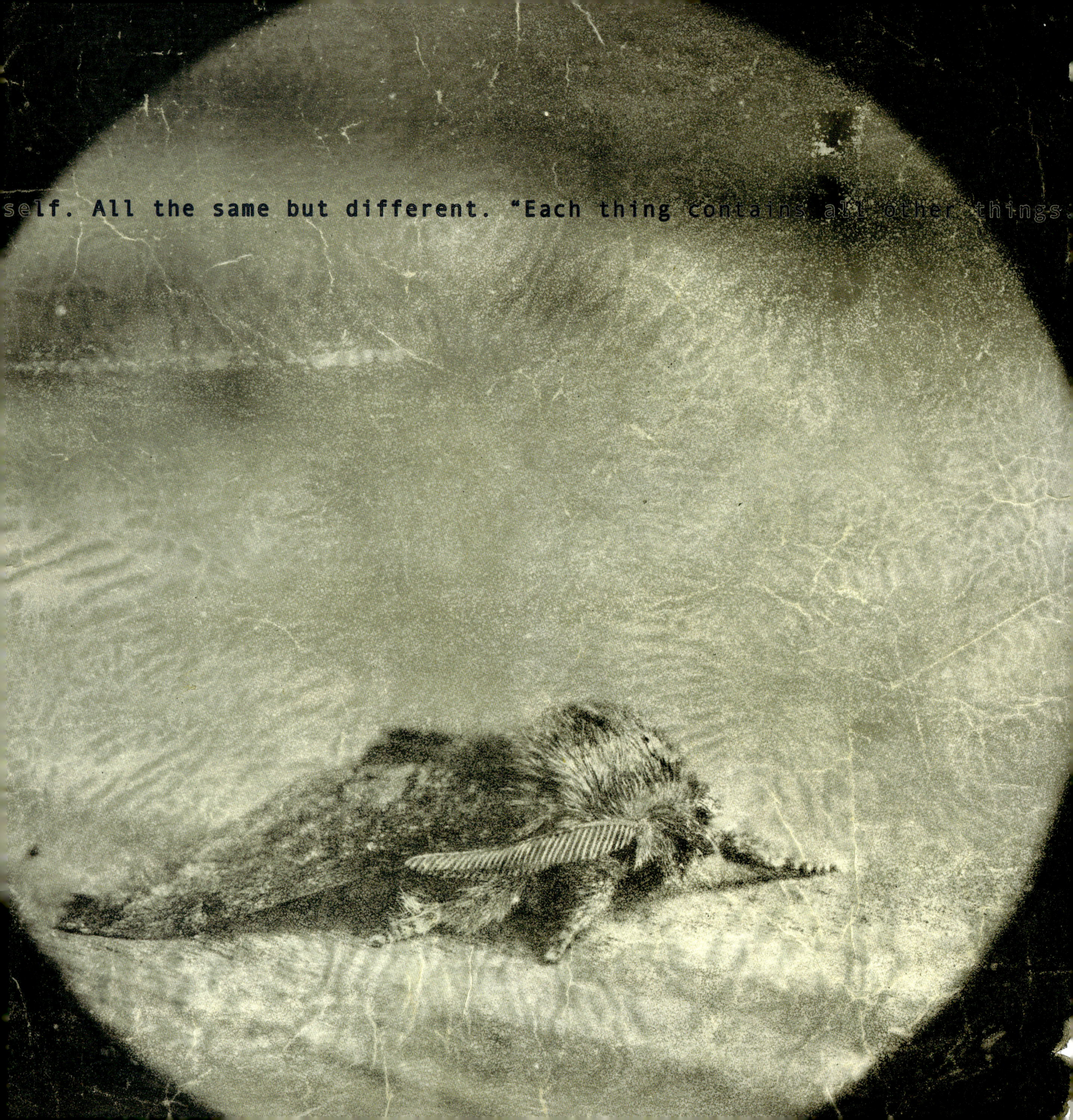

self. All the same but different. "Each thing contains all other things.

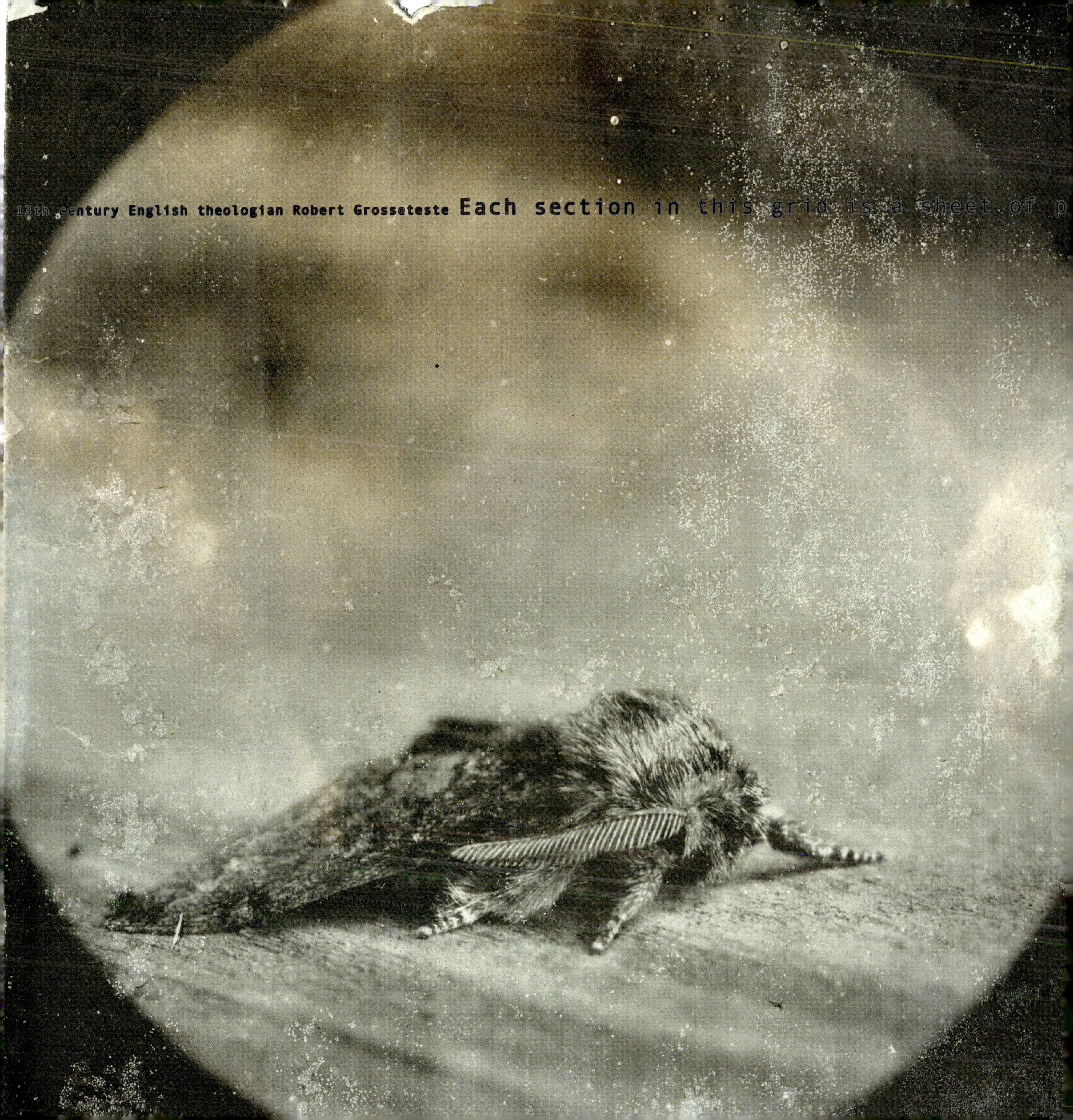
13th century English theologian Robert Grosseteste Each section in this grid is a sheet of p

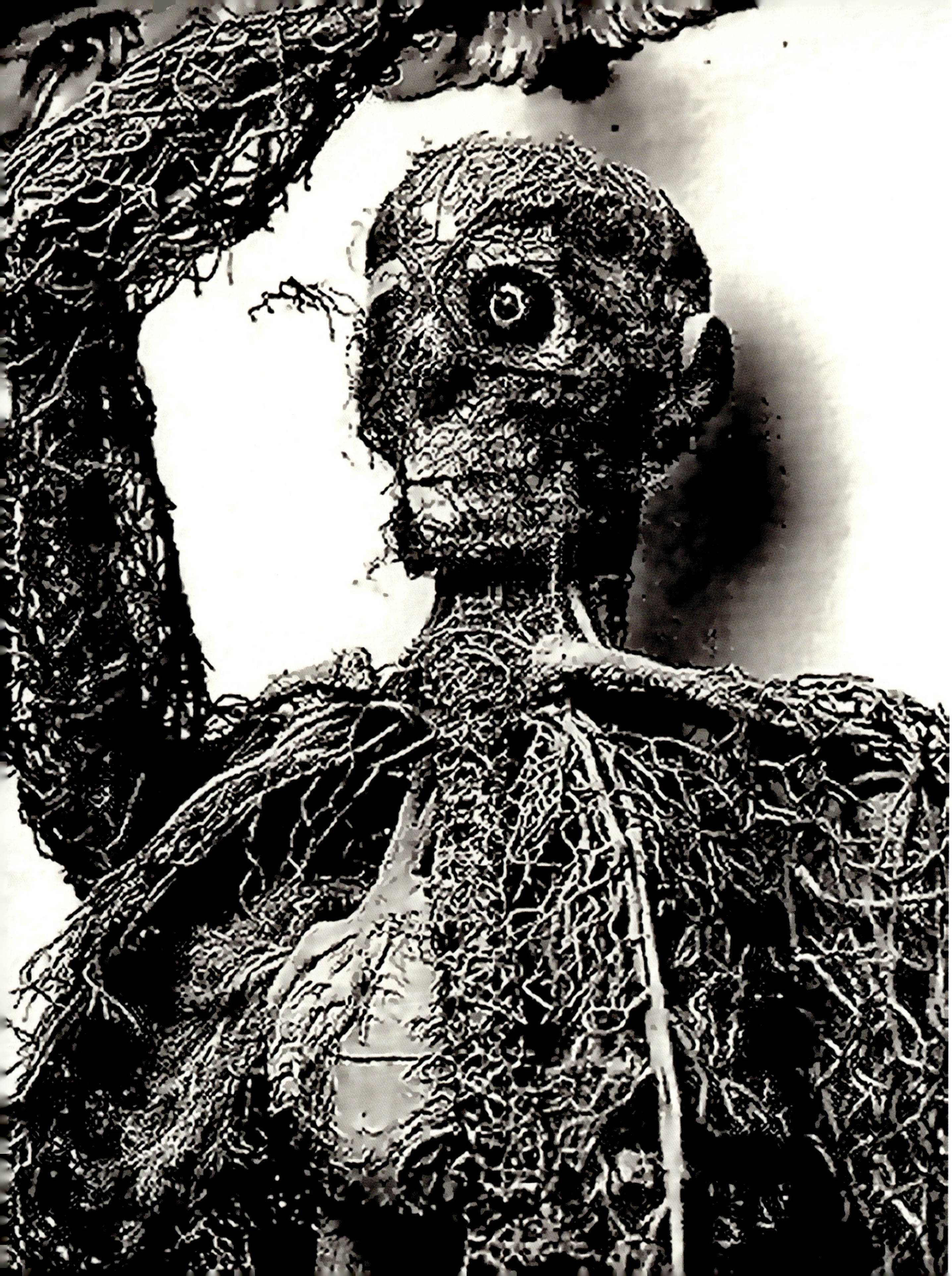

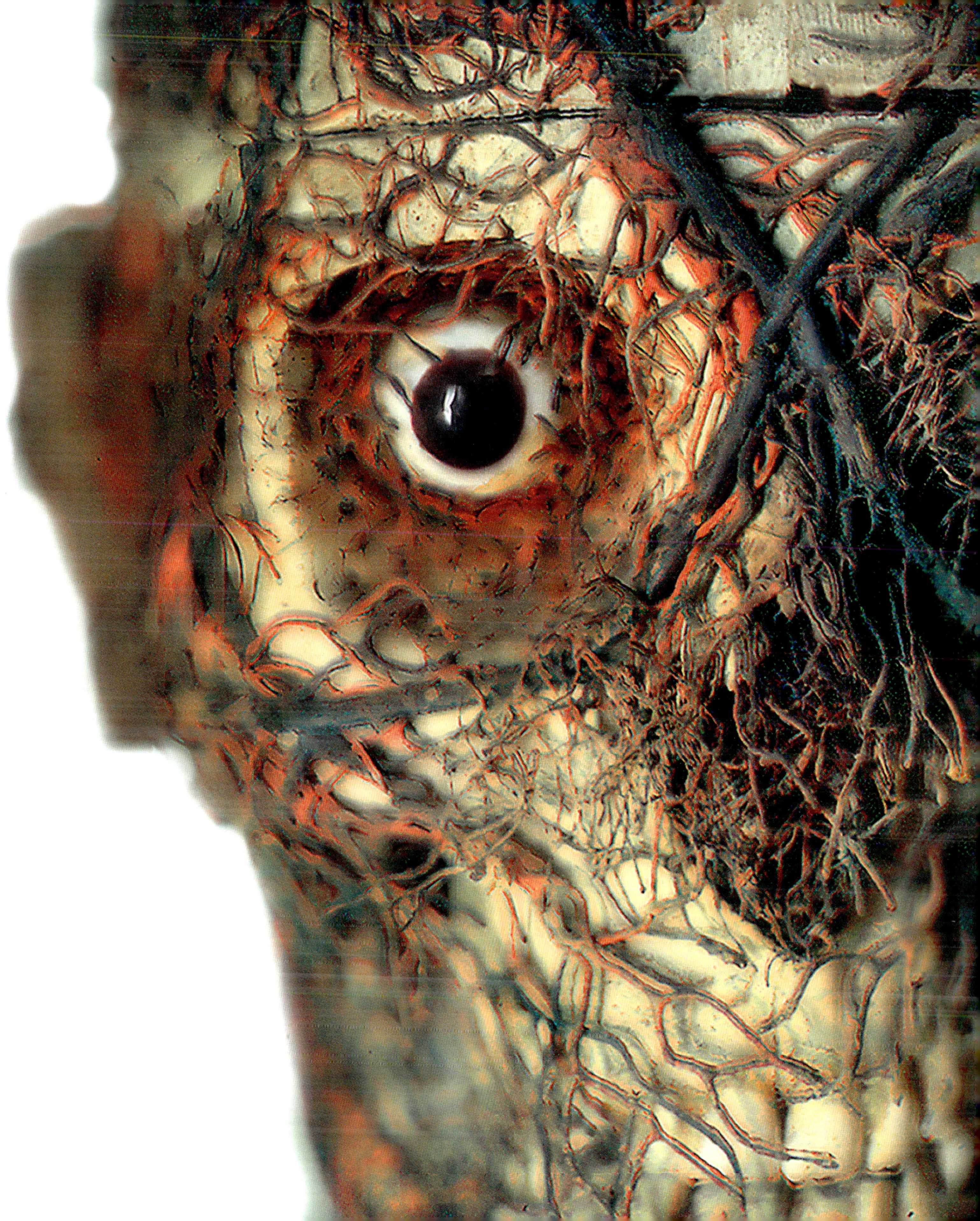

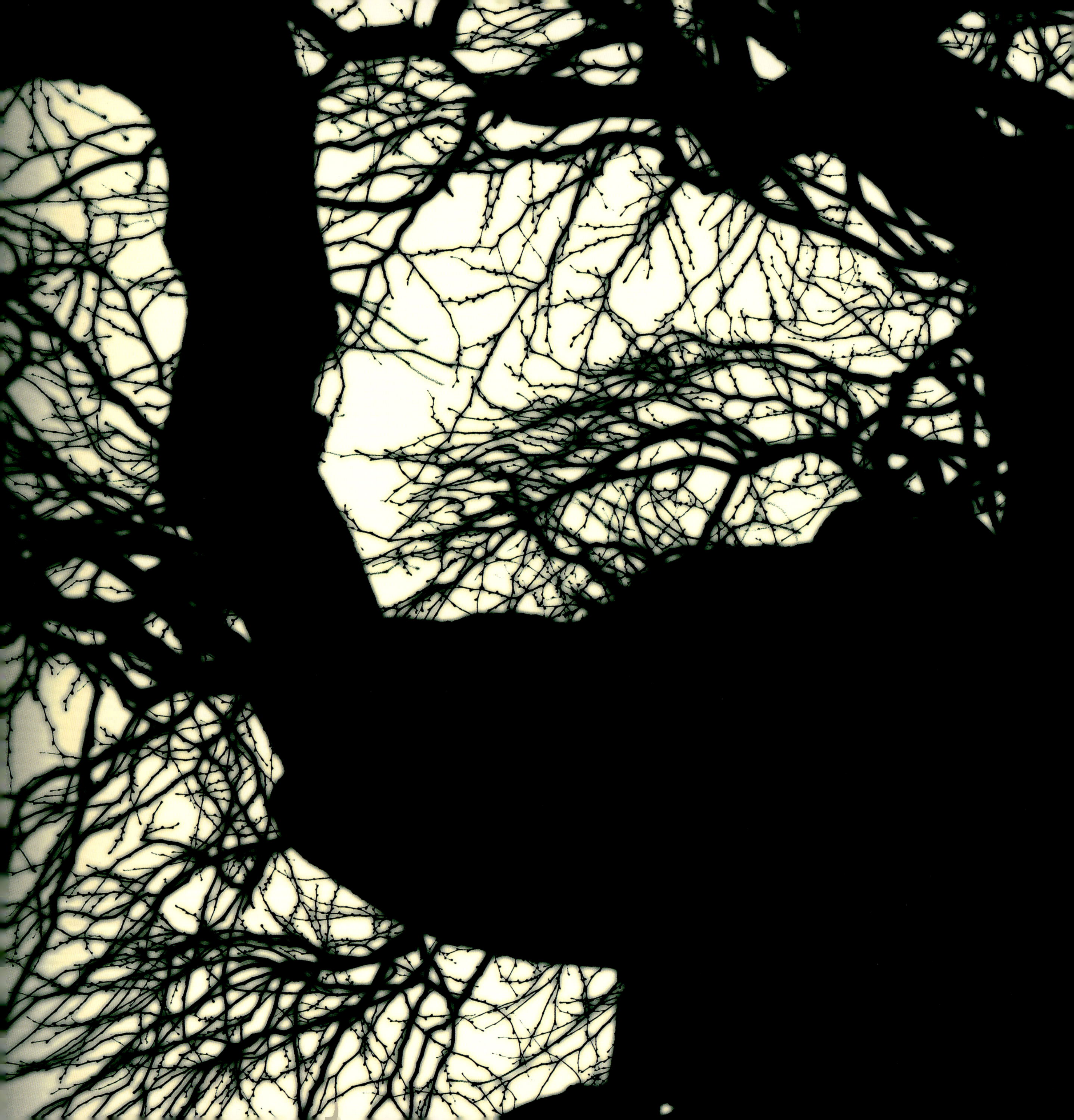

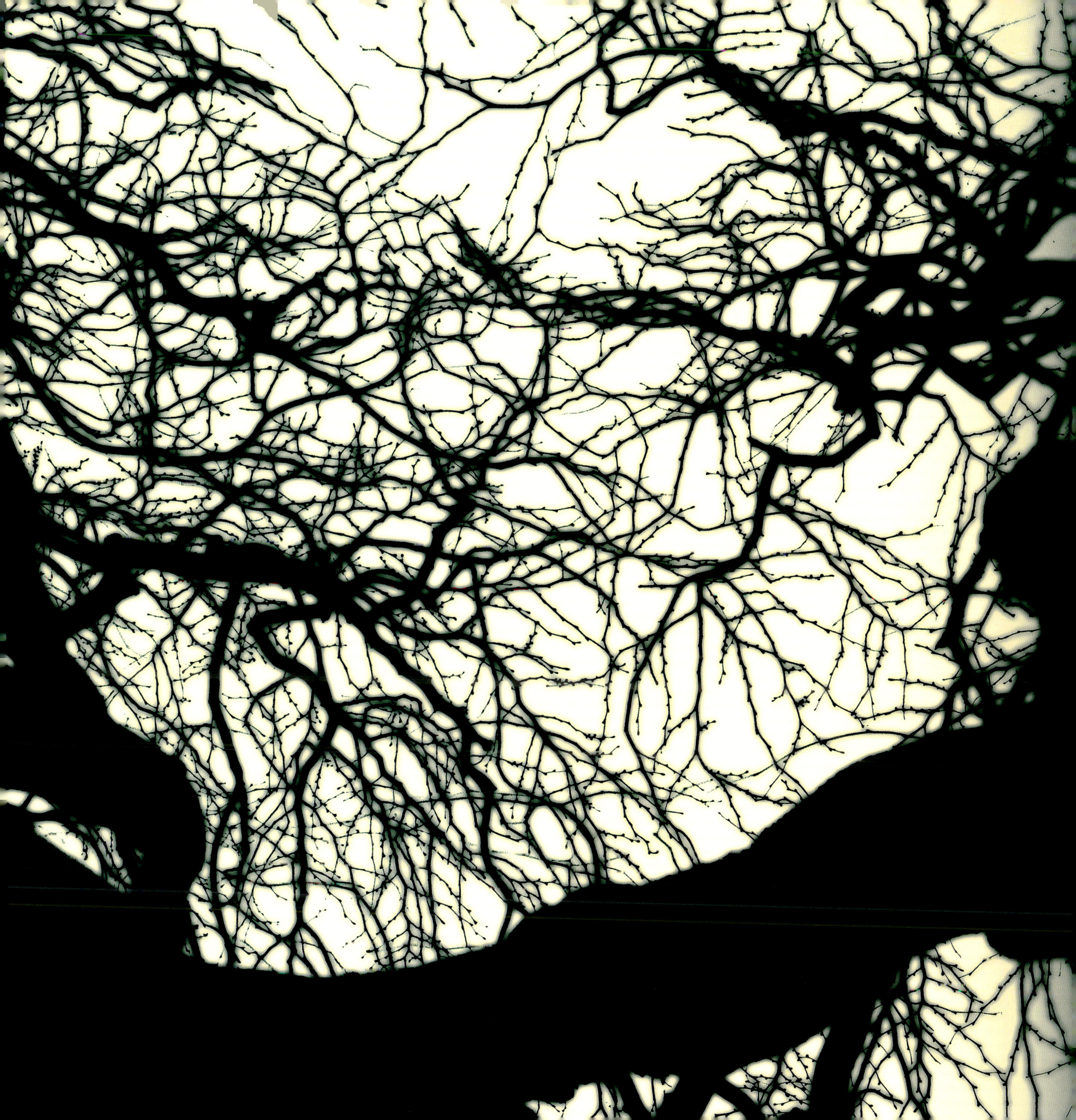

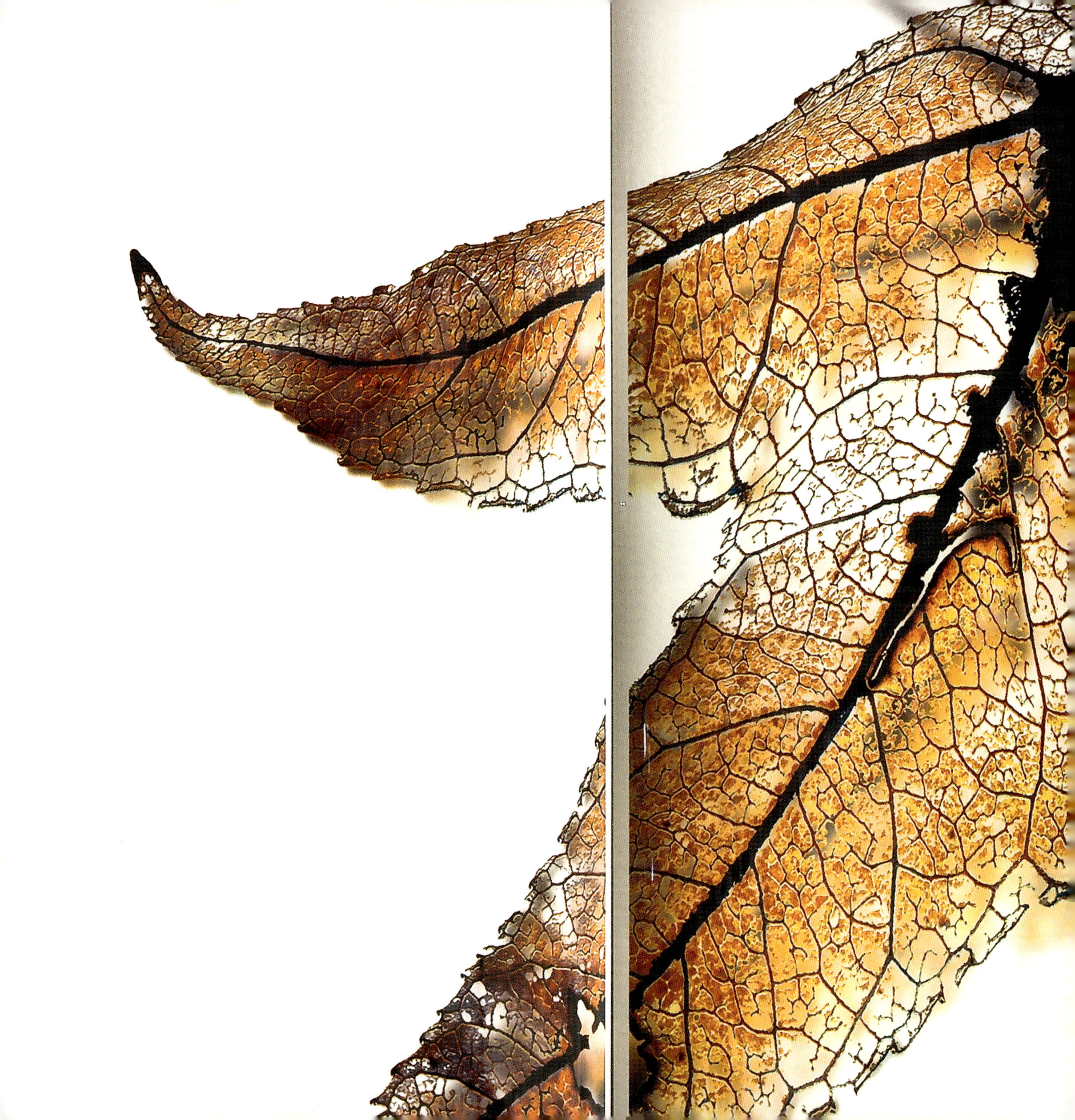

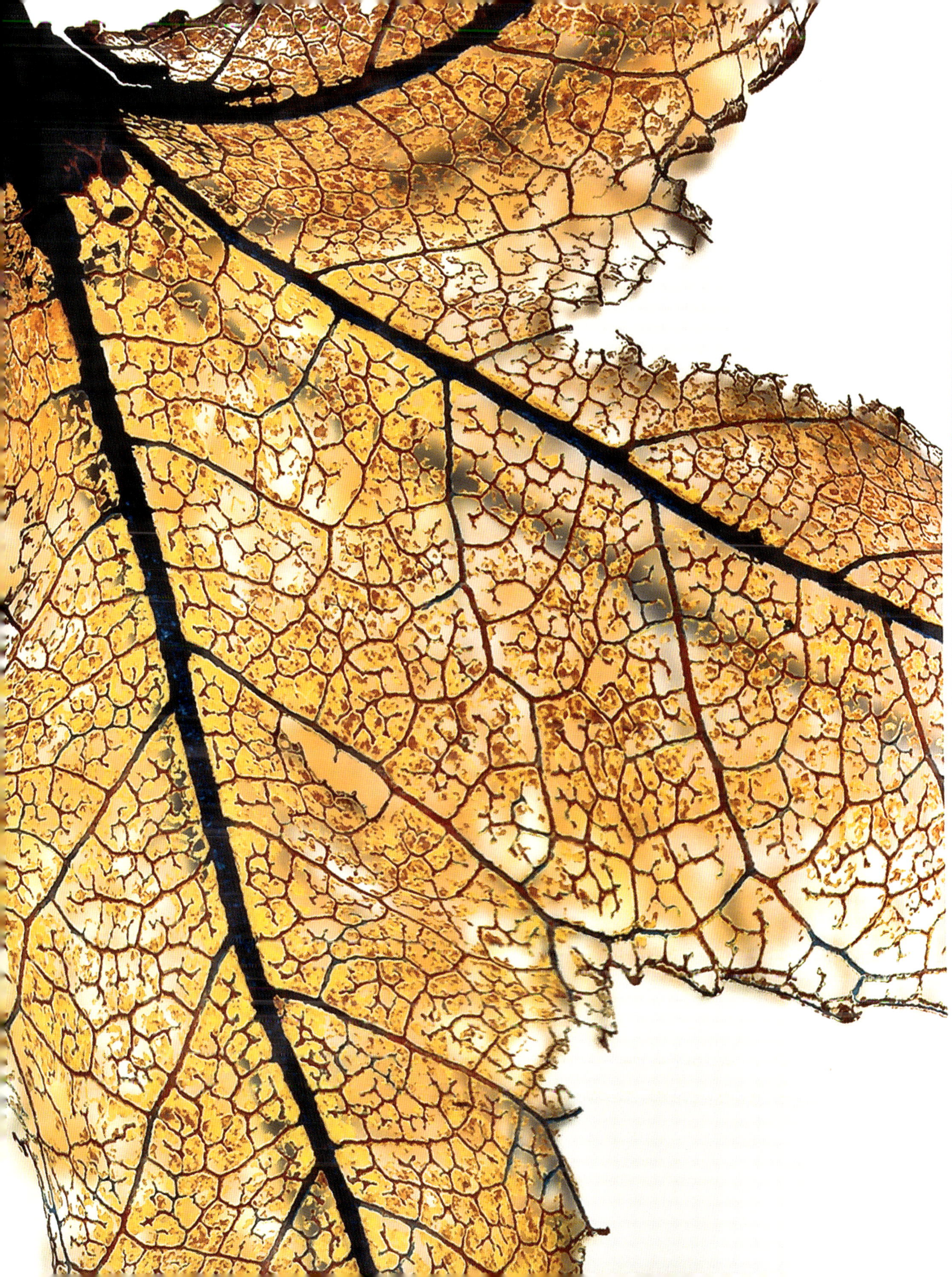

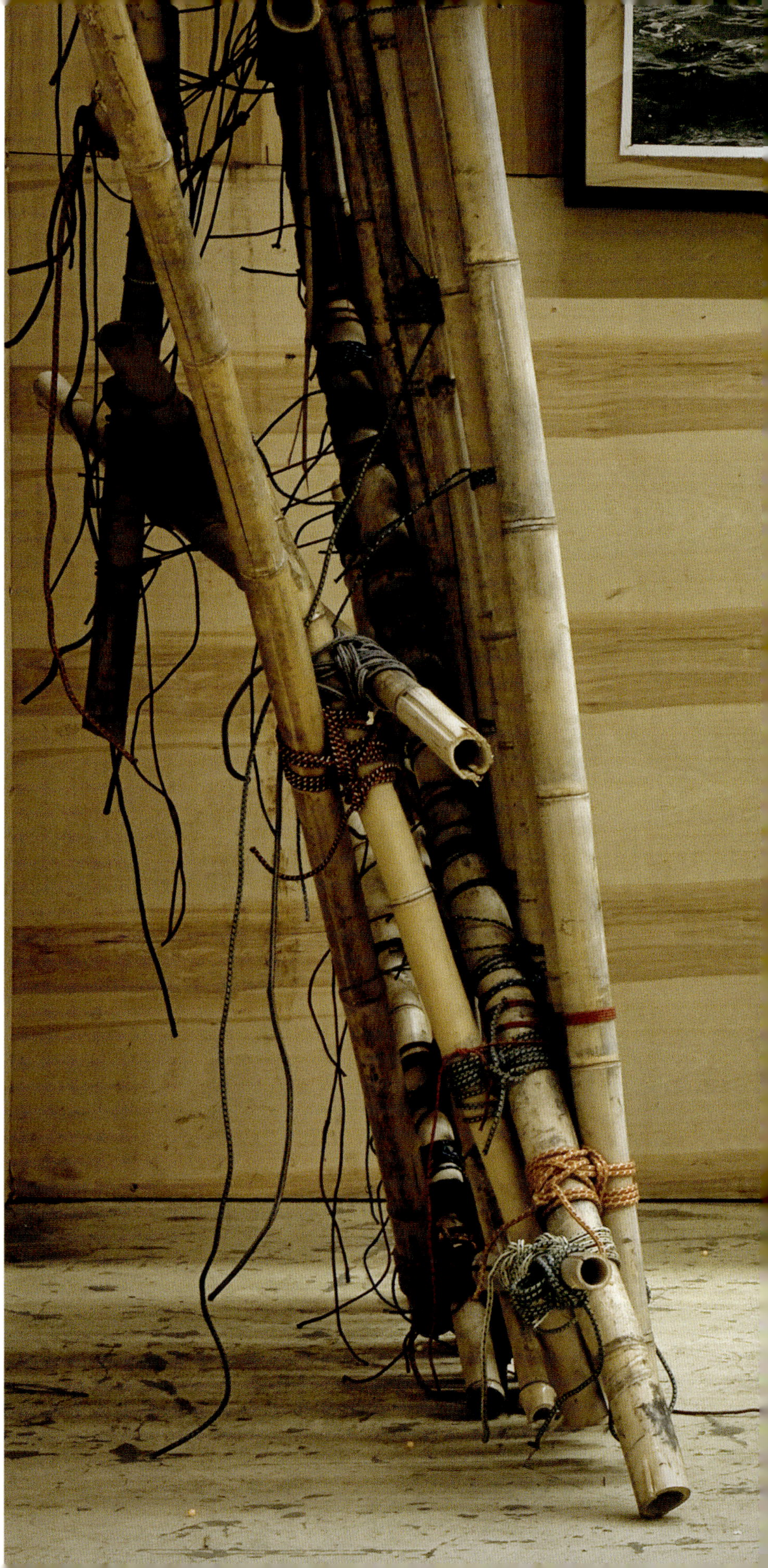

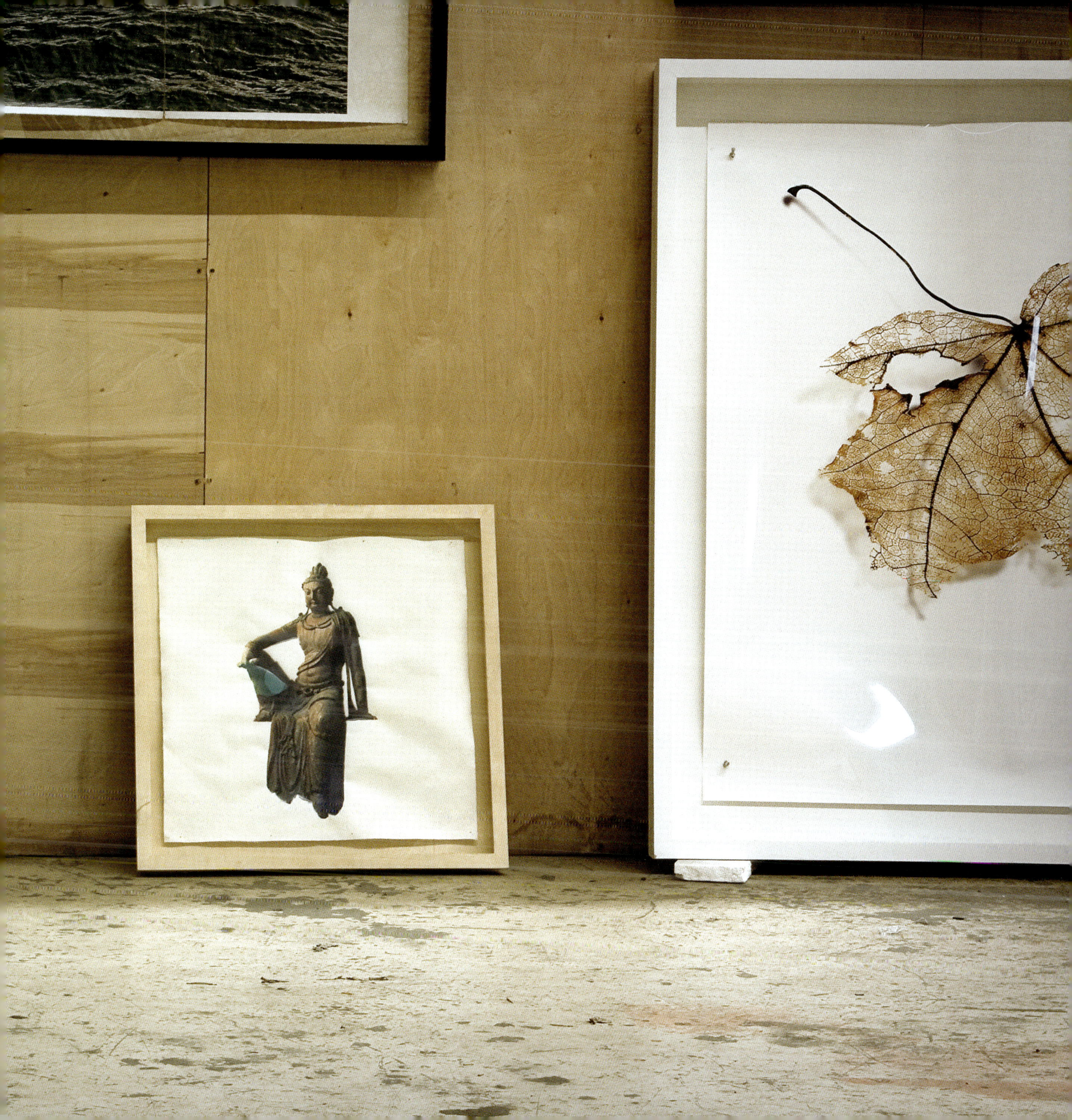

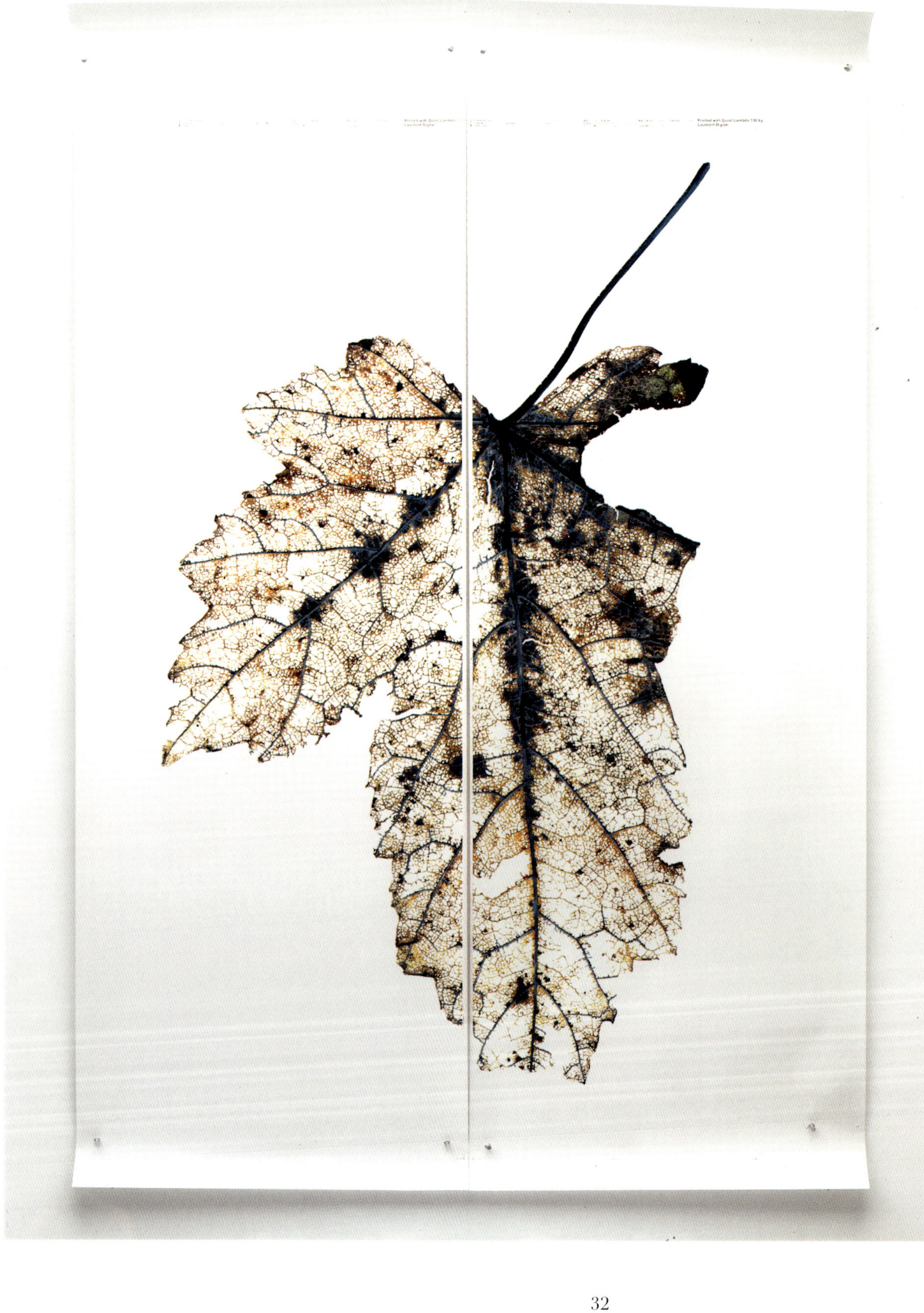

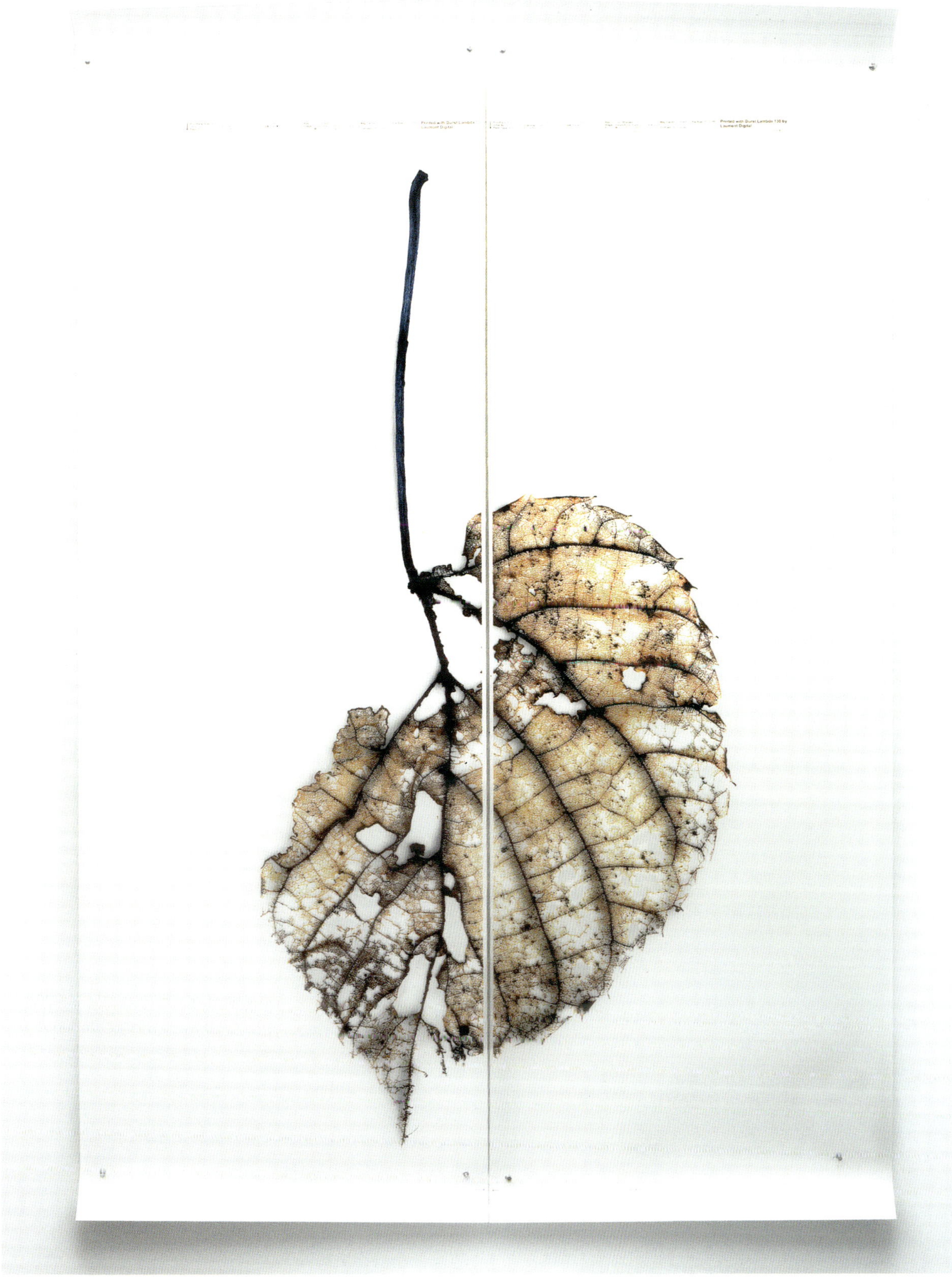

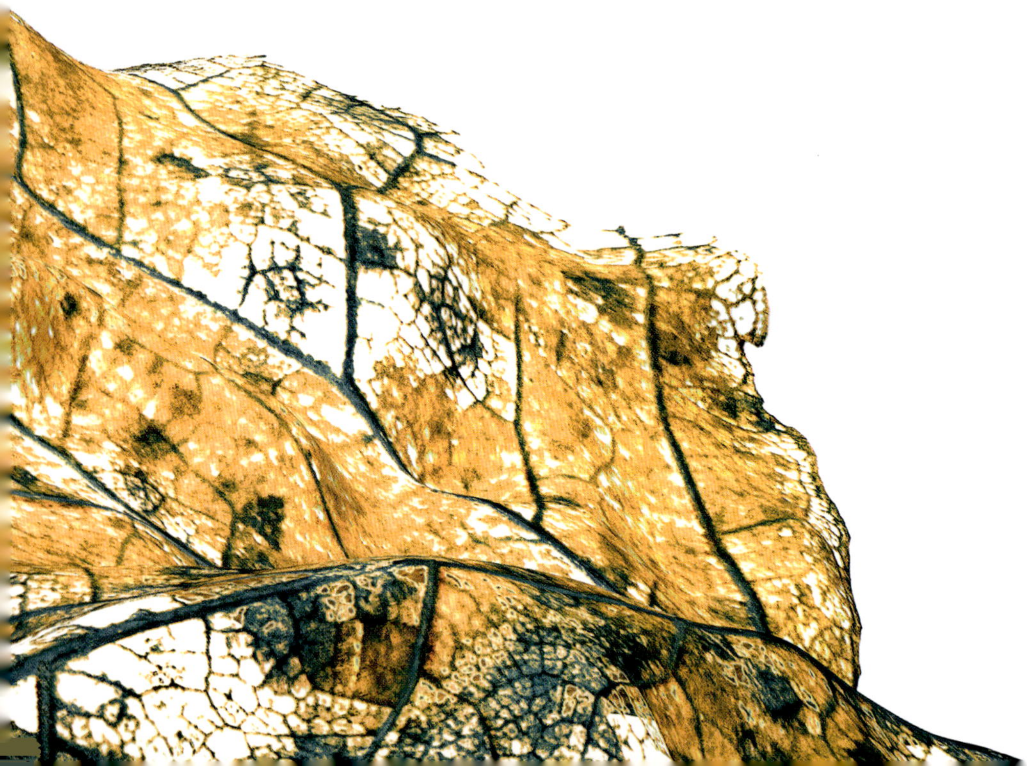

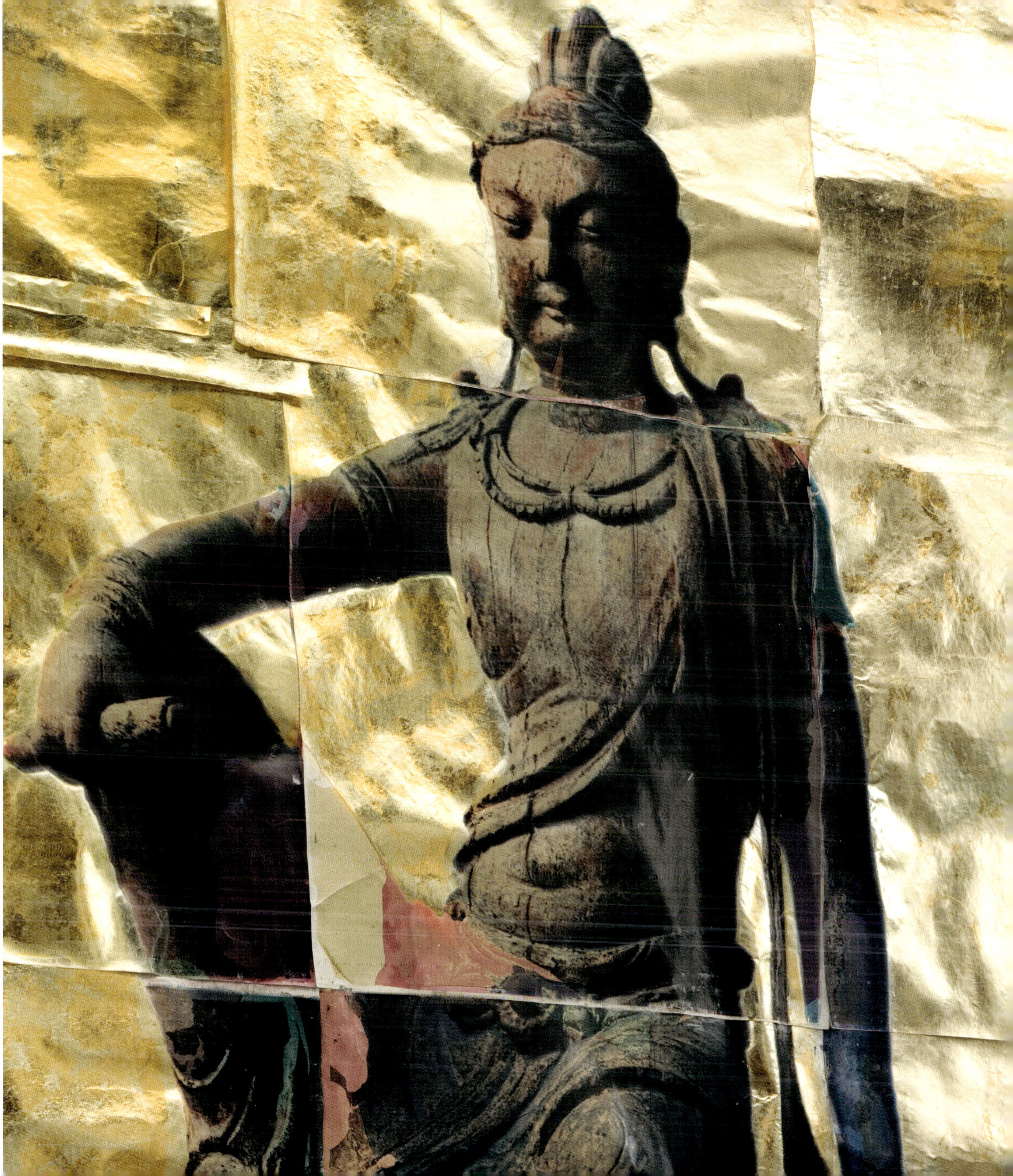

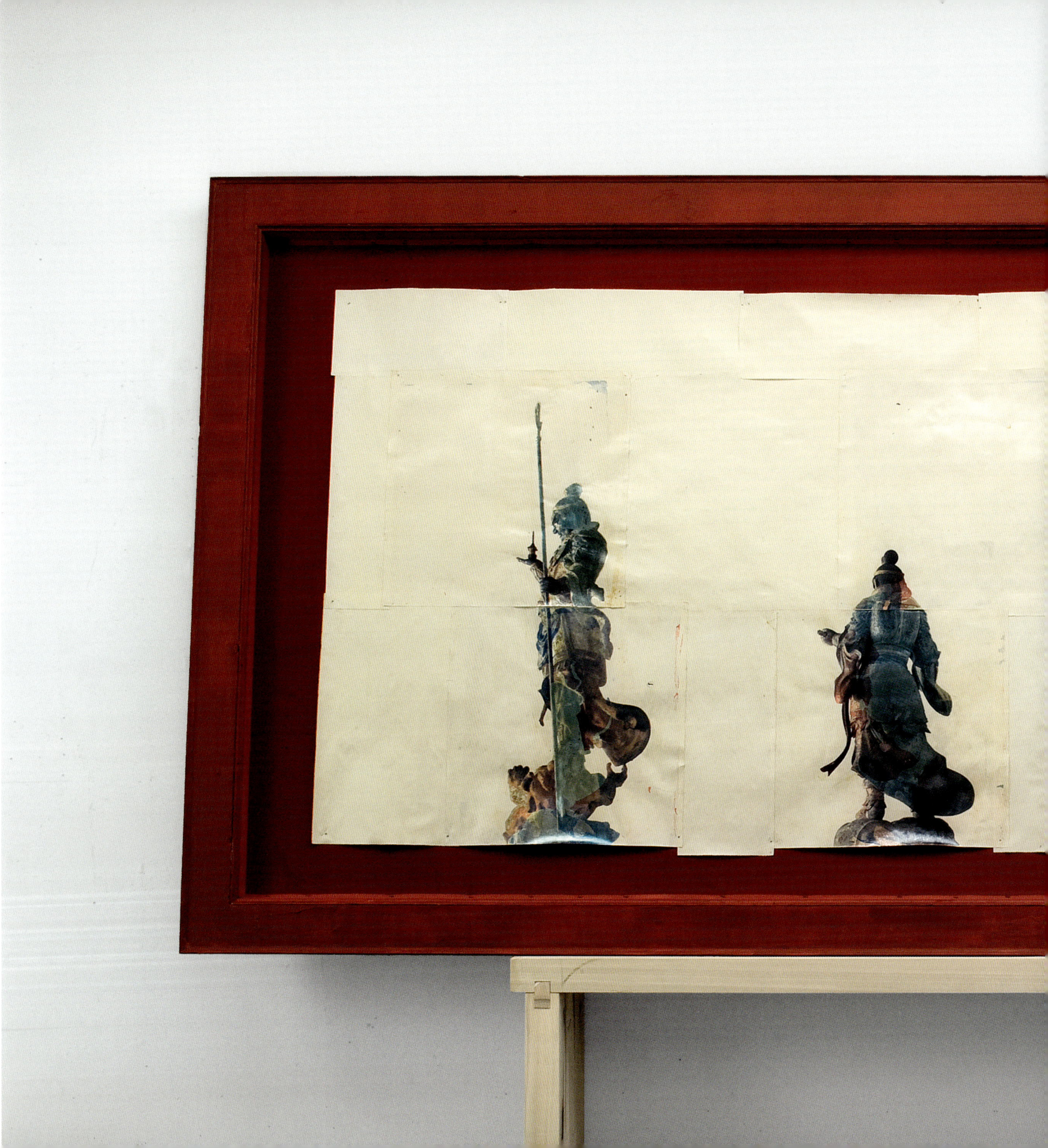

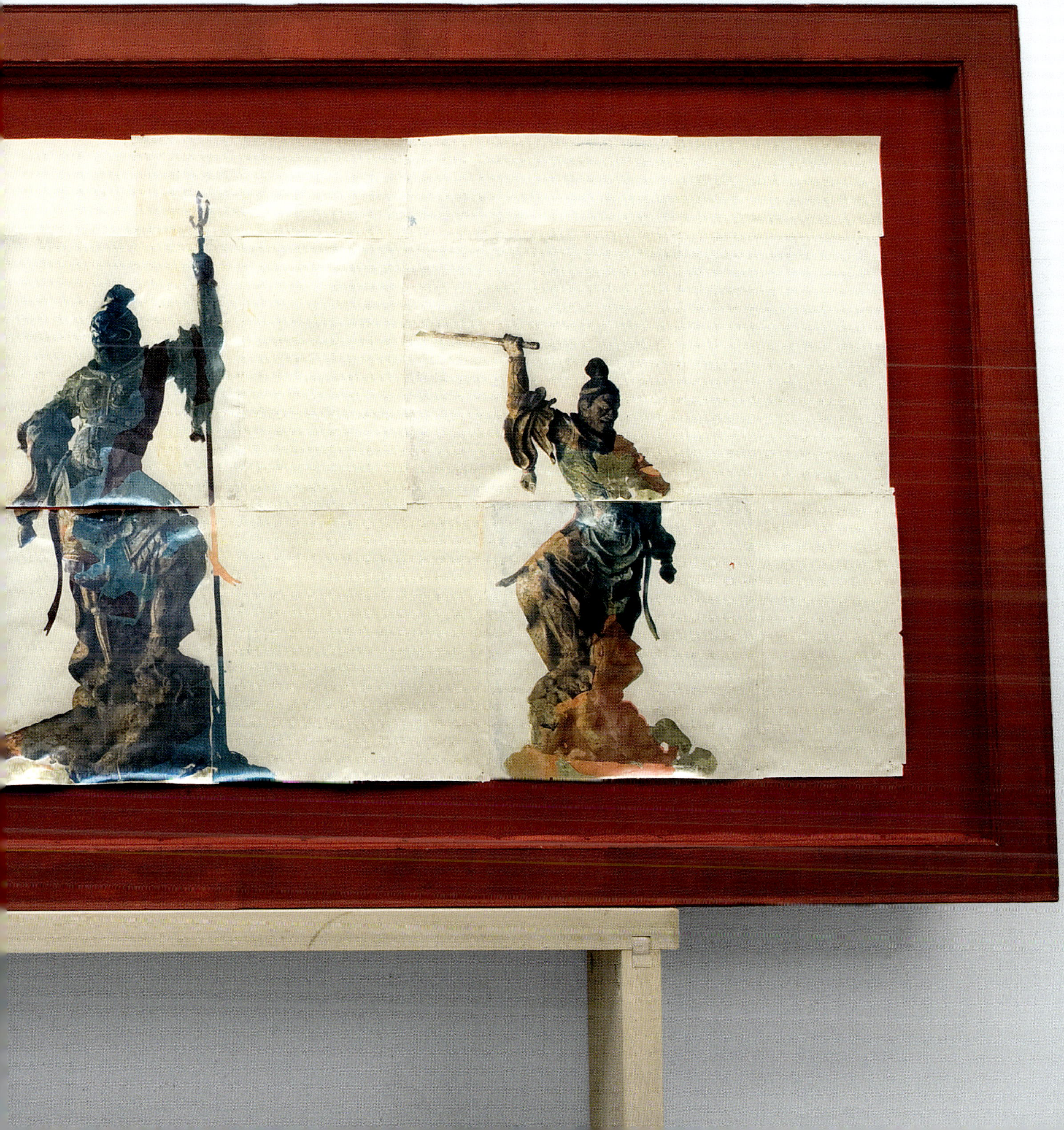

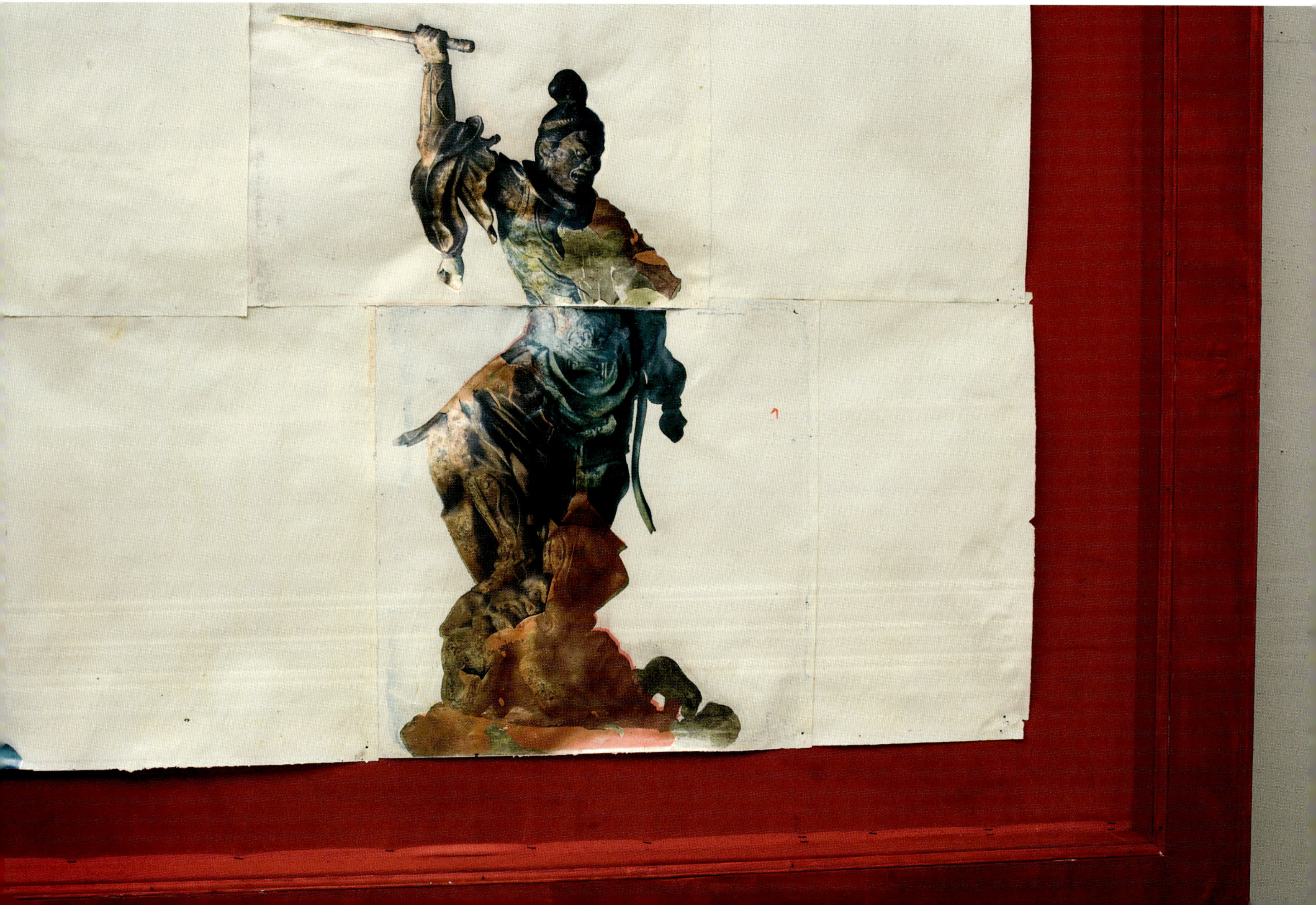

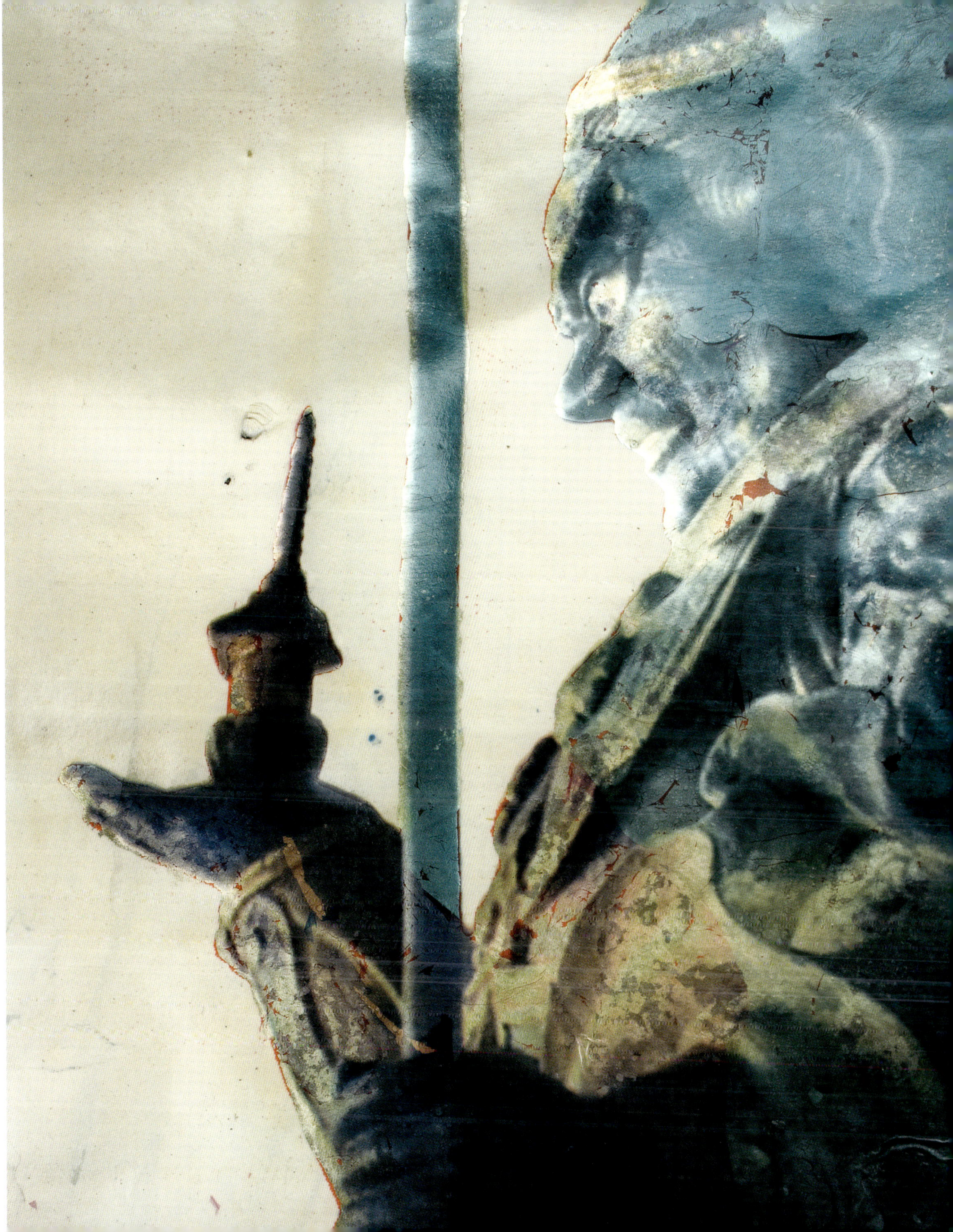

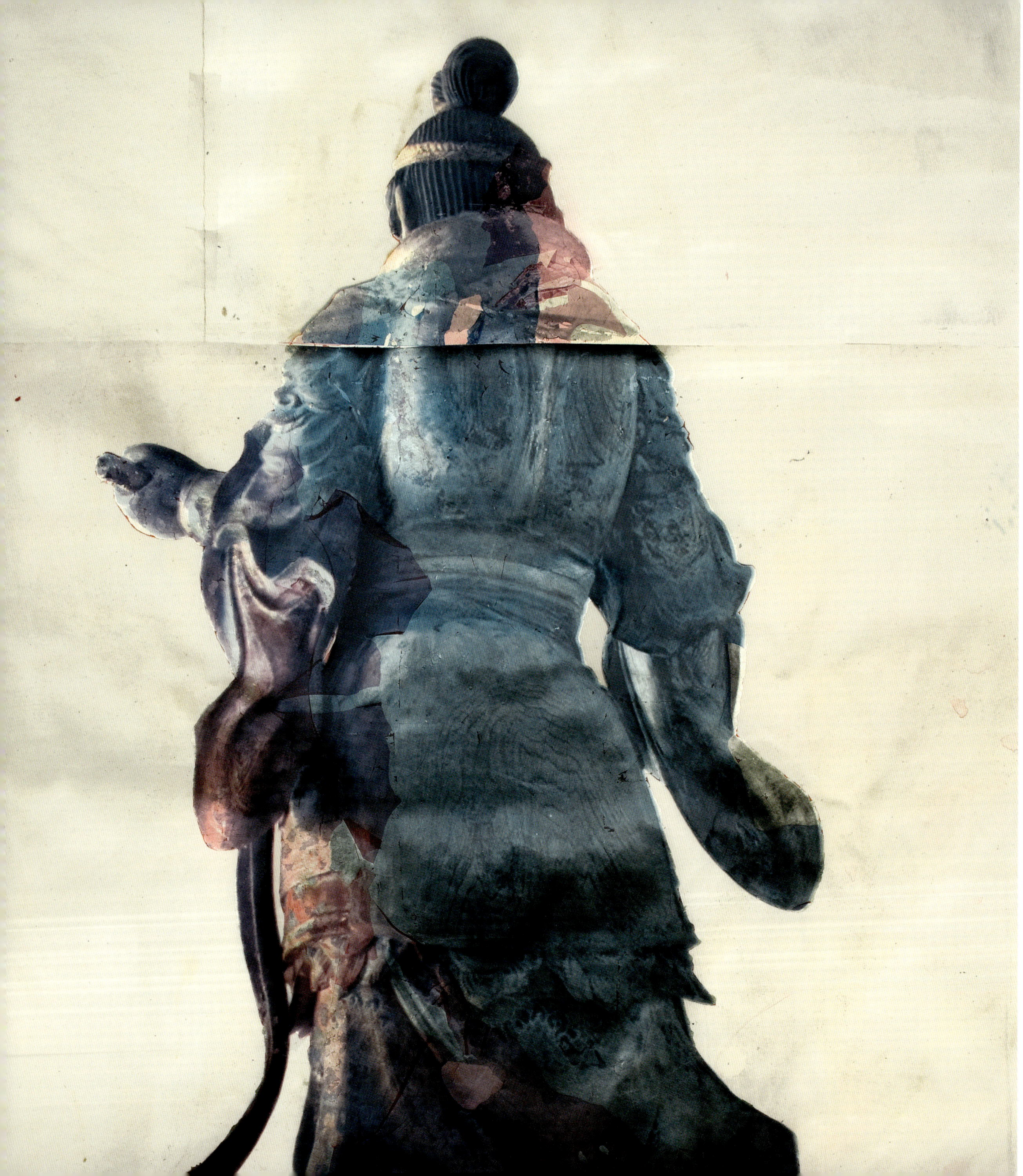

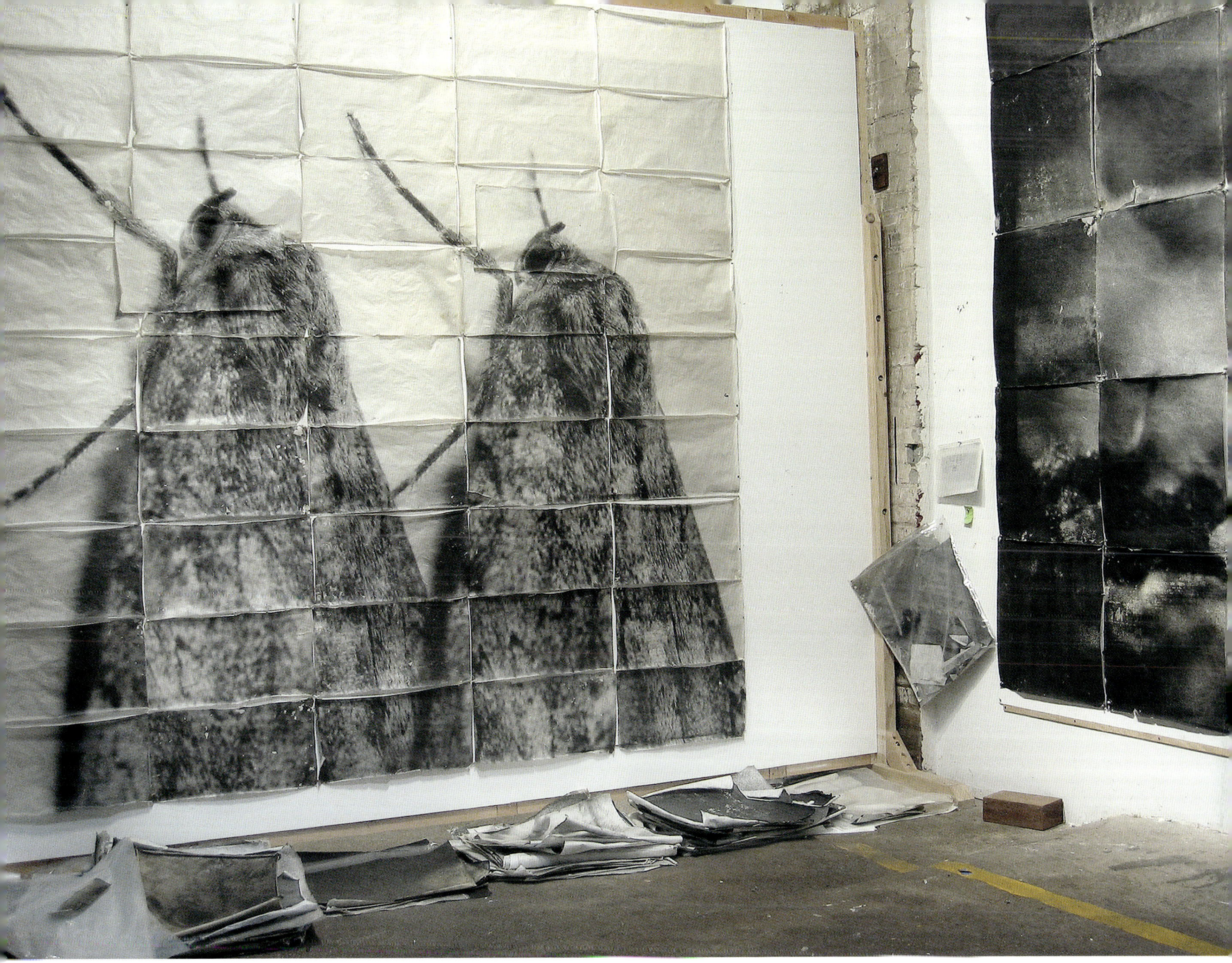

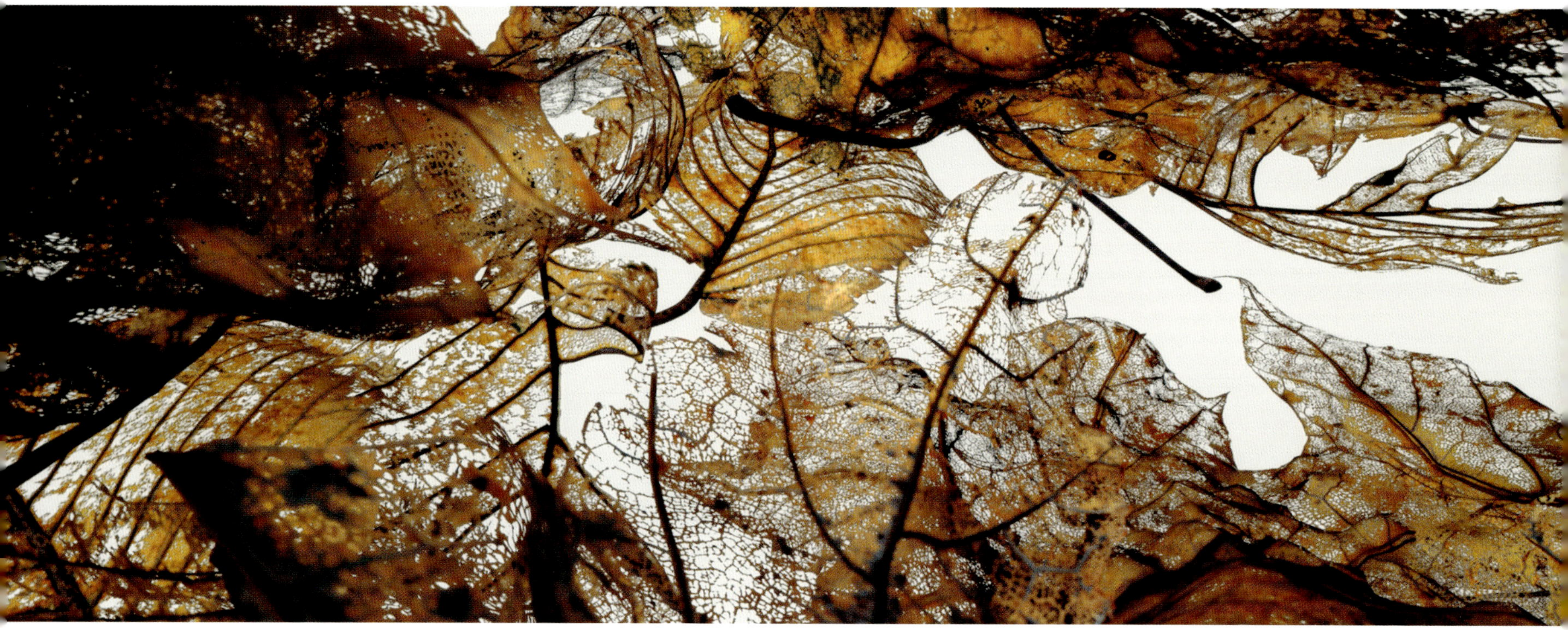

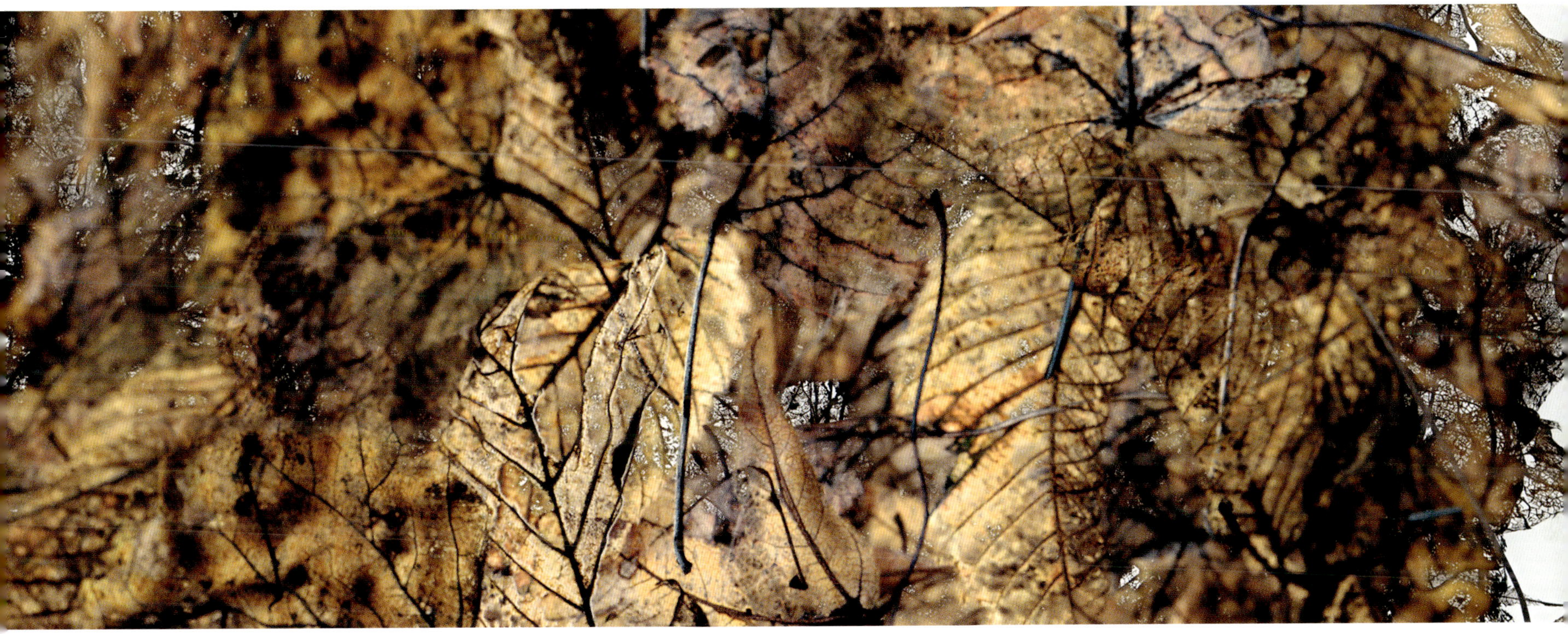

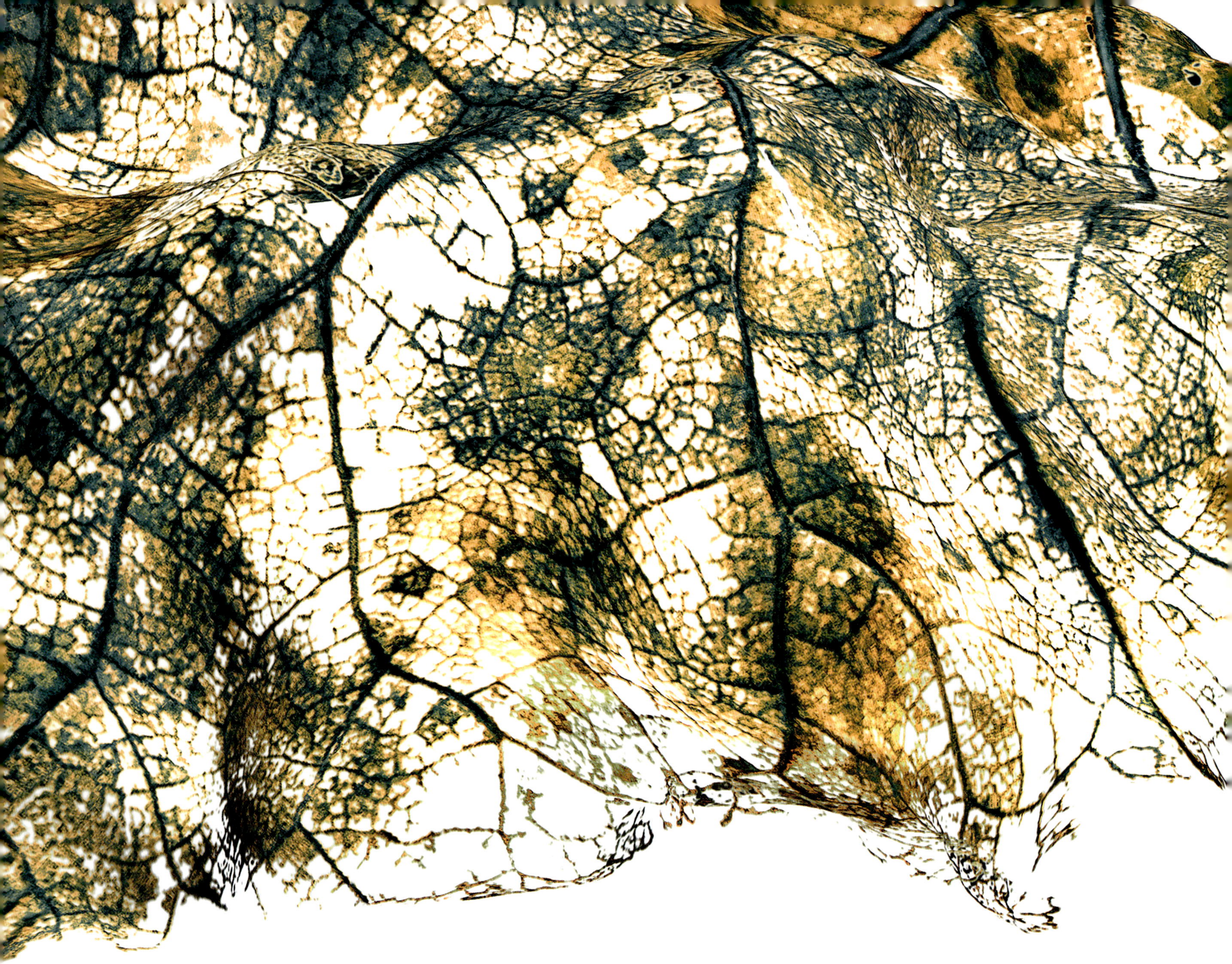

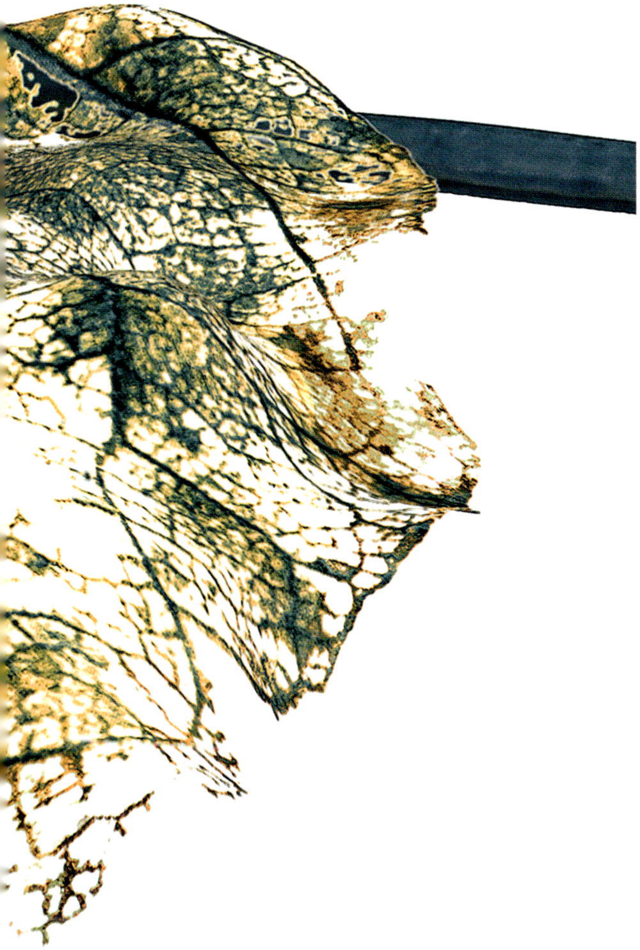

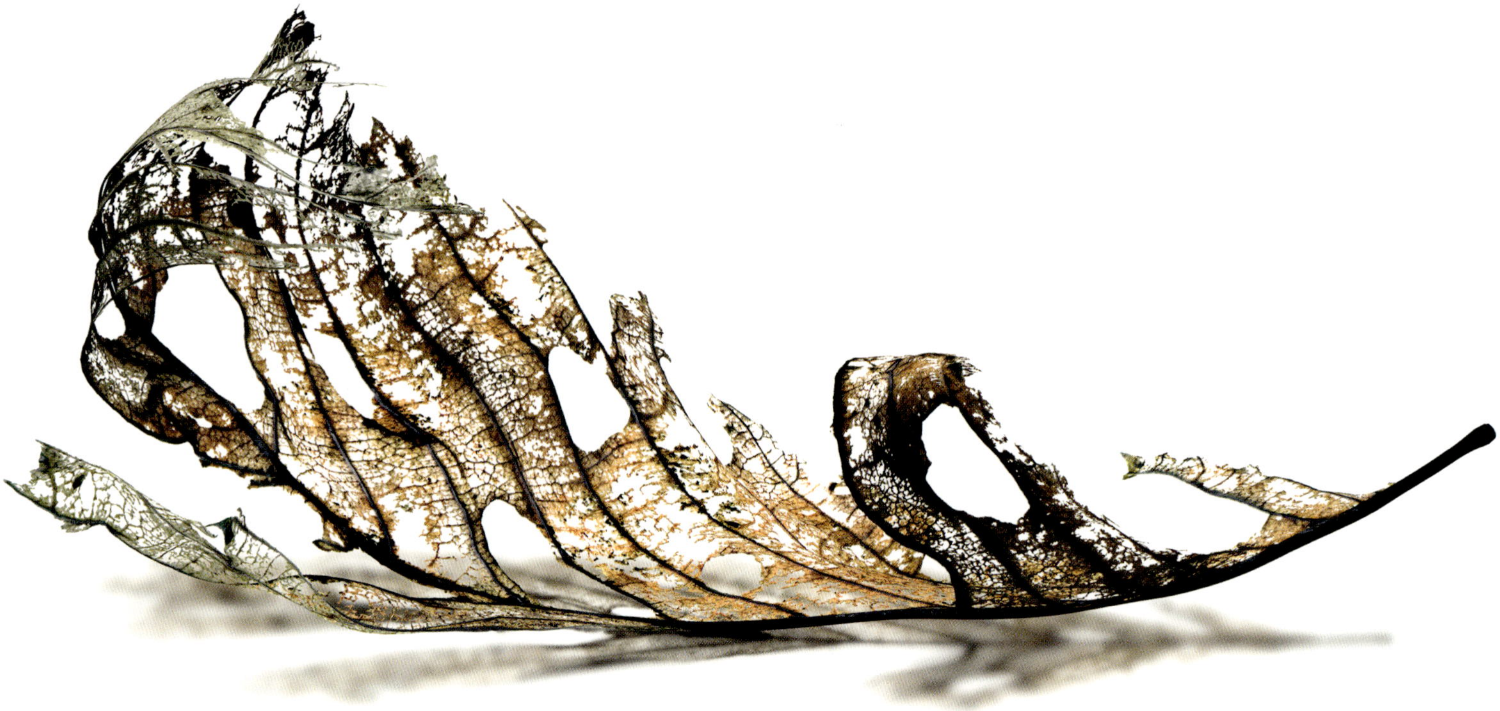

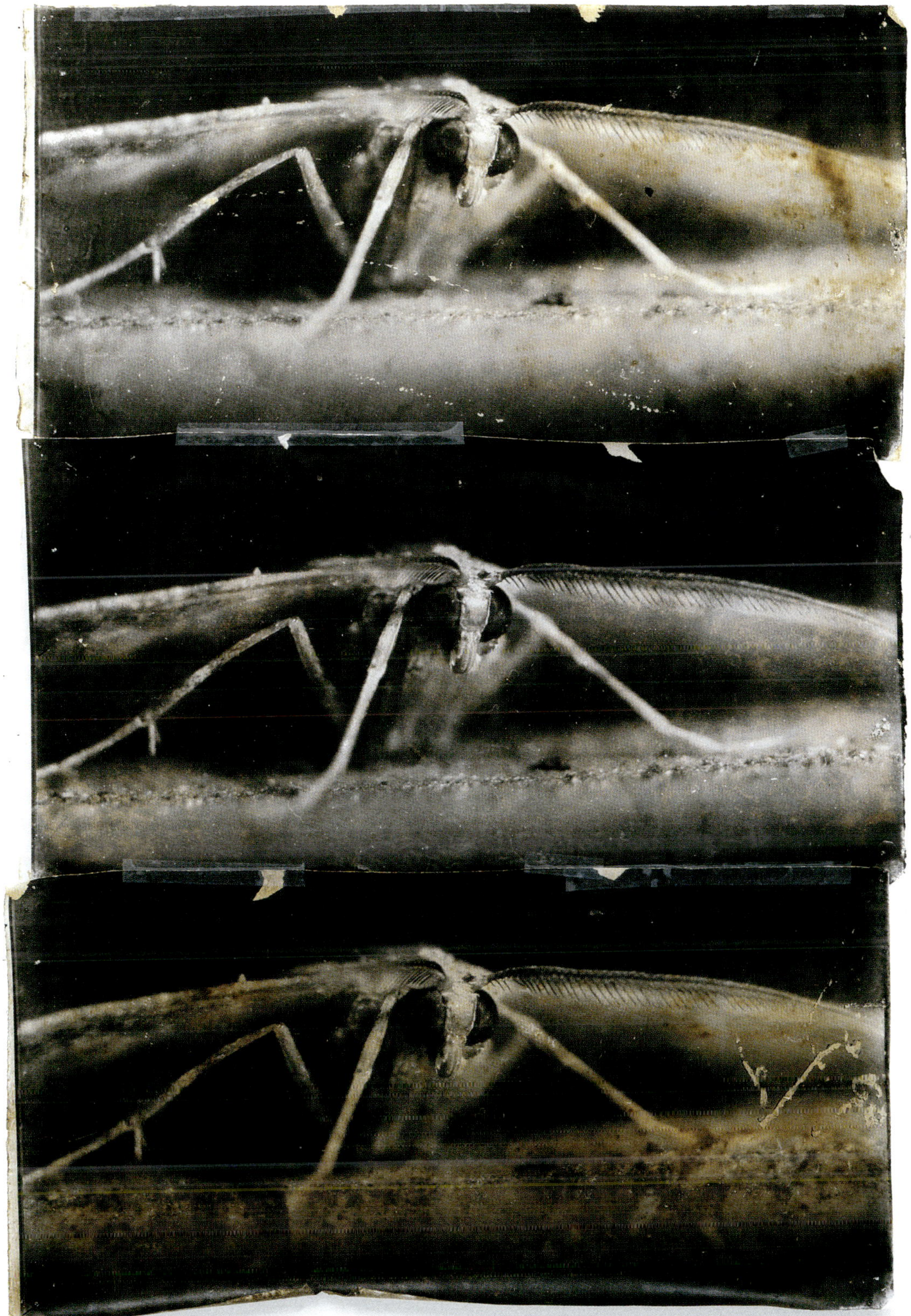

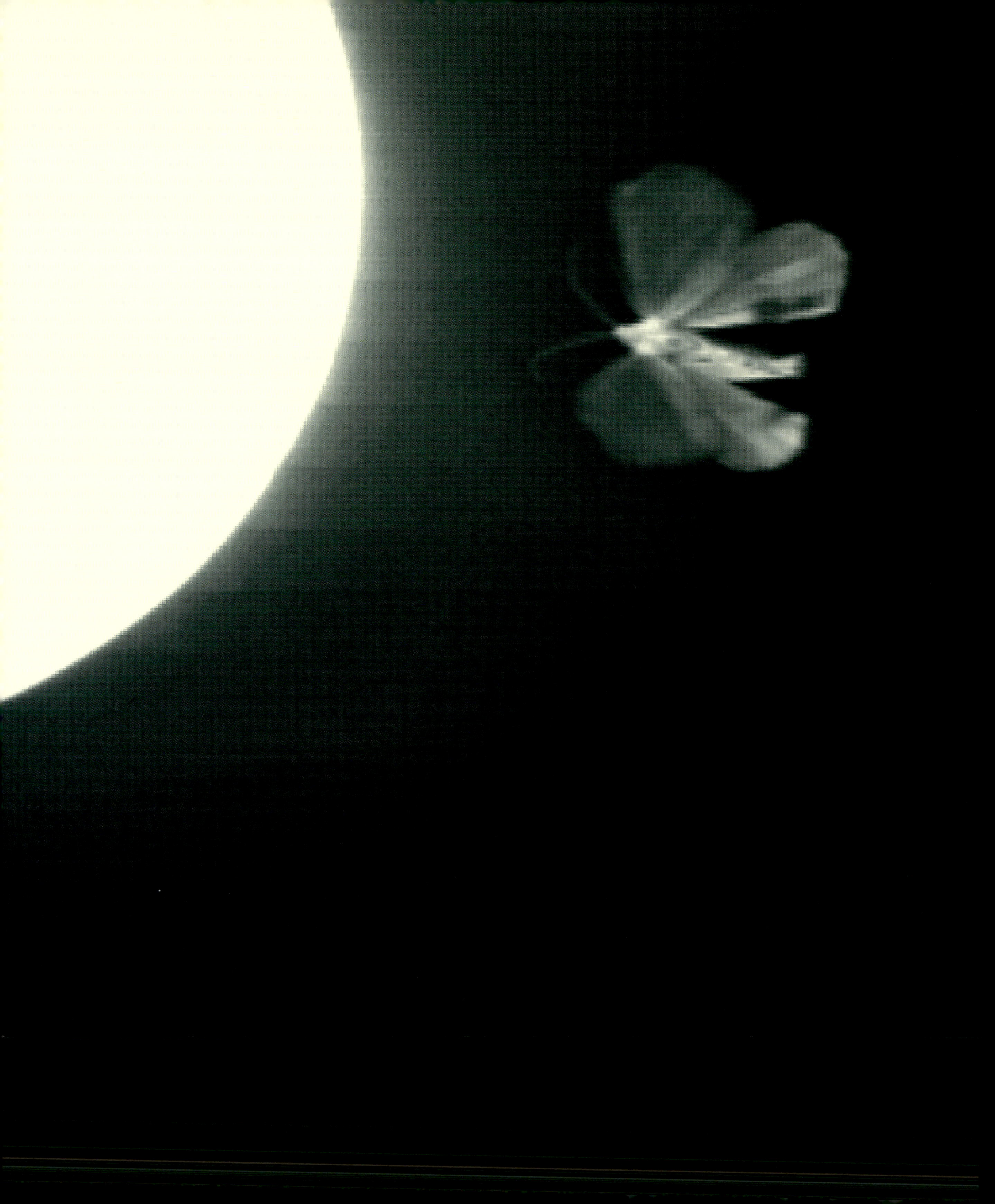

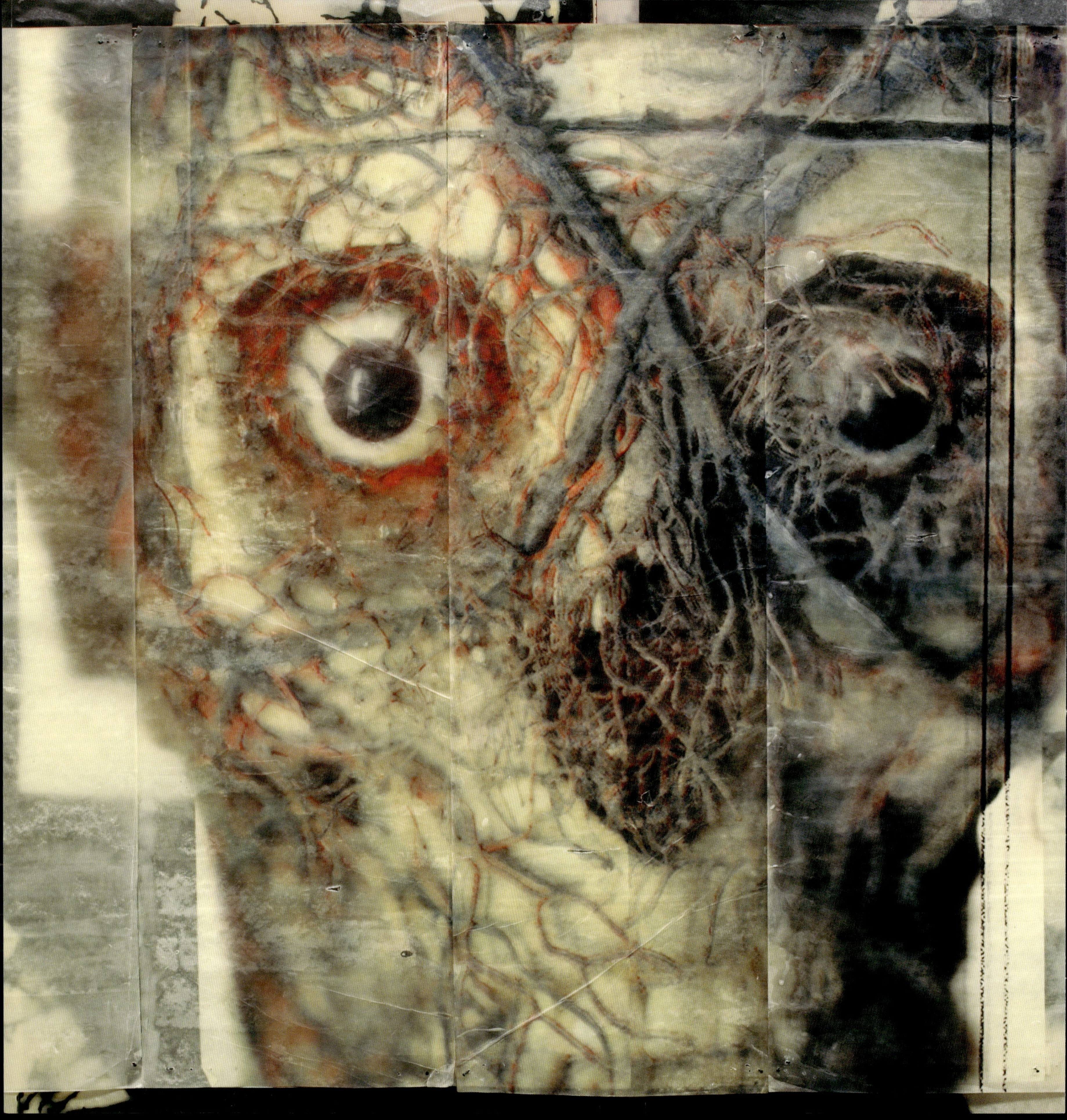

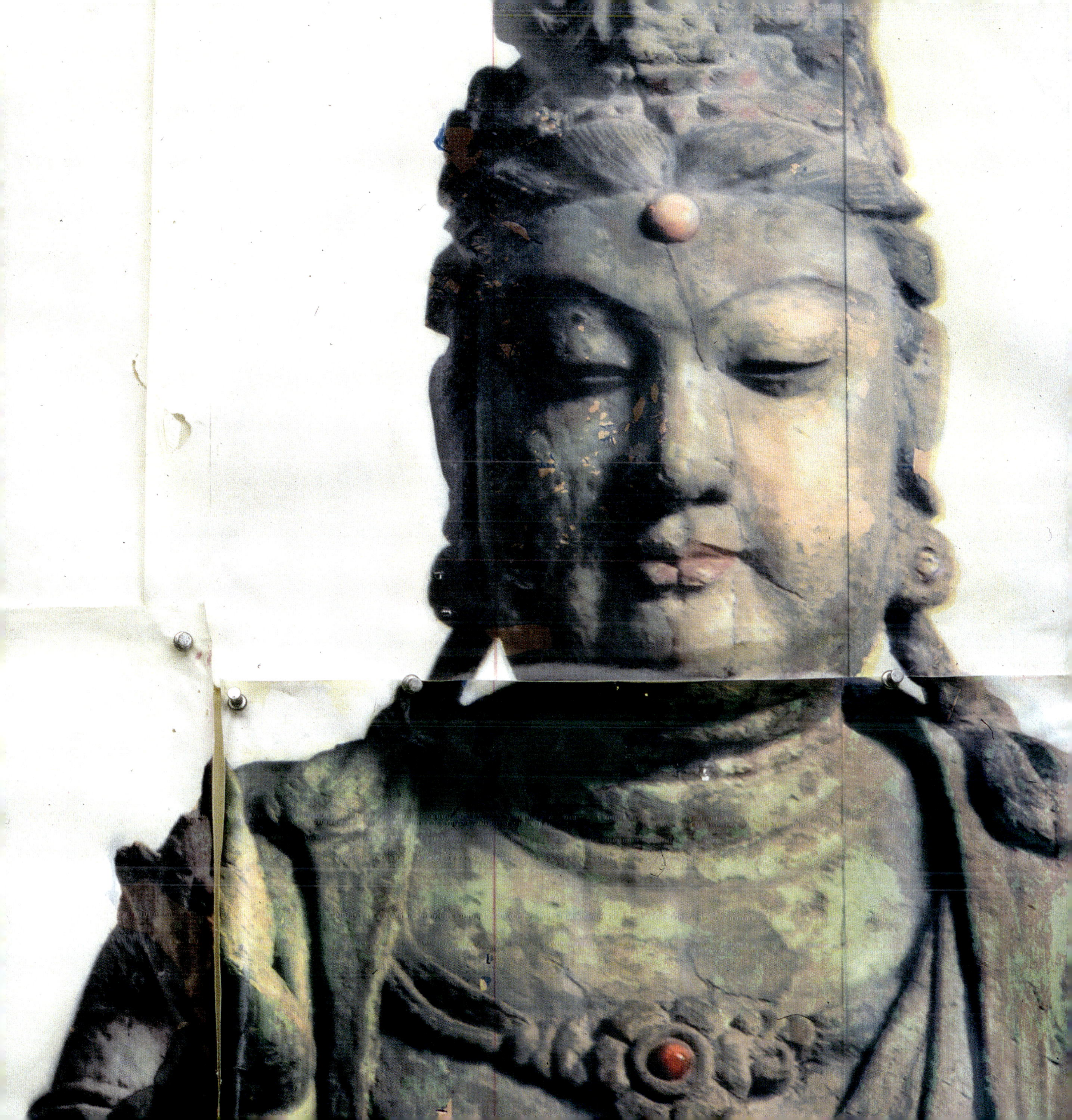

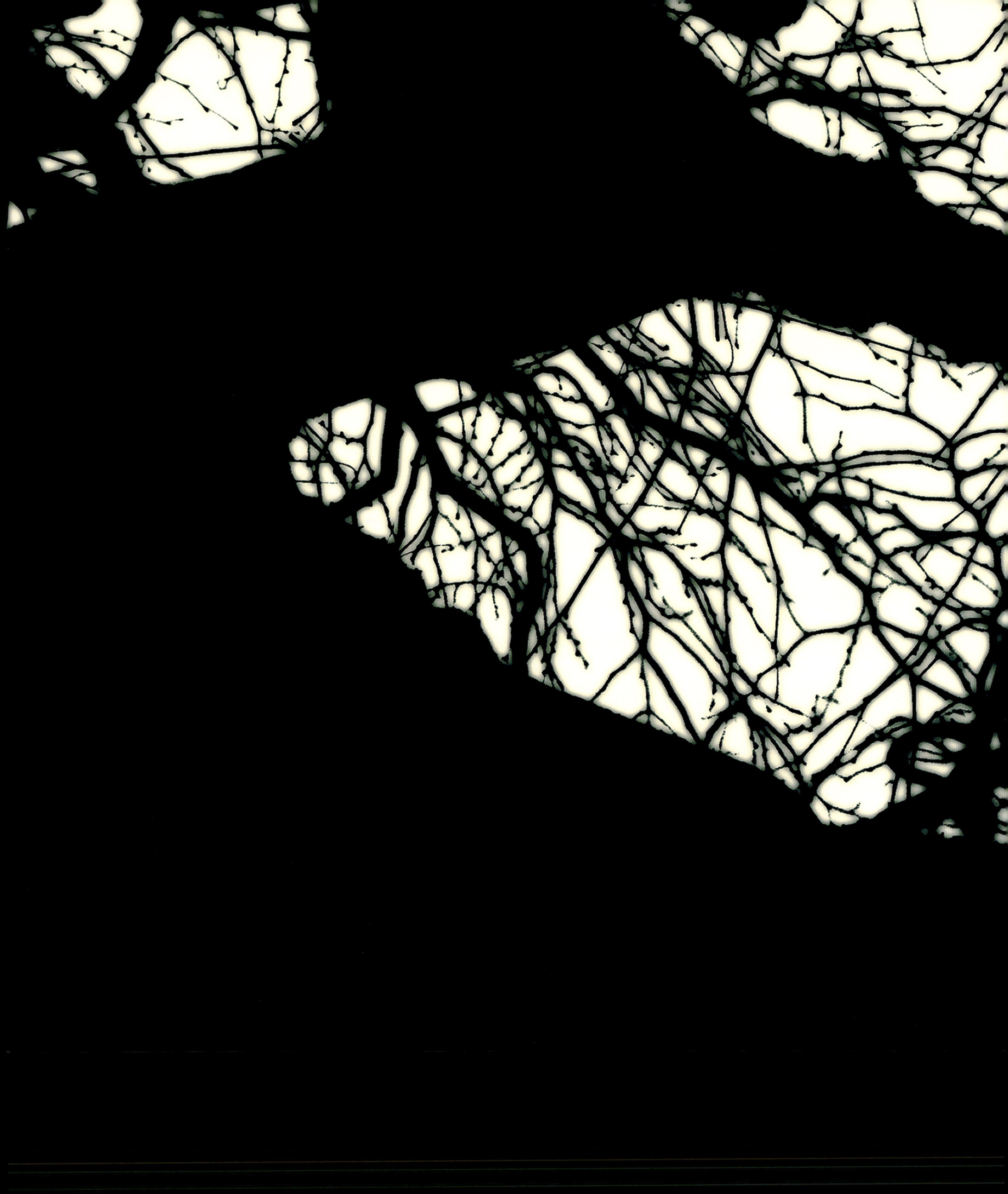

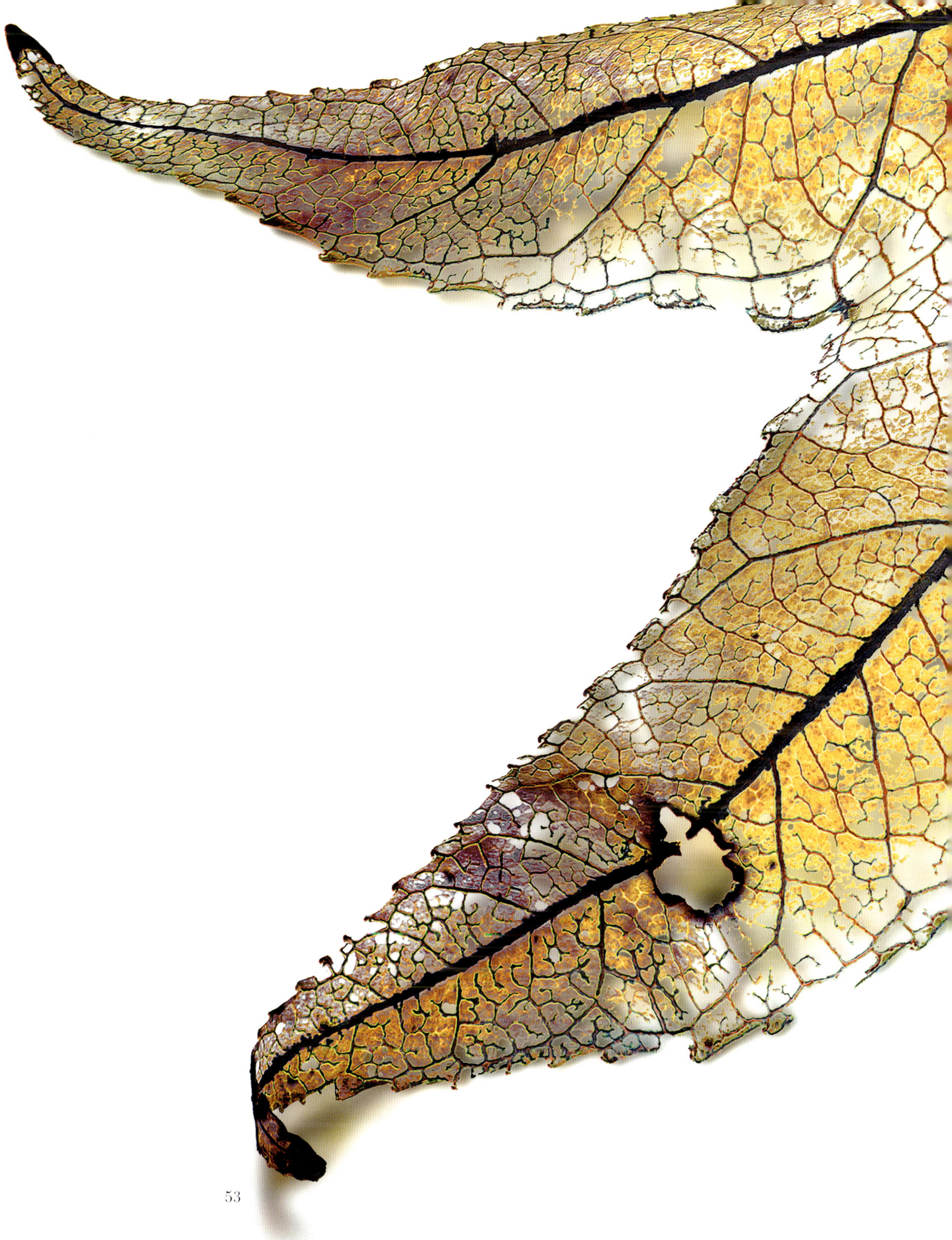

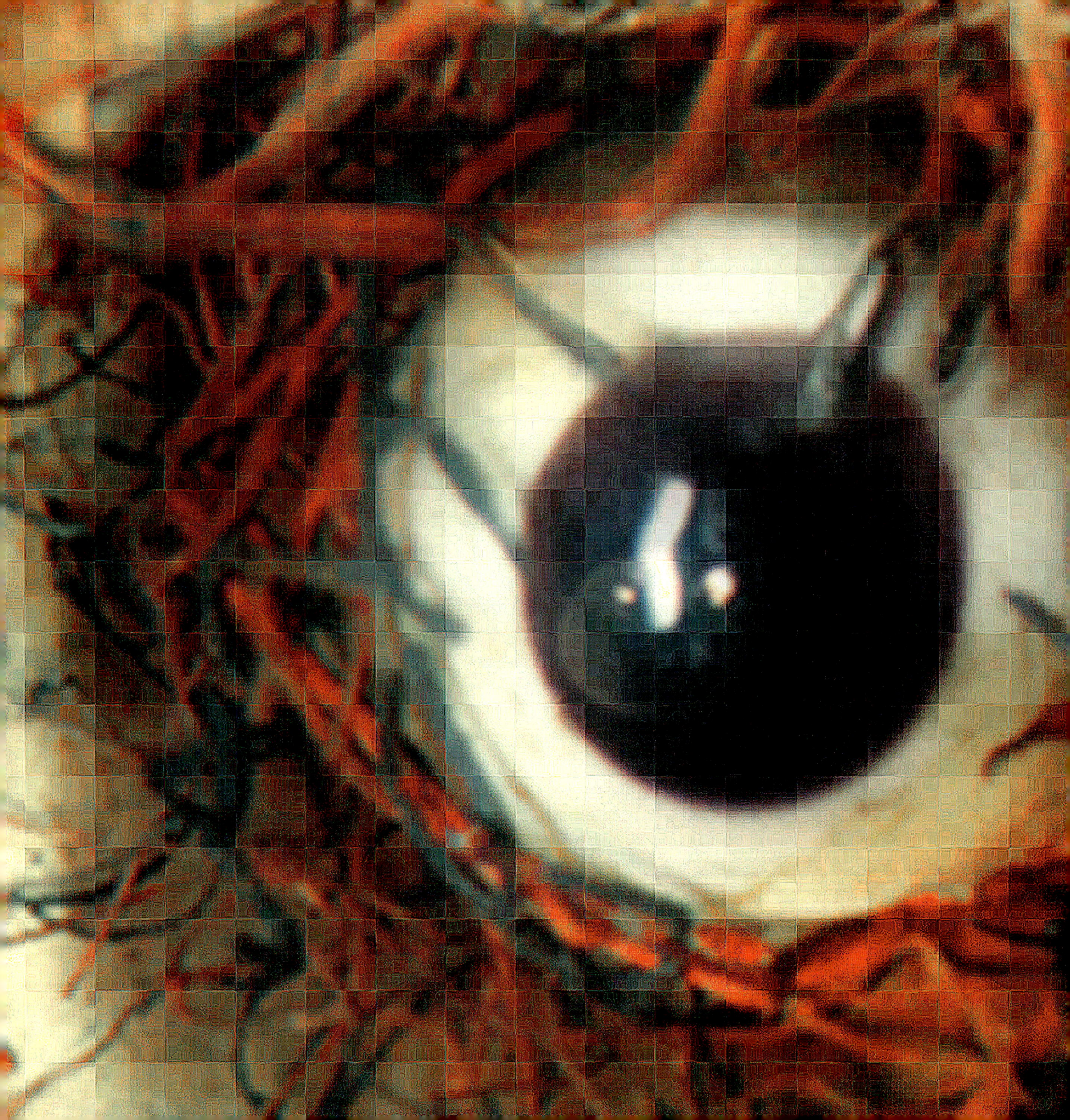

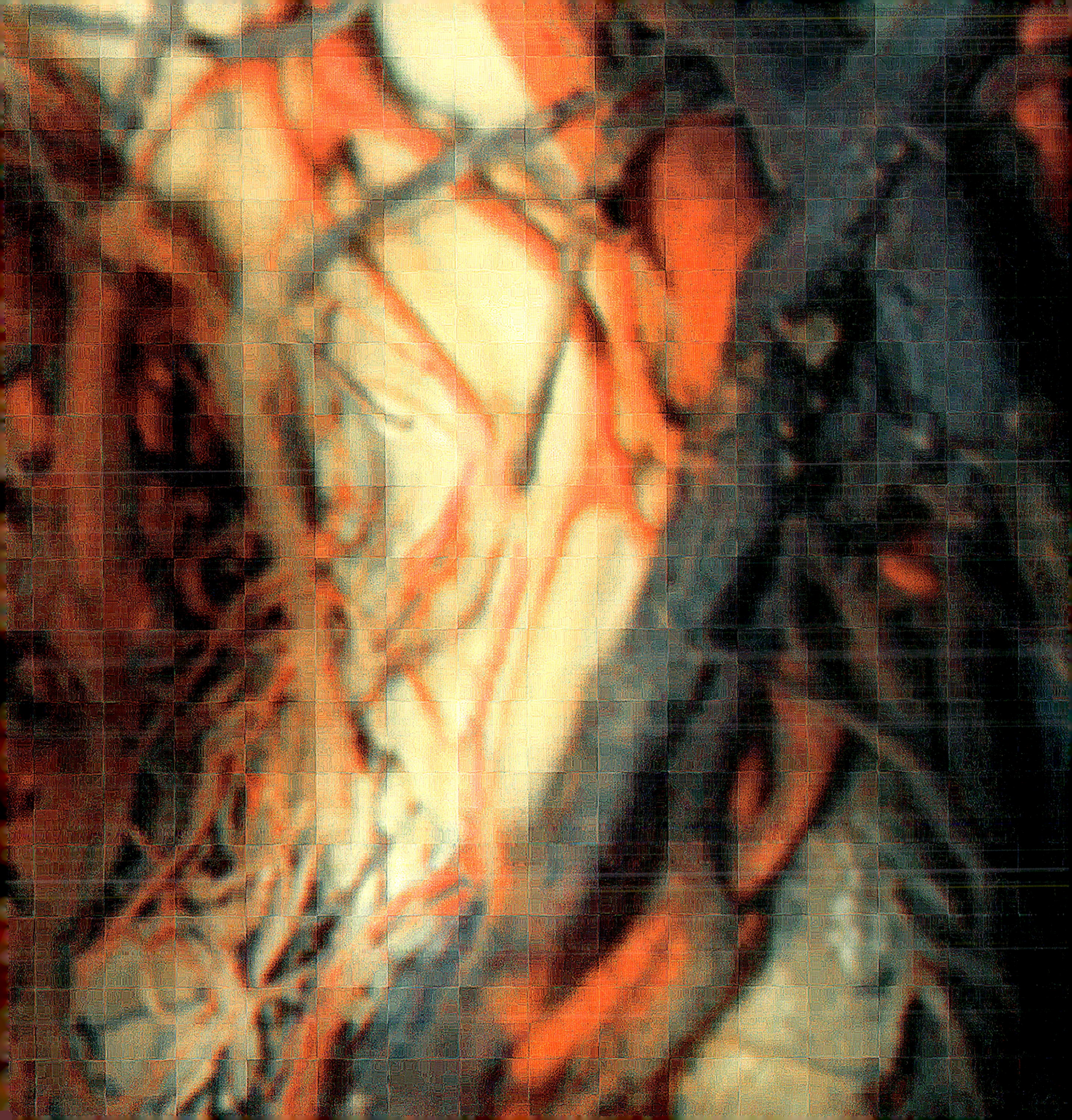

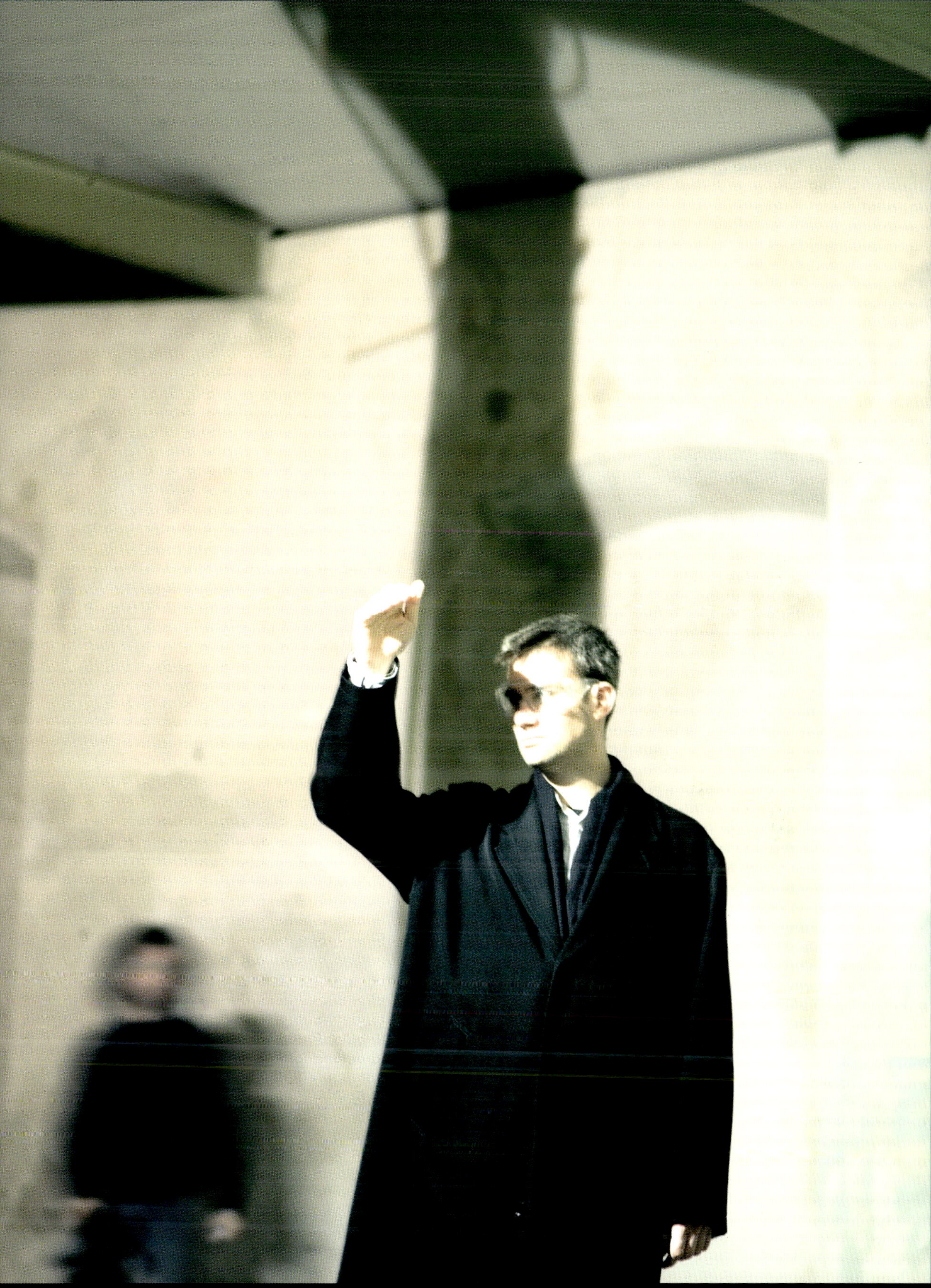

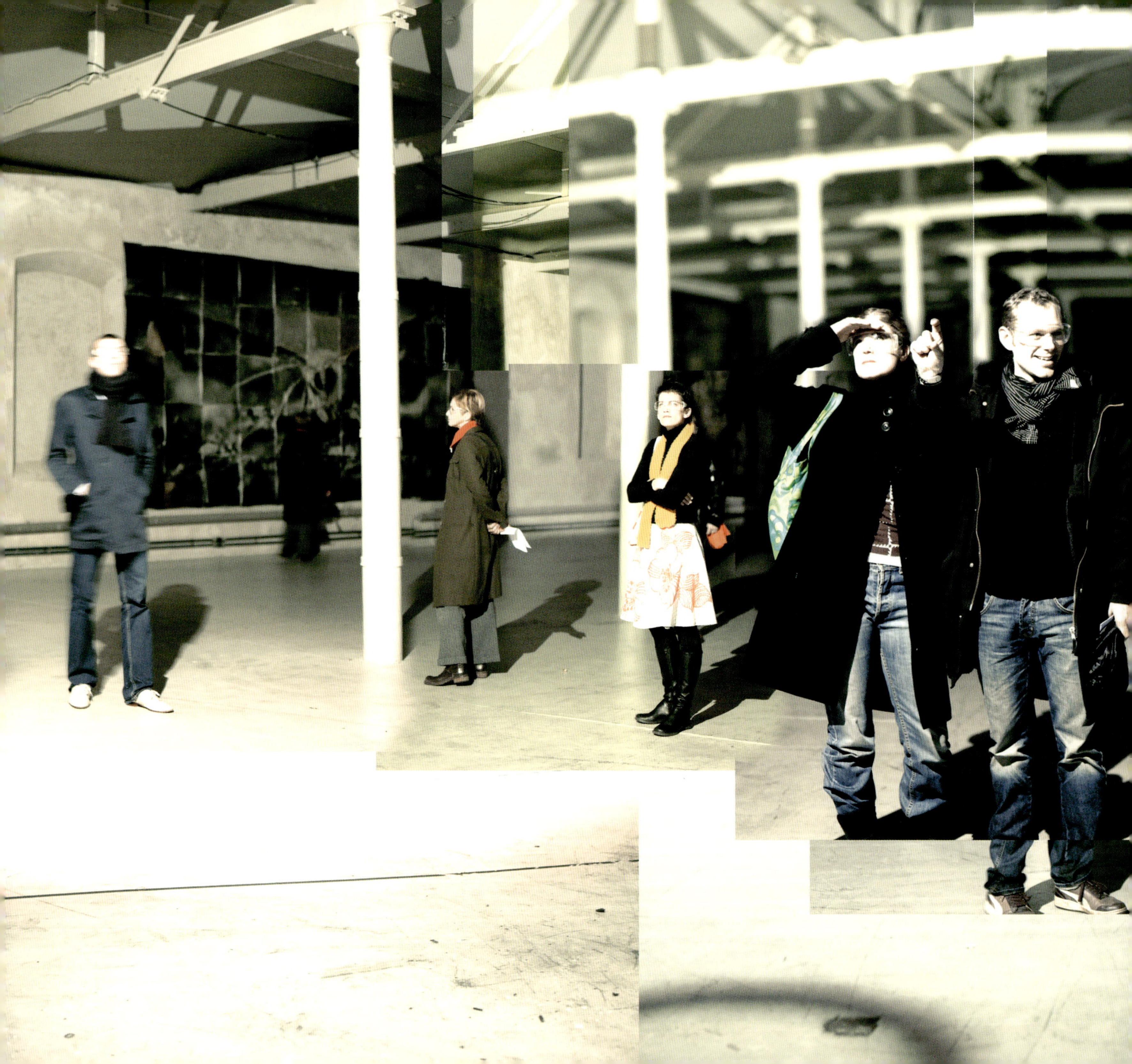

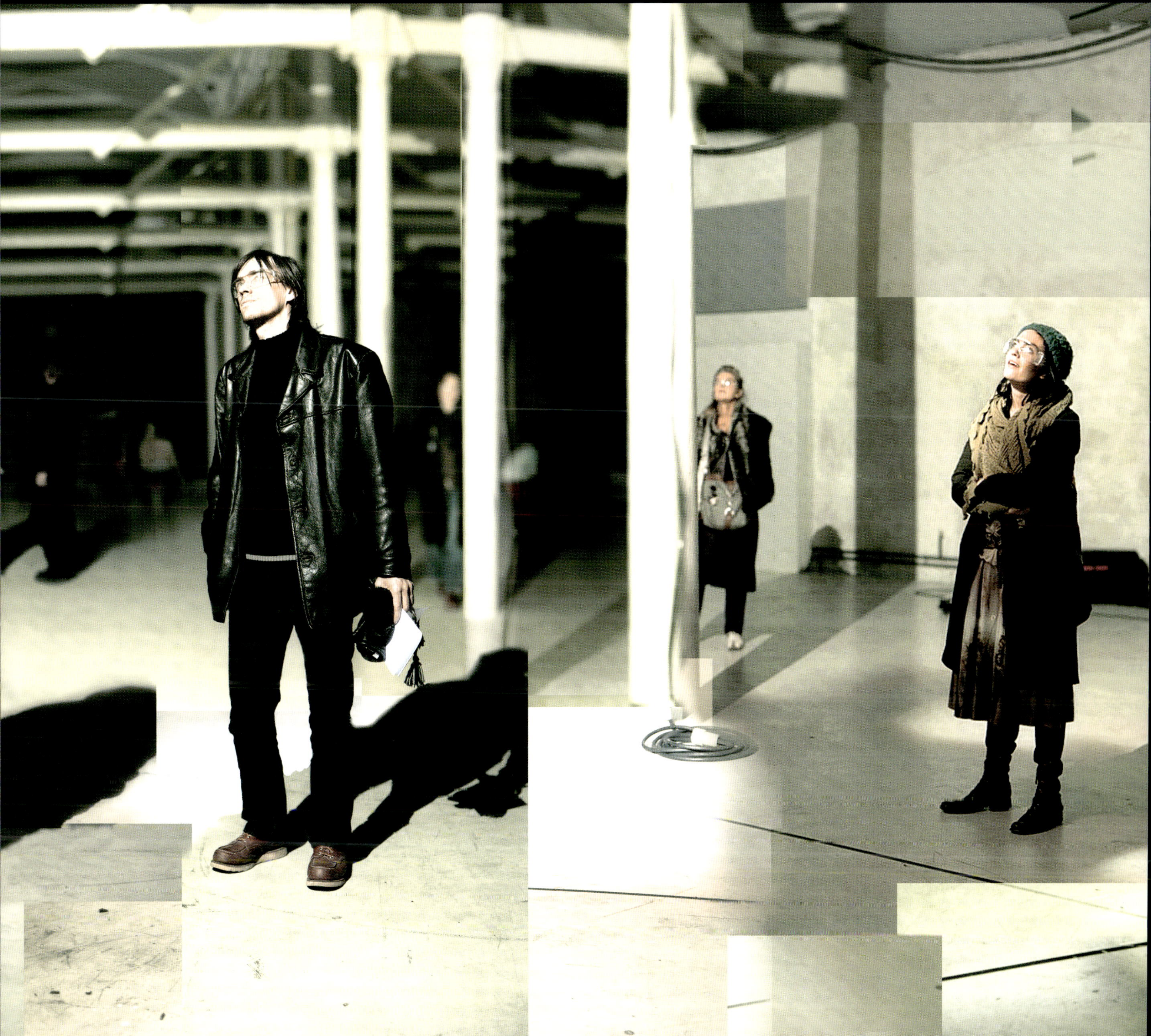

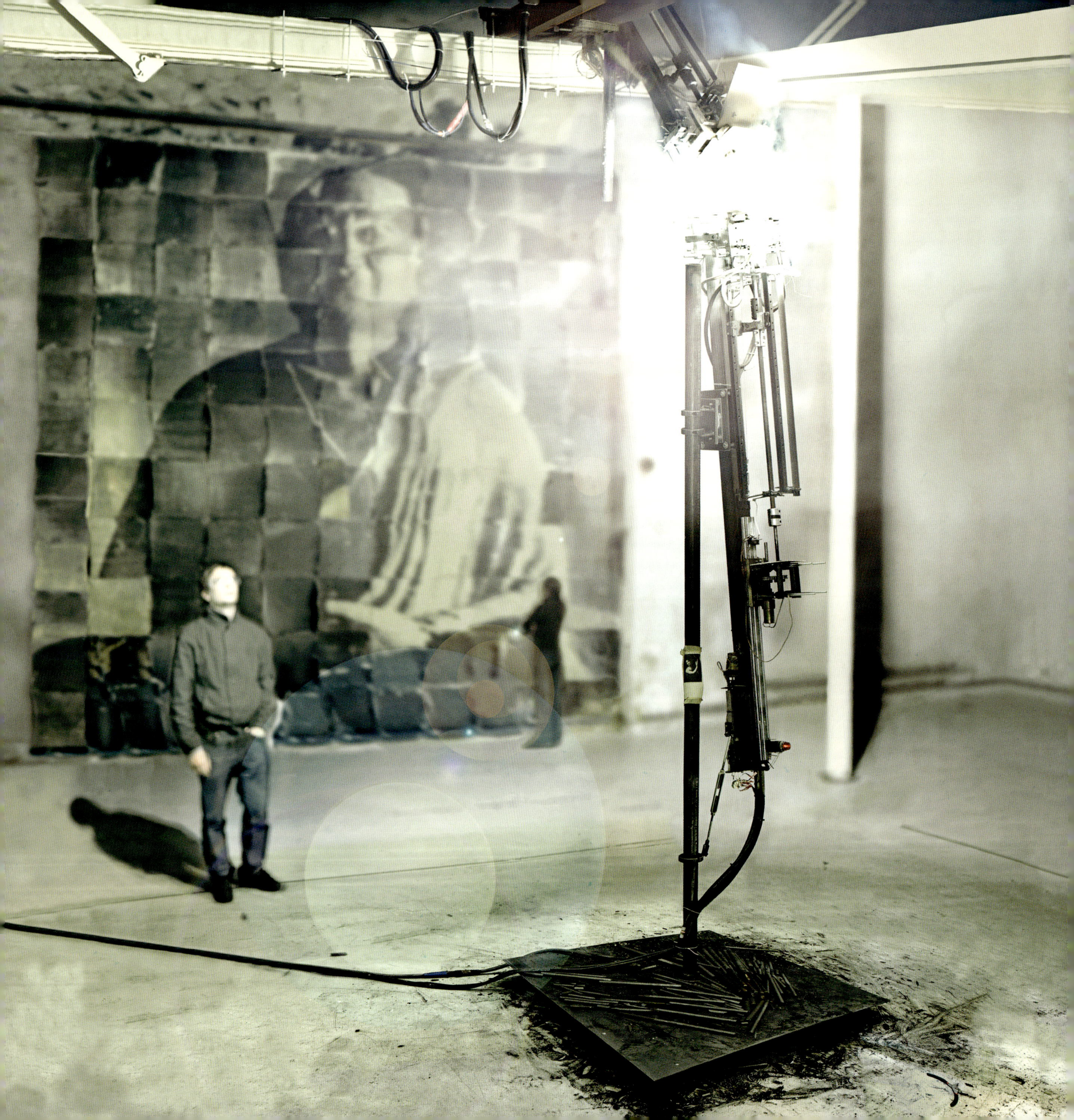

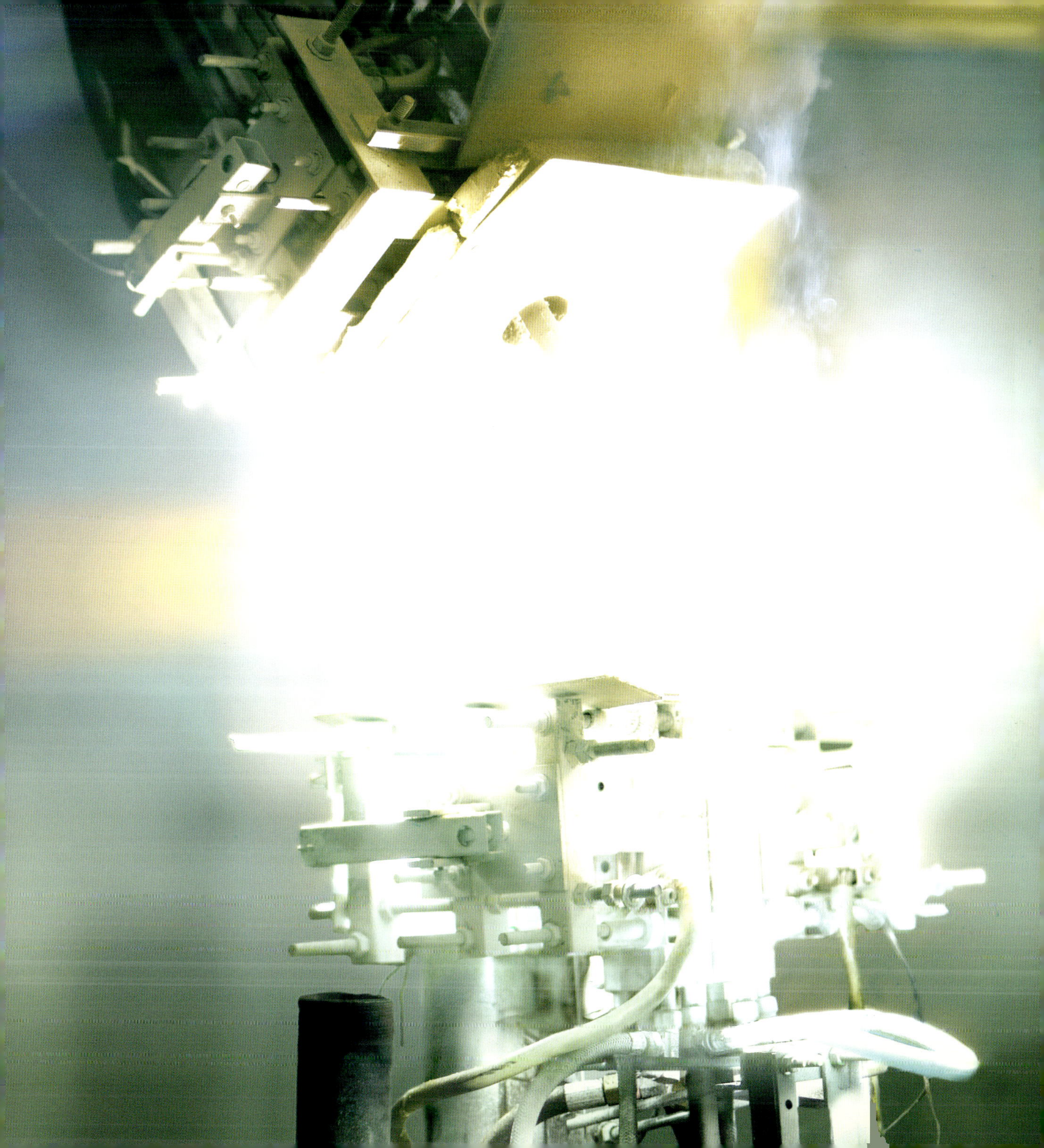

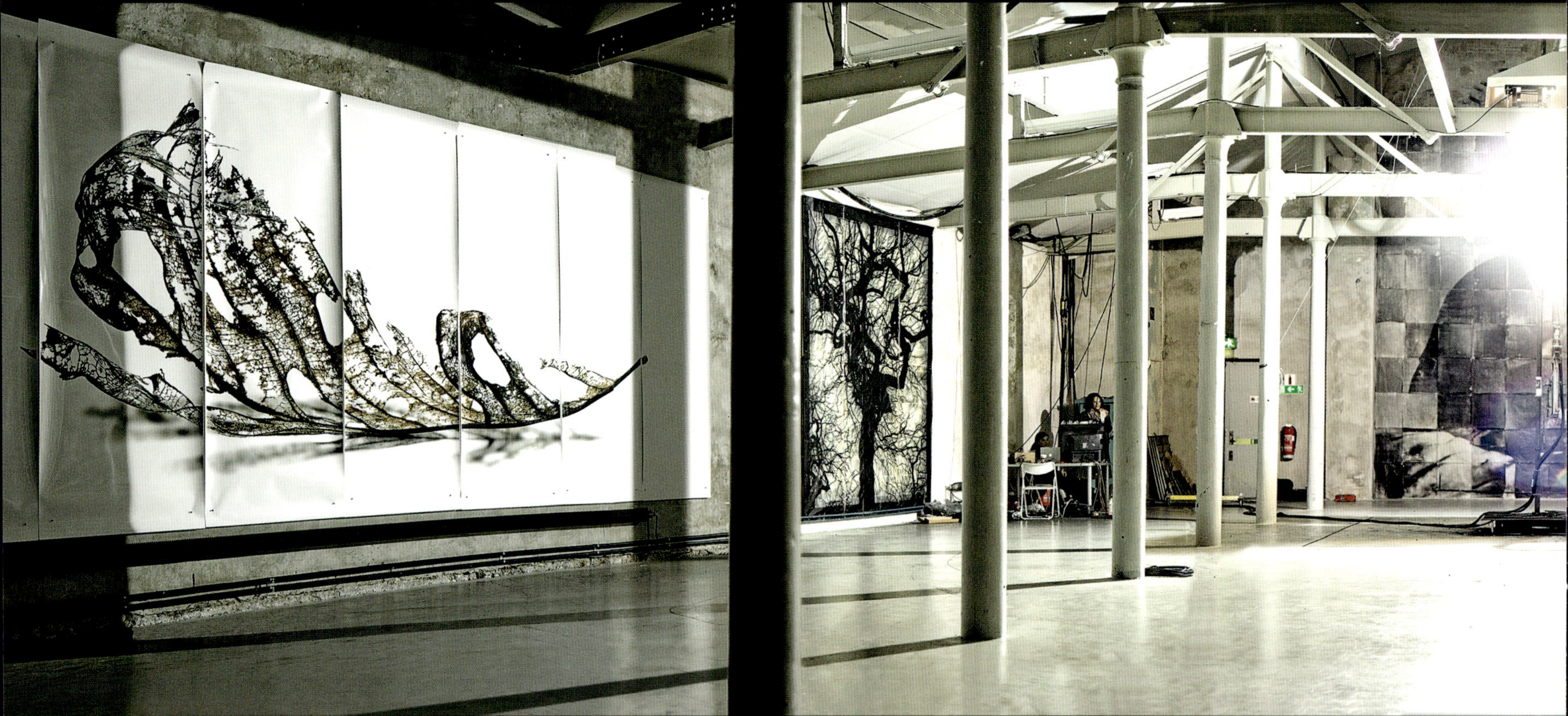

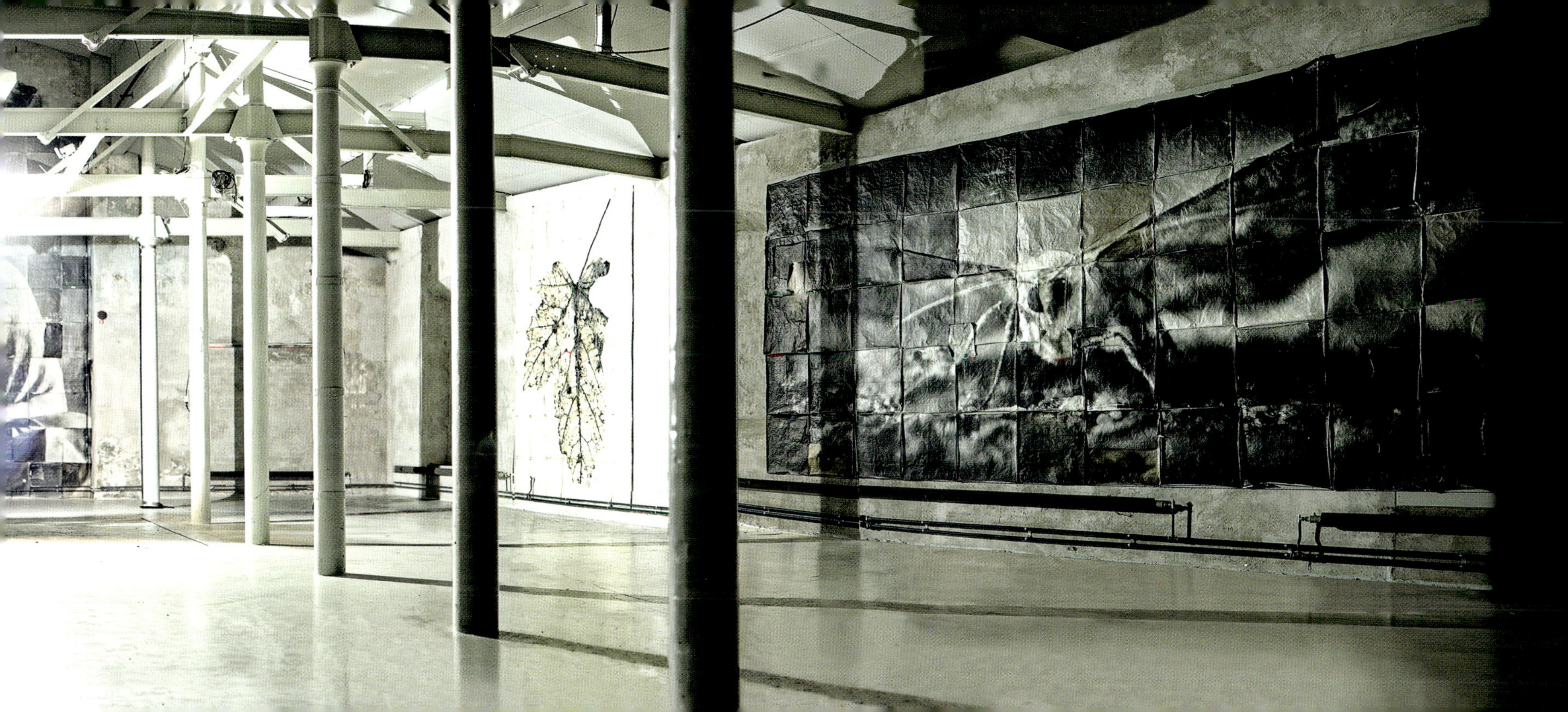

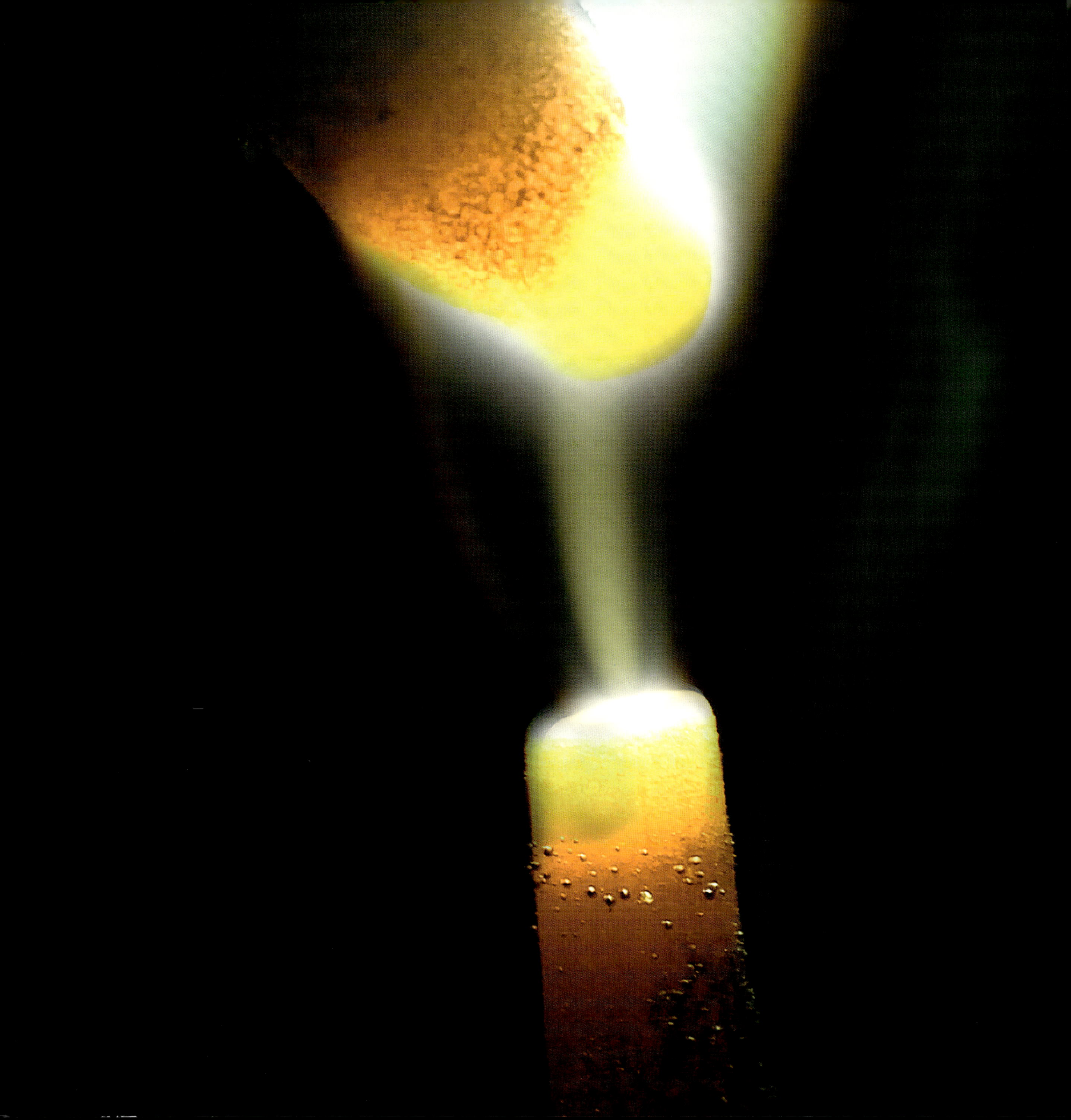

M + D
STARN

LEONARDO'S
ST. JOHN
OR
THIS
IS MY
MIDDLE
FINGER

Leonardo's St. John
or
This is my middle finger

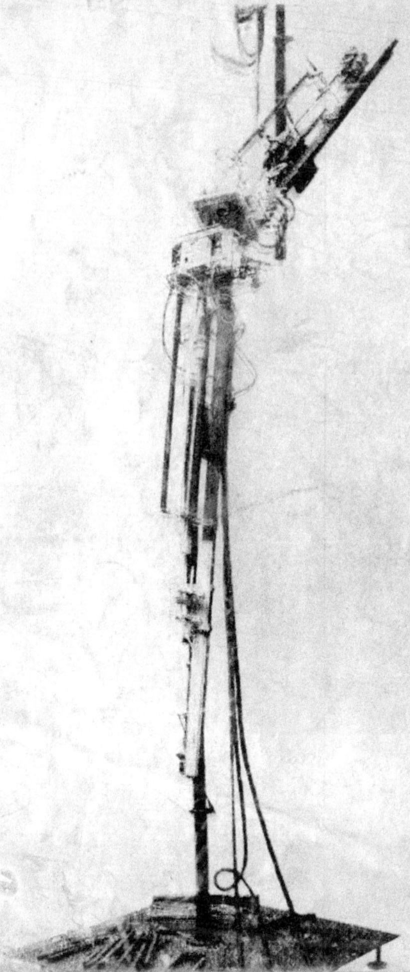

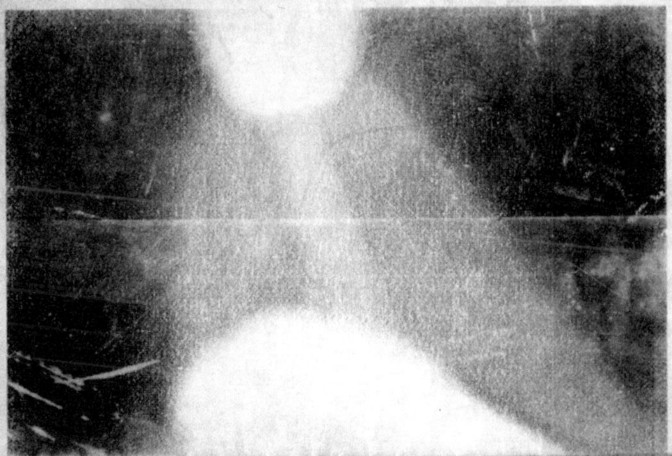

The keeper of the arc lamp needs to wear SPF 50 sunblock otherwise will be badly sunburned by the end of the day. all visitors to the lamp must wear polycarbonate eye protection for their retinas. Like the sun, … *my middle finger* emits the full spectrum including harmful UV light/radiation at close proxity.

An arc lamp is a device that produces light by the bridging of electrons through the air with a high current maintained between two carbon rod electrodes. The rods are touched and then slowly drawn apart; as the rods separate the electrical current remains attached and in an arc flows across the gap in an intensely brilliant and violent ionized path. A current of 44,000 watts of electricity bursts forth from one carbon rod into the other producing a tempeature of 6000 degrees (the melting temp of steel is more than 3000 degrees cooler.) The tips of the carbon rods are heated to incandescence, also creating light. The rods are slowly vaporized during the process and the lampkeeper needs to regularly adjust to maintain the arc.

carbon is black:

Black is the complete absence of light, an emptiness, and necessarily emptiness is waiting for anything or everything to fill it.[1] Emptiness implies the potential for existence and change. This emptiness is black; an absence of light meets our eyes, even while there is light going past our eyes. Light itself is invisible as it travels, it cannot be seen except when something is in its path, then light is reflected off its surface and the presence of light becomes noticeable. An astronaut in space seems surrounded by black, but he or she is surrounded by light in emptiness and with nothing for the light to bounce off of-empty space swallows all light. The sun shines invisibly, and the photons spread out in all directions. Light travels as blackness through empty space but if we look at the sun we see its photosphere, we see the explosion of plasma. **Black is emptiness, the complete absence of light.**

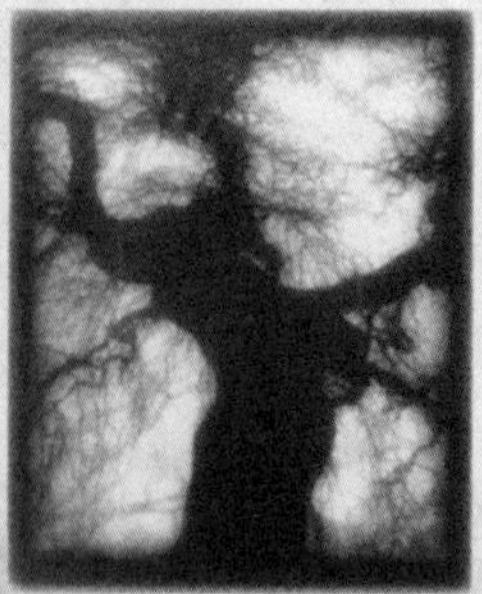

1. Sunyata-Emptiness, The Sanskrit root su also conveys the concept of being swollen with possibility. It is most important not to confuse emptiness with total nothingness.

But Black is the complete collection of light, when looking at a black object you see no light reflected from it, the wavelength s of light have been absorbed into the molecules of its surface giving you none back. Something that appears to be white has no light absorbed within it; snow or piece of

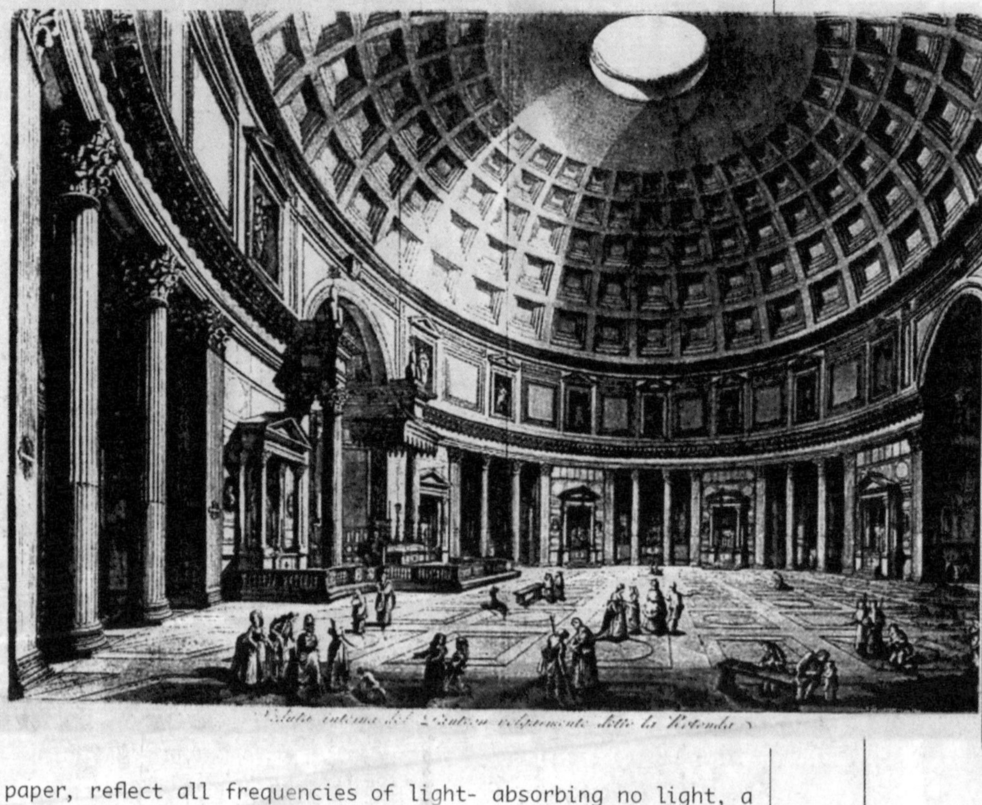

paper, reflect all frequencies of light- absorbing no light, a green leaf actually absorbs all colors except green. A piece of charcoal, carbon distilled from a tree, absorbs all frequencies, the entire spectrum of light, and is black. **Black is complete absorption of light.**[2]

2 Molecules are made of atoms and atoms contain electrons. It is often useful to think of these electrons as being attached to the atoms by springs. The electrons and their attached springs have a tendency to vibrate at specific frequencies. Similar to a tuning fork or even a musical instrument, the electrons of atoms have a natural frequency at which they tend to vibrate. If a light wave of a given frequency strikes a material with electrons having the same vibrational frequencies, then those electrons will absorb the energy of the light wave and transform it into vibrational motion. (The light waves that are not of the same frequency of the atoms of the object will reflect off the surface and we see only that frequency of light [color] 'painting' the surface of the object.) (Atoms that absorb all frequencies of light and reflect no light, such as carbon atoms, are therefore black.)

Black is, contradictorily, both the lack of and the collection of light. Both the void and the reservoir of what we need. A black hole, where light and we are pulled without choice. Suction filled with everything - but still a void. At night, a dilated pupil is starved for light-opened wide to swallow as much as it can. The holes in the sphere of your skull let illumination into your mind. Trees are built of light, light turned into carbon through photosynthesis.[4-5]

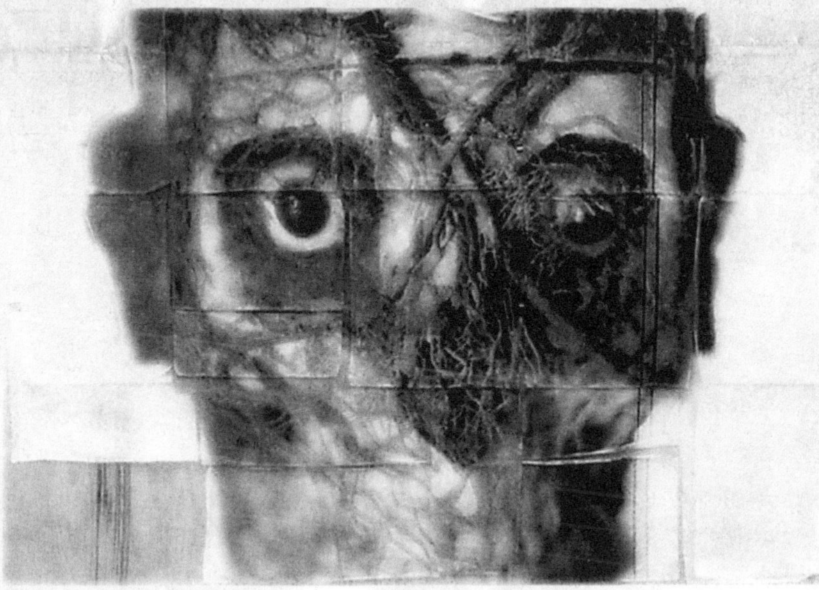

a sculpture made in 1763 in Naples; an alchemical experiment, in contemporary reports supposed to have been created by injecting a servant with a metallic solution of mercury mixed with lead which slowly coursed throughout the body and eventually "metalicized" the entire circulatory system. The soft flesh was then dissolved revealing the solidified myriad veins , arteries and capillaries leaving the skeleton and eyes caged within.
The Alchemist was the Prince of Sansevero, Raimondo di Sangro, it was said that he could also create blood and had discovered how to make an eternal flame (with crushed skull, phosphorus and magnesium). Alchemy is the search for the pure, symbolized as gold[5B], the search is performed through *Solve* and *Coagula*- meaning to dissolve and to solidify. The first step is to rip apart and look deep within, the dark,at the Black, the blackest black there is- the *nigredo*, eventually leading to discovery and to the whitening- the *albedo*. Take off the skin- it ain't no sin to look beneath there is light flowing in the veins.

Light is power, knowledge, it is what you want, it is what you need, it is satisfaction, fulfillment, truth, and purity. It is history, the future, the past, it is contradiction, spirituality, God, Satan, your body, your soul, time. Light is what we fear and hate. It is outside Plato's cave, it is

arbon is present the atmosphere as bon dioxide, this m of carbon is sumed by plants ing photosynthesis. breathe the air the atmosphere to d our bodies oxygen ough our blood eam, the waste duct of the oxygen's sage through our lies is carbon xide. This same bon is in turn noved from the in the cells of leaves. Through torespiration, ht is inhaled and ivates the process manufacturing kness from light.

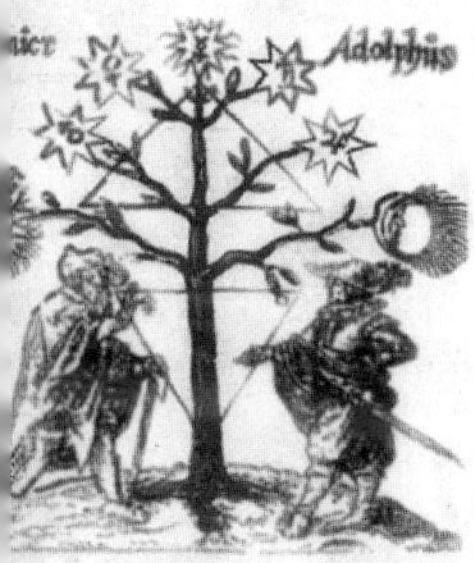

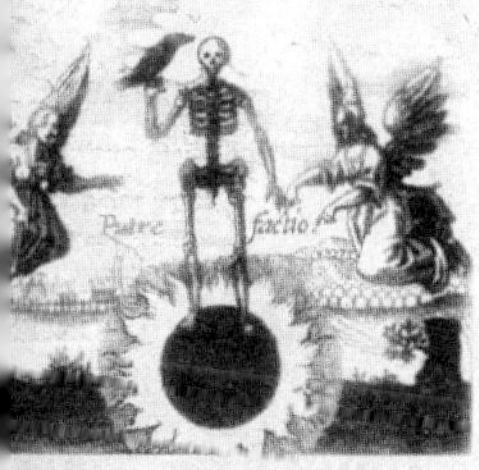

carbon dioxide inhaled on the erside of the f, oxygen is aled leaving the ck carbon, which s through the ns creating the y of the tree. es are built of ht; light turned o carbon through tosynthesis-a nsformation of ht into dark sical matter- an hitecture of inky ck darkness. Trees more carbon than thing else.

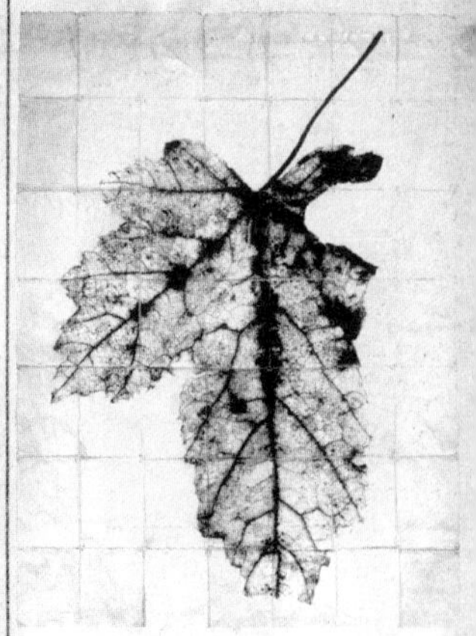

5 *Black Carbon, pulsing and streaming through the veins. is the absorption of light and is the light that controls me. Our veins are filled with the light, the light is us. We are buckets of blood flowing through miles of tangles.*

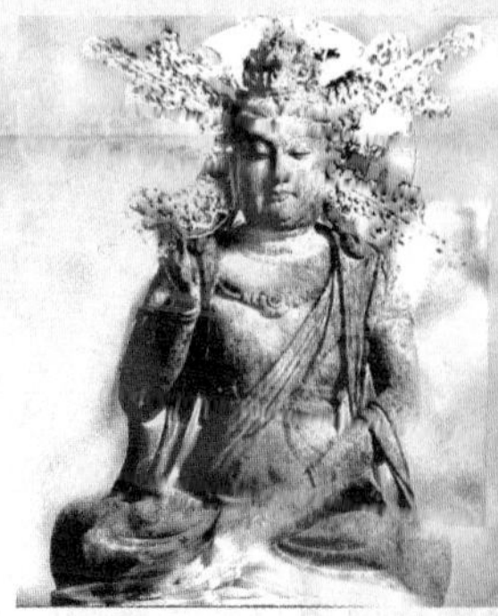

5B *gilded Buddha image, gold equals light, light equals everything. fullspectrum....*

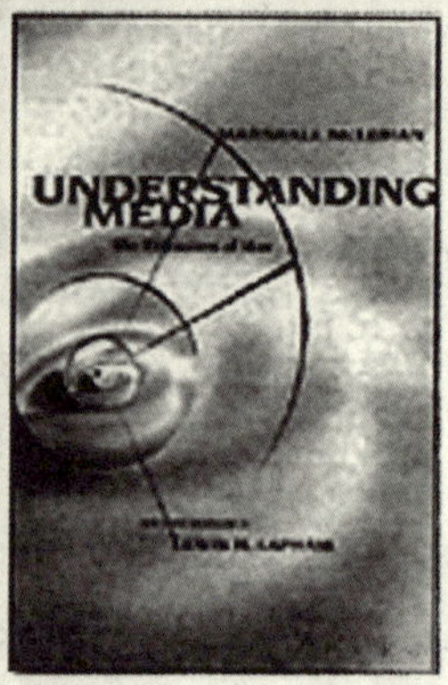

Mcluhan's information, Light is language, Light is thought, light is what attracts us, light has gravity. Light is what controls every decision and action we take. The Sun pulls the planets around itself, the back porch light pulls the moth from the darkness.6 Trees are made from light and grow towards it.7 The gravity of light is so broad and vast it is not noticed. We exist in it we are pulled by all these

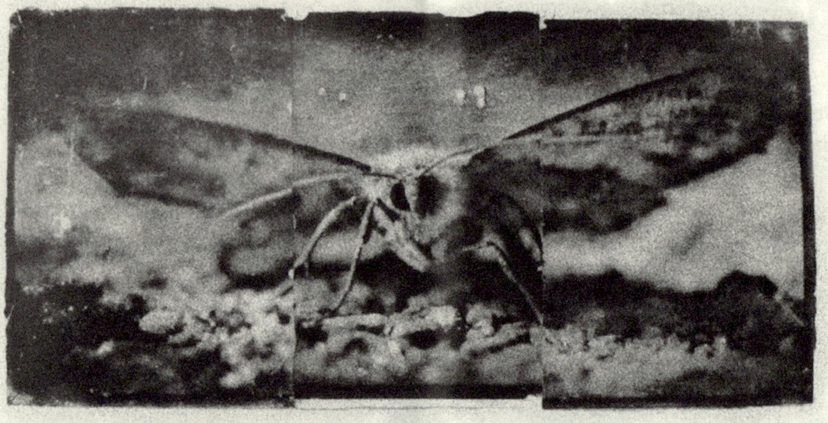

controls simultaneously, like the oceans held to the Earth, but pulled towards the Moon. We are always falling to the gravities we have made or were given to us.

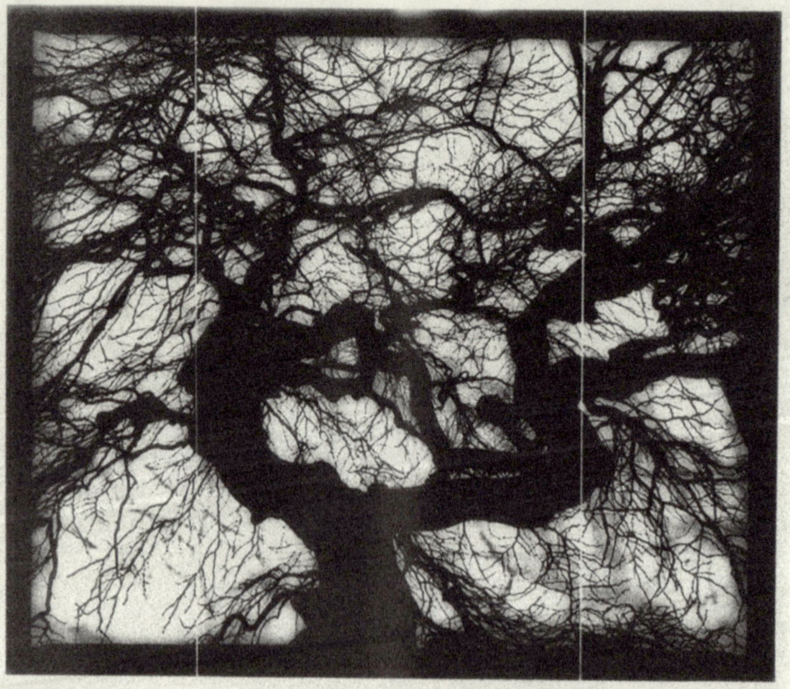

The structure of thought is not sequential. It is layers upon layers of ideas, memories and emotions all connected or able to connect. None of the ideas necessarily comes first. It is rhizomatic; connections happen at any point, there is no hierarchy, it is separate and connected. Yet there is

6 *When looking into the deep, velvety black eyes of moths you see emptiness (the true nature of reality) and (the absorption of) light. Moths choose darkness but search for light. The light that is love and hate, the void and reservoir of desires,*

7 *The black body of the trees is the black of written information, is the black ink on the pages of books through thousands of years of transcribed thought and creation. the trees are containers of comprehensive information and layered knowledge. The interconnectedness of trees are like dendritic neurons in the brain, a network of information and links. The layered dendritic branches are in relation to the complexities of knowledge, understanding, memory and imagination; Trees are light written in the calligraphy of the sun.- "One day when the Emperor Hiuan-Tsong, of the Tang Dynasty-, says the Taokia-ping-yu-che, "was at work in his study , a tiny Taoist priest, no bigger than a fly, rose out of the inkstand lying on his table, and said to him. 'I am the Genius of ink; my name is Hei-song-che'-tchoo [Envoy of the Black Fir]; and I have come to tell you that whenever a true sage shall sit down to write, the Twleve Divinities of Ink will appear upon the surface of the ink he uses.'" L-Encre de Chine,- by Maurice Jametel. Paris, 1882 black is the complete absorption of light.*

order to this confusion like capillaries in your body or in a leaf. These dendritic forms make structure and force fluid, dynamic and broad. The completely black tree colapses like a shadow, destroying the heirorchal structure enabling movement between all points, like space and matter in a black hole. All locations become accessible to one another in this way the mind interprets the constant feed of information. Your mind decodes and understands based on a lifetime of constructions, memories, desires and learning. Vision is a humble construction, pieced together with tape- every minute of your life. The structure of thought is a living dendritic accumulation of intersections and layers. The fingers untangle what the eyes can't.

Carbon is black:

Towards the end of the Enlightenment, at the turn of the 18th to the 19th Century, empirical science was gaining momentum, and alchemy was being pushed further into the shadows. Empirical science's first order of business to understanding the universe was to identify what exactly it and we all are made of. In 1800 Alessandro Volta invented the battery- the first sustained electric current, leading to experiments in Electrolysis. In electrolysis, electric current is immersed in liquid compound elements through two conductors – the anode (positive charge) and the cathode (negative charge). Atoms in the liquid compound are then attracted to the conductor of the opposite charge – rendering the compound elements into their pure states.[8]

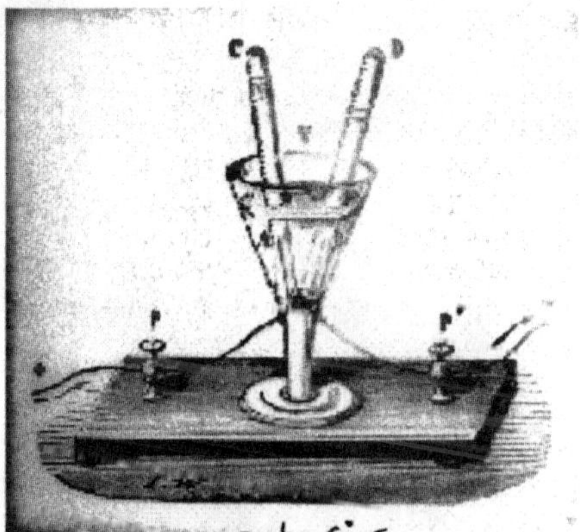

elecrcolysis

At this time, science, philosophy and art were closely aligned, there was no wall between them yet; this was the early days of the Industrial Revolution, and there was a recognition of powerful and new way of not only understanding the world but molding it to our needs. Natural Philosophers were the heros showing the way and there was an enormous appetite for science among the public. Humphry Davy, a young chemist in London who had formulated the theory of electrolysis and had discovered many elements had come to personify this new science. Davy was not only a great chemist, he was a fascinating lecturer, giving sometimes explosive demonstrations at the Royal Institution, which were so popular that all the people coming in their carriages made the Albemarle Street entrance so crowded that it became the first one-way street in London.

8 This discovery reordered the conception of the universe; it proved that matter itself is not inert, it is charged and held together by electrical forces. In the time since Newton there had been only one force, gravity, holding the stars and planets together, but electrolysis showed there was a second cosmic force operating at the tiny distances within the invisible, almost unimaginable, world of chemical atoms. Gravity may be the guiding force of Mass; but it was now known that electricity is the guiding force of Matter.

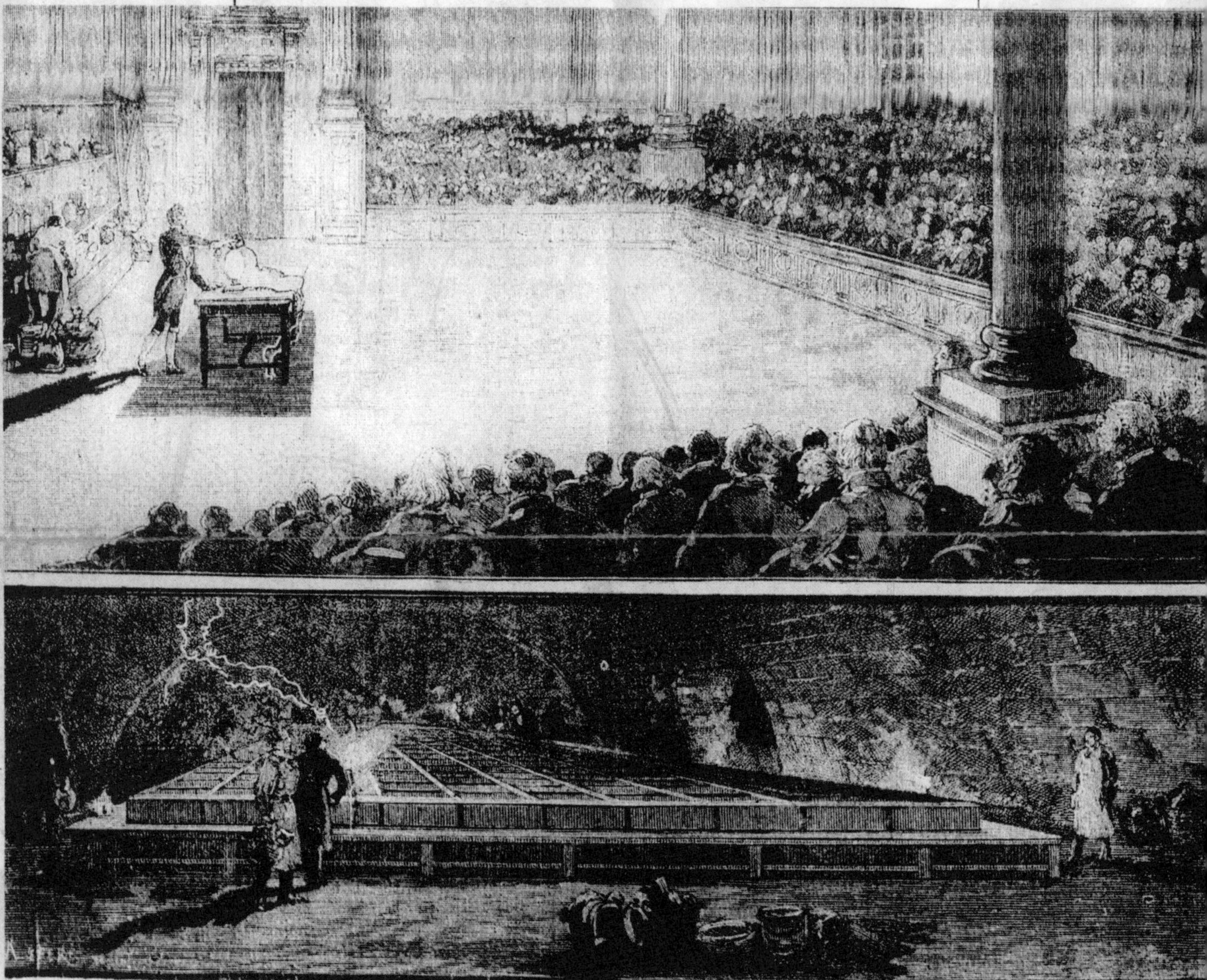

FIG. I. — EXPÉRIENCE DE DAVY A LA « ROYAL INSTITUTION »

In 1804, the largest battery ever created was made for Davy-it consisted of two thousand cells and filled the huge basement of the Royal Institution lecture hall. Upstairs he connected the current to two pieces of charcoal (pure carbon) and an explosion of light quivered and clashed between them. Davy wrote, 'an arc so vivid that even the sunlight compared with it appeared feeble'.[8B]

He did not furtherdevelop this use, but the carbon arc lamp was the first light that lit the cities of the world (Paris in 1841), the housing of the carbon arc lamps are still in use on the Brooklyn Bridge (but were long ago modified to incandescent light)[9] and Edison's first light bulb in 1879 had a filament thread made of carbon.

8B *#this is the very first creation of what we call "artificial light" as opposed to candles, lanterns etc… Although it is a semblance of the plasma in the Sun with its flow of free electrons, it is created through human intervention altering the natural state of things producing another state of nature.*

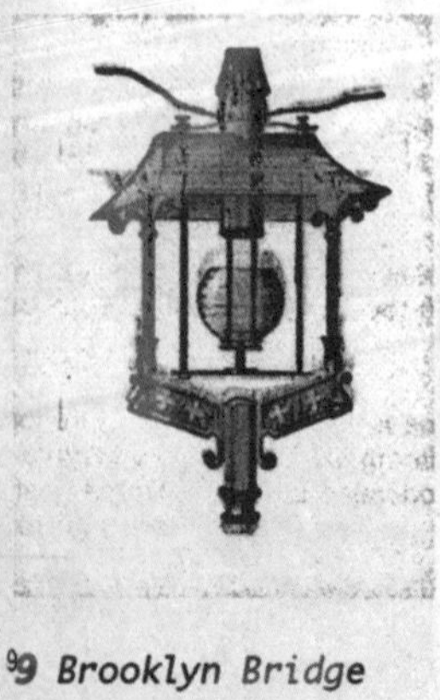

9 Brooklyn Bridge Arc Lamp fixture

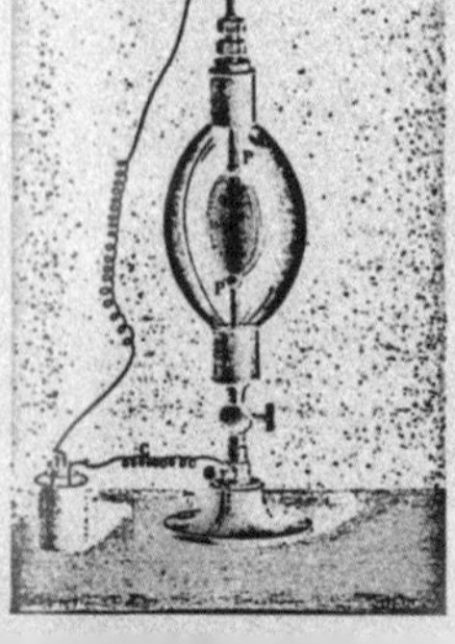

The sun has unfathomable depths-1,000,000 Earths would fit inside. The tremendous violence of constant explosion will continue another four billion years. The reality set in motion by those enormous fires exists as cycles of birth and decay. . Physics and art turn the light of the Sun into knowledge and creation, and the light of consciousness into theorems, words and images.

The triumph of science is discovery, rendering previous knowledge obsolete and antique. The heights reached with all that knowledge, faith and art are ephemeral.The Sun's force and size and age dwarfs our achievements and goals, the fire burns and destroys all efforts to encompass it. Its light absorbs the dimmer lights.

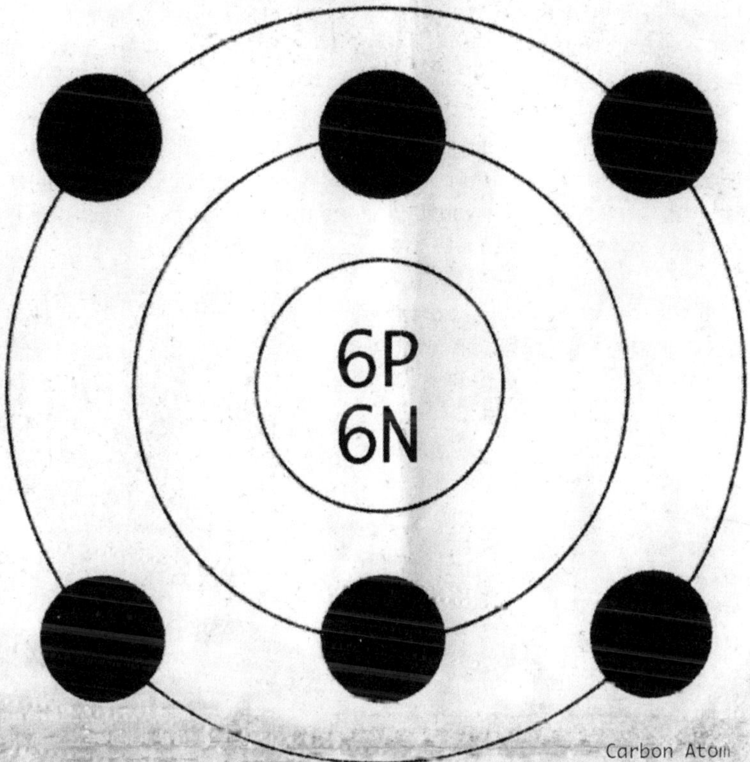

Carbon Atom

***10** Carbon Carbon, C, is a non-metallic element found in Group IVb of the periodic table. Carbon has two main allotropic forms (i.e. diamond with a relative density of 3.52 and graphite with a relative density of 2.25). *Atomic Number : 6 *Atomic Mass : 12.0115 *Melting Point : 3550 degC *Boiling Point : 4200 degC *Density : 2.25 (graphite) There are two stable Isotopes of carbon, having mass numbers 12 and 13, and four radioactive isotopes (mass numbers 10, 11, 14, and 15). Carbon-14 is used in carbon dating.*

Chemically, Carbon is unique in its ability to form many compounds containing chains and rings of carbon atoms. This property is responsible for the vast number of Organic Compounds.

Carbon compounds which incorporate other elements including hydrogen, oxygen and nitrogen are essential for life, as we know it. Without Carbon, life would not exist.

ATOM Carbon has the highest melting point of any element, a characteristic that makes it excellent as a source of thermal radiation or incandescent light. carbon in its graphite form is black and therefore an excellent absorber and emitter of light. In physics a black body is a theoretical object that absorbs 100% of the radiation (including visible light) that hits it. Therefore it reflects no radiation and appears perfectly black. In practice no material has been found to absorb all incoming radiation, carbon absorbs all but about 3%.

At a particular temperature the black body would emit the maximum amount of energy possible for that temperature. This value is known as the black body radiation.
It would emit at every wavelength of light as it has absorbed all incoming radiation. The maximum wavelength emitted by a black body radiator is infinite. Objects at around room temperature emit mainly infra-red radiation which is invisible to us. The sun emits most of its radiation at visible wavelengths, particularly yellow. Stars are approximate black body radiators. Most of the light directed at a star is absorbed. It is therefore capable of absorbing all wavelengths of electromagnetic radiation, so is also capable of emitting all wavelengths of electromagnetic radiation. Most approximate blackbodies are solids but stars are an exception because the gas particles in them are so dense they are capable of absorbing the majority of the radiant energy.[12]

12 *Lying on the beach and glancing up for an instant, I get a black sun burned into my eyes. It seems so small. A negative of the sun. Now there's a black hole in front of and through everything I look at.*

I came across something about Apollo butterflies, a species found in the Canadian Rockies. They're controlled by the sun. While the sun shines they fly in groups, and when a cloud covers over, together, they drop to the ground. When the sun reemerges, they rise up again, only to fall with the next cloud. Up and down all day long, they seem to create an idiotic poetry of puppets. Creating an embarrassing metaphor for ourselves; enlarging our perspective, we see the dominance of the sun over the Earth and humanity, revealing that we are nothing more than a meaningless silhouette, a shadow, and shadows have no control. diagram version of 'size of earth' We are slaves to gravity: No matter how much influence we exert to go higher, gravity pulls us down, again and again. Gravity binds us to history, politics, and economics; but it also ties us to the sun, a far more omnipotent force. The sun is knowledge, fulfillment, and satisfaction. The sun lights up the proceedings.
Too bright to look at, it is truth, purity. It is knowledge held at an unattainable height - eight minutes above us at the speed of light.

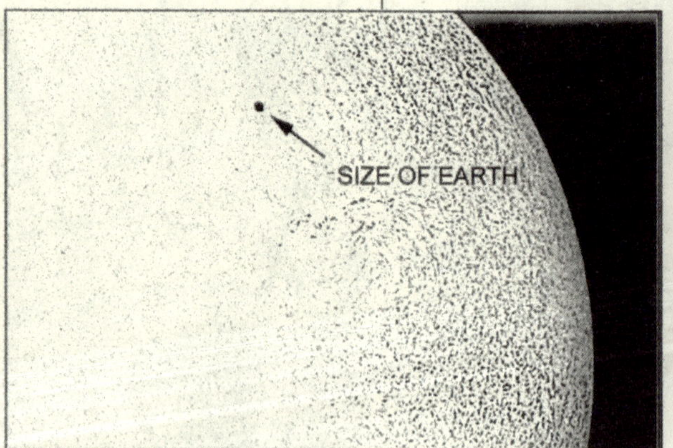

Comparative scale between the Sun and planet Earth

Carbon appears black when it is cold because it absorbs all light that hits it (reflects essentially no light) and because the thermal radiation that it emits below 750 F is invisible to our eyes. But when carbon is hot enough, its thermal radiation drifts up to the portion of the spectrum that is visible to us and we see it as glowing.

That doesn't mean that he carbon isn't 'black', it's just that black doesn't mean exactly what we normally think it does- at high temperatures black carbon is still molecularly black but our eyes see its temperature; and its temperature, its thermal

radiation, is 'white'. Though it is still black,- at 6,000 F black looks white, the black carbon rods of Leonardo's St John are so white they are too bright to even look at.
Carbon is releasing light at the same time it is black- but our vision, our perception of the thermal radiation, reveals (or presents) a negative of the black.

All carbon atoms in the universe were originally created in a star, but during that early state of creation, the nuclei and electrons are separate and essentially unattached, this is plasma. Plasma is often called the 'fourth state of matter' the other three being solid, liquid and gas. a plasma is a distinct state of atomic structure in which nuclei are stripped of electrons.

Within the incredible heat of a star atoms are not stable, but as they migrate towards the surface and the relatively cooler temperature of 100,000 degrees, carbon nuclei start collecting electrons and become complete atoms of carbon.
Billions of years later, some of those same carbon atoms were "distilled" from trees into charcoal and then consequently purified and pressed into carbon rods for us.

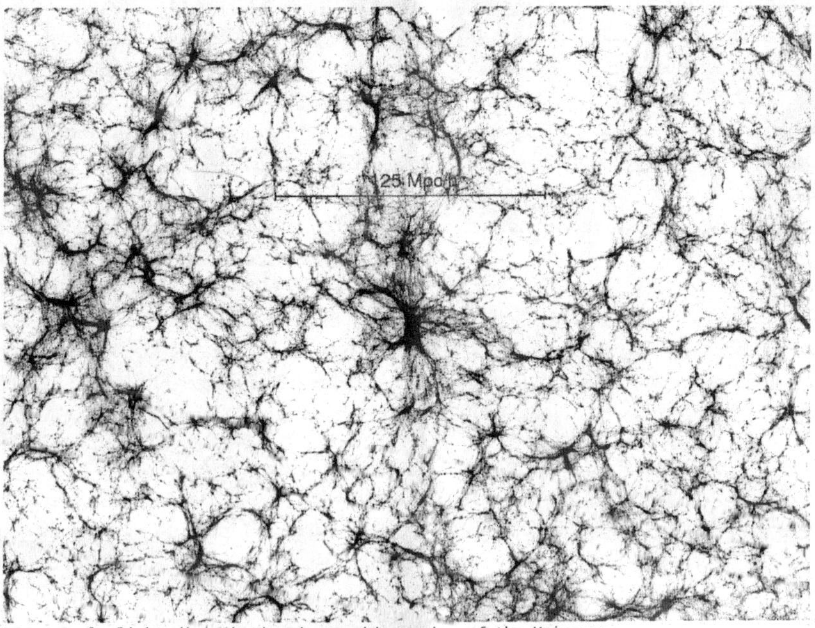

Large-scale light distribution in a cubic region of the Universe
Max-Planck-Institut fur Astrophysik

Most of the mass of the universe is contained in stars, which are of course largely plasma, actually plasmas are estimated to constitute more than 99 percent of the visible universe.
This means the state of atoms in our little world (basing our perception and experience of reality and existence) can be seen as a kind of deviation of the general state of matter. We are an aberration. Our reality is a separate reality.

"False imagination teaches that such things as light and shade, long and short, black and white are different and are to be discriminated; but they are not independent of each other; they are only different aspects of the same thing, they are terms of relation not of reality".-Buddha.

"[Niels] Bohr advocated the use of both pictures, which he called complementary to each other. the two pictures are of course mutually exclusive, because a certain thing cannot at the same time be a particle (i.e., substance confined to a very small volume) and a wave (i.e., a field spread out over a large space), but the two compliment each other."-Werner Heisenberg.

"For we see that these apparently opposite terms of one and many, form and formless, finite and infinite, are not so much opposites as complements of each other; not alternating values...but double and concurrent values which explain each other; not hopelessly incompatible alternatives, but two faces of the one reality." -Sri Aurobindo. "All those who have truly understood quantum theory...look uponit as a unified description of atomic phenomena, even though it has to wear different faces." -Niels Bohr

"The no-mind not-thinks no-thoughts about no-things." -Buddha

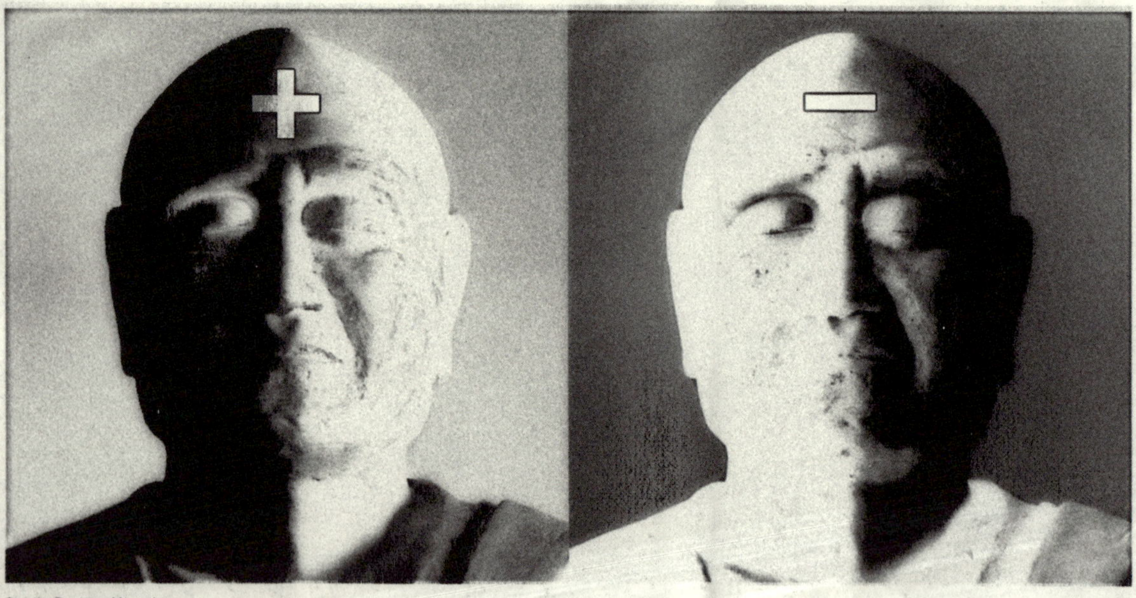

Ganjin Positive Negative

*The gold worn by time
He's a negative Dark
where there should be
light Bright where h
should be dim An 8th
century monk called
Ganjin. Light flows
though his veins. He'
a man he's a god he's
empty His useless
blind eyes see the
light inside the blac
Black is nothingness?
Or emptiness?
Or an empty vessel
filled with light.
emptiness filled with
everything. Emptiness
drunk on everything.*

"The oneness of duality: not two, and not one. This is the most important teaching: not two, and not one. Our body and mind are not two and not one. If you think your body and mind are two, that is wrong; if you think that they are one, that is also wrong. Our body and mind are both two 'and' one. We usually think that if something is not one, it is more than one; if it is not singular, it is plural. But in actual experience, our life is not only plural, but also singular. Each one of us is both dependent and independent." -Shunryu Suzuki

In ***Leonardo's St. John or This is my middle finger***, high voltage electrical current flows through the carbon rod on top (the negative electrode) and is connected momentarily to the lower carbon rod (the positive electrode) and instantly they heat up and electrons separate into the air (called thermionic

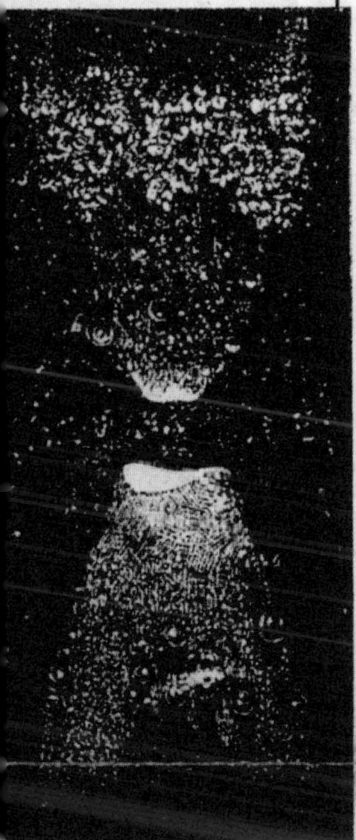

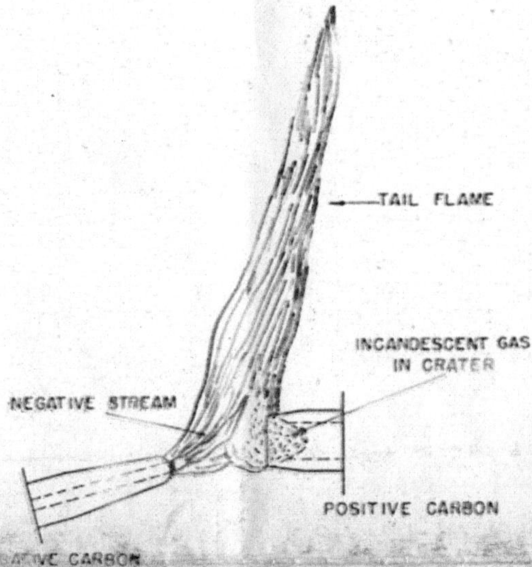

Fig. 68. Section View of Normal Arc

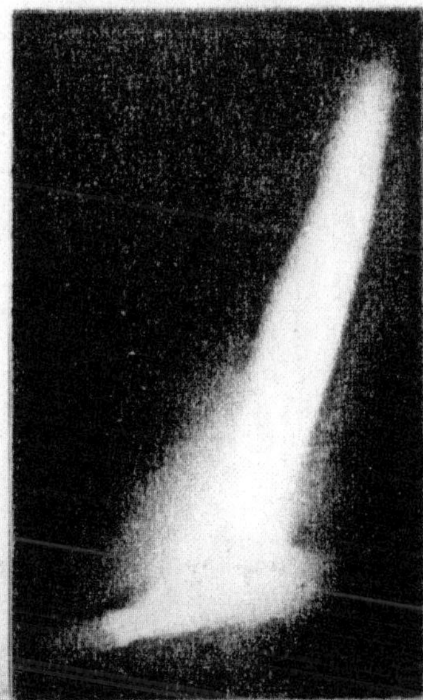

Fig. 69. Normal Appearance of Arc

emission) creating a dense, hot plasma.
The charged atoms accelerate in the strong electric field between the electrodes and crash into one another. When a collision is violent enough, it can knock electrons off of atoms or molecules and create an electron ion pair. Those electrons and ions in *...my middle finger* then accelerate in the electric field and they, in turn, can create more collisions and charged pairs. Its a run-away cascade of destruction. Plasmas are notoriously unstable - the cascades can easily get carried away, it's hard to stop the plasma from becoming so dense and electrically conducting that you can't provide enough electric power to handle it (or it melts down the point of electrical contact with the carbon rods.) The heat and violence of the energetic collisions in the arc strip off one or two of those electrons from most of the carbon atoms in the arc and they partially return to the bare-nuclei state of the star, releasing light from black.

Black carbon is both an ideal absorber and ideal emitter of light; the physics of absorbing radiation (both visible light and other waves) and the physics of transmitting exactly the same radiation are time-reversals of one another. Basically, if you run the 'movie' backward, absorption becomes emission. In the heat and electric current of the arc, the carbon atoms sublime, meaning they release into the air, most of the light you see from *my Middle Finger* is from carbon atoms burning. The incandescent carbon sublimed from the rods are particles in that flame. The fact that you can see the whole spectrum in the arc's light shows that it contains approximate tiny black bodies, carbon particles too small to see but to bright to look at.

Light, of course, classically represents seeing the truth, intelligence, information, thought.. in age of the *Enlightenment* Descartes studies of consciousness 'cognita ergo sum'.

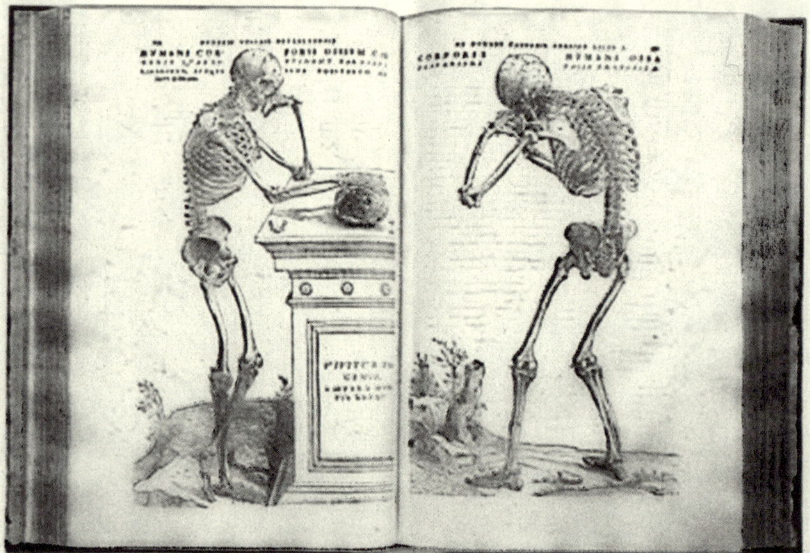

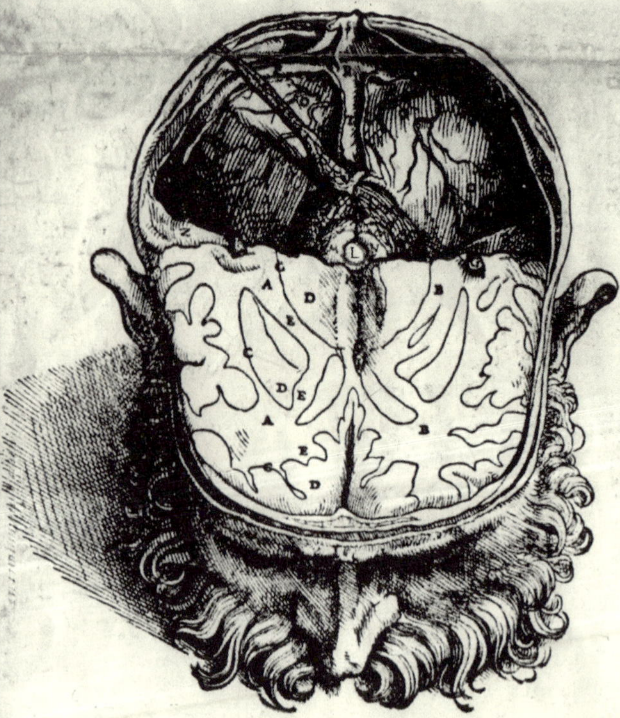

"L" Pineal gland

The center for his concept of consciousness, his 'I' was located deep in the middle back of the brain; the Pineal Gland (it is marked "L" in this diagram by the great sixteenth-century a natomist, Vesalius.) It is the only organ in the brain that is mid-line, rather than paired with left and right versions. Smaller than a pea, it sits in a splendid isolation on its stalk. coincidently Descartes pinpoint of the 'light of consciousness' is actually still known as a kind of seer in the brain, a 'third eye', the third organ in the body that rsponds to light Exposure to bright light and darkness is the strongest factor in signaling the pineal gland to secrete melatonin, among other things, and is responsible for setting our biological clocks and sleep and wake cycles.

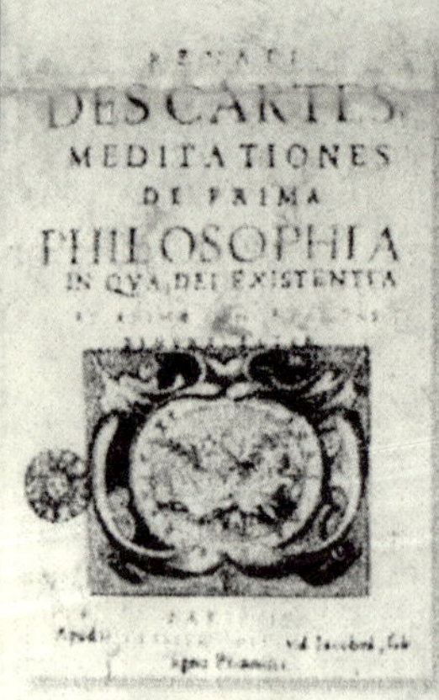

Descartes

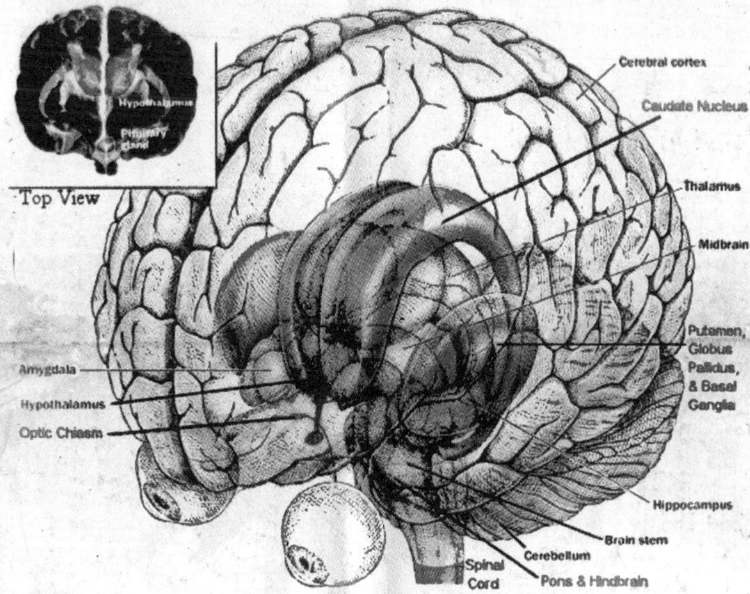
Hypothalamus
Pituitary Gland
Top View
Cerebral cortex
Caudate Nucleus
Thalamus
Midbrain
Putamen, Globus Pallidus, & Basal Ganglia
Amygdala
Hypothalamus
Optic Chiasm
Hippocampus
Brain stem
Cerebellum
Spinal Cord
Pons & Hindbrain

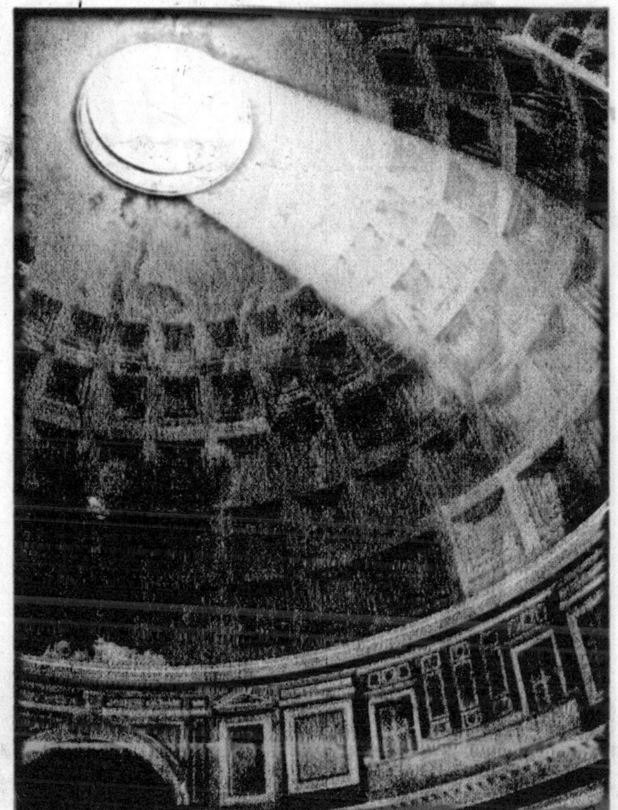

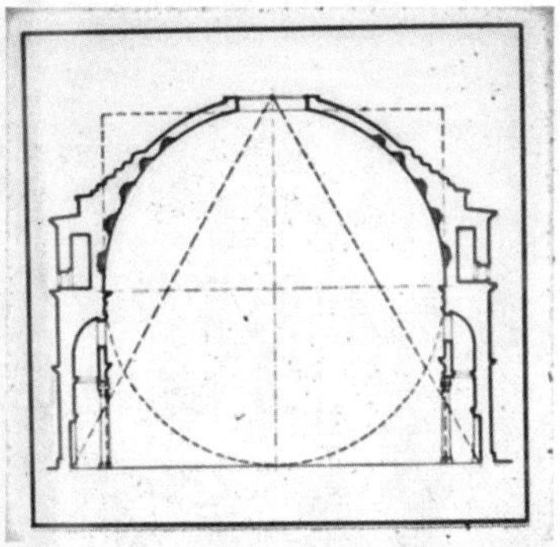

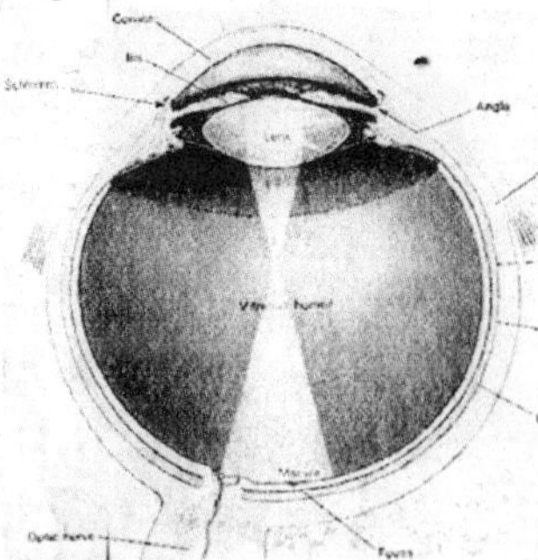

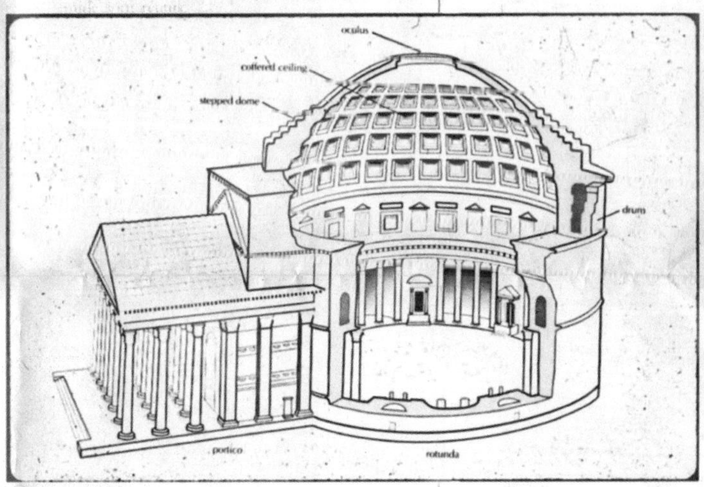
oculus
coffered ceiling
stepped dome
drum
portico
rotunda

Carbon is black

Carbon is the unbending desire to go after the unattainable, a state of un-fulfillment and longing for betterment, the conditions that hold us and drive our desires are the light that pull us, and that we push ourselves towards. Light is always the desired object or state of being. It is our intelligence, conscious of our own consciousness. Black is the absorption of light and the void of light, this is literally true, but also our enigma. The coincidence of opposites, the floating razor's edge between two truths. The carbon that flows through our veins is light and is the carbon that is absorbed in the leaf veins, pumped through the arteries of the leaves into the reaching branches of the trees, the absorbed light of thought that is the trees. The desire for the light through the tens of thousands of years of human existence.

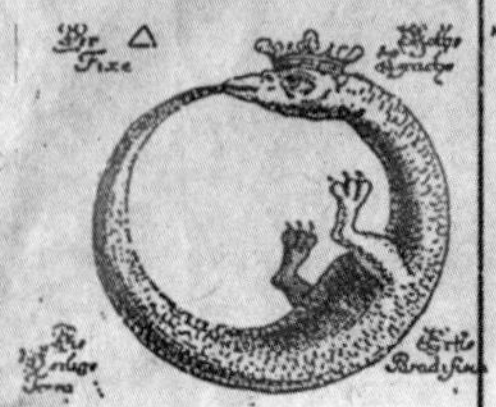

The reaching for that light through science, Davy's pure science, in 1804 the discovery that we can release the light; bring the light to our eyes, into the sphere of our skulls by running electricity through the carbon, releasing the sun's energy from the carbon. There is a happy thrill in knowing some of the secrets and the light of these secrets is my middle finger. In the shadow of earth, where one side has turned from the sun, carbon is burning brightly, illuminating the night. As Mcluhan said, the world has changed. Creating a sun, bringing the light in a full circle; the carbon is that embodied light, absorbed as black, and then released as light again, a spiral of information and impression illuminating the metaphors that are facts.

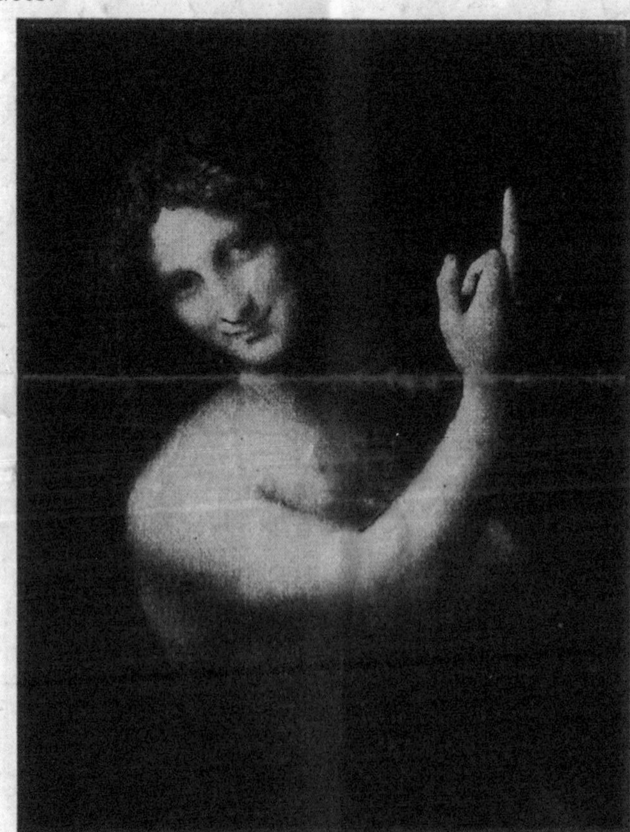

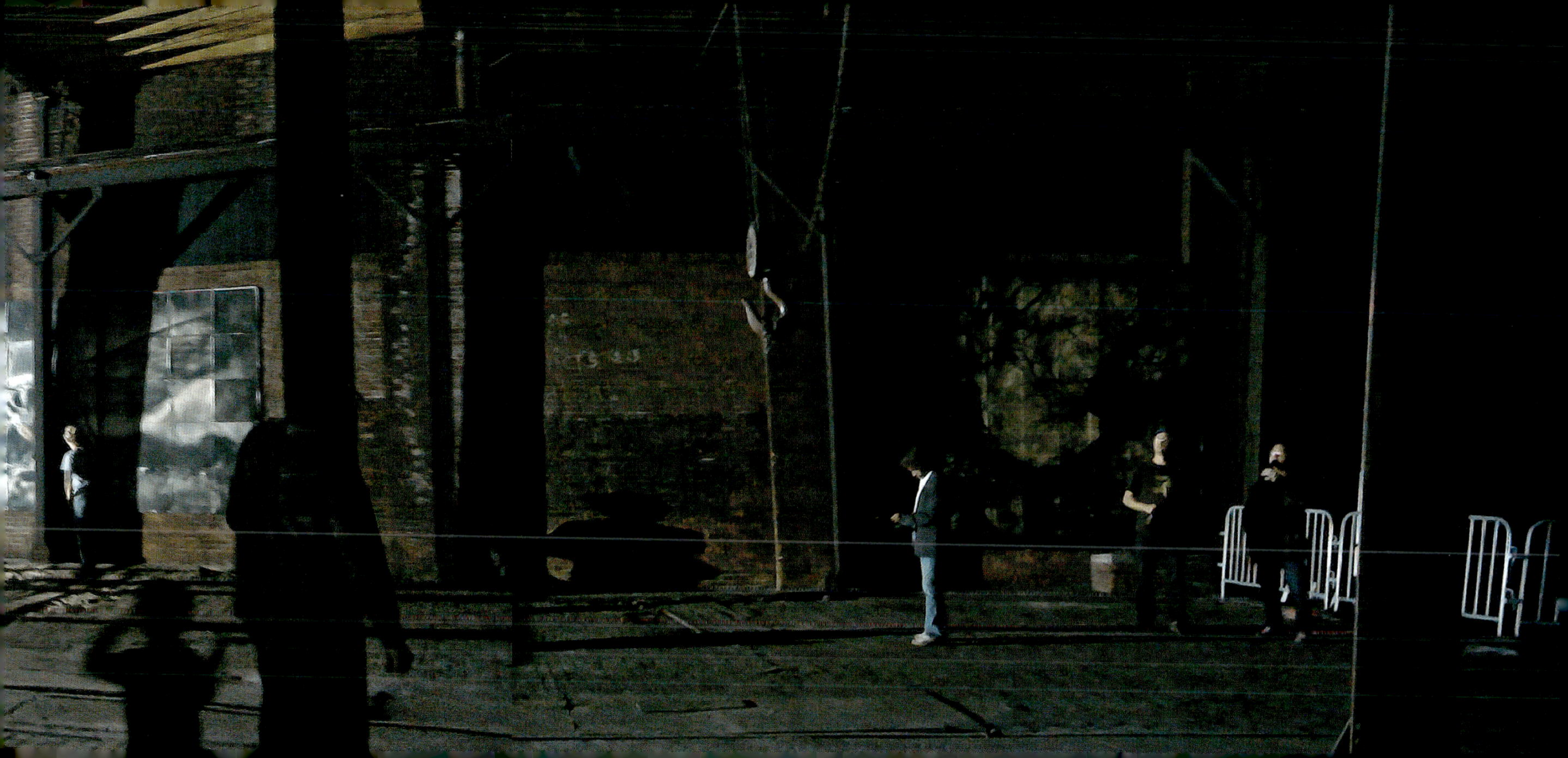

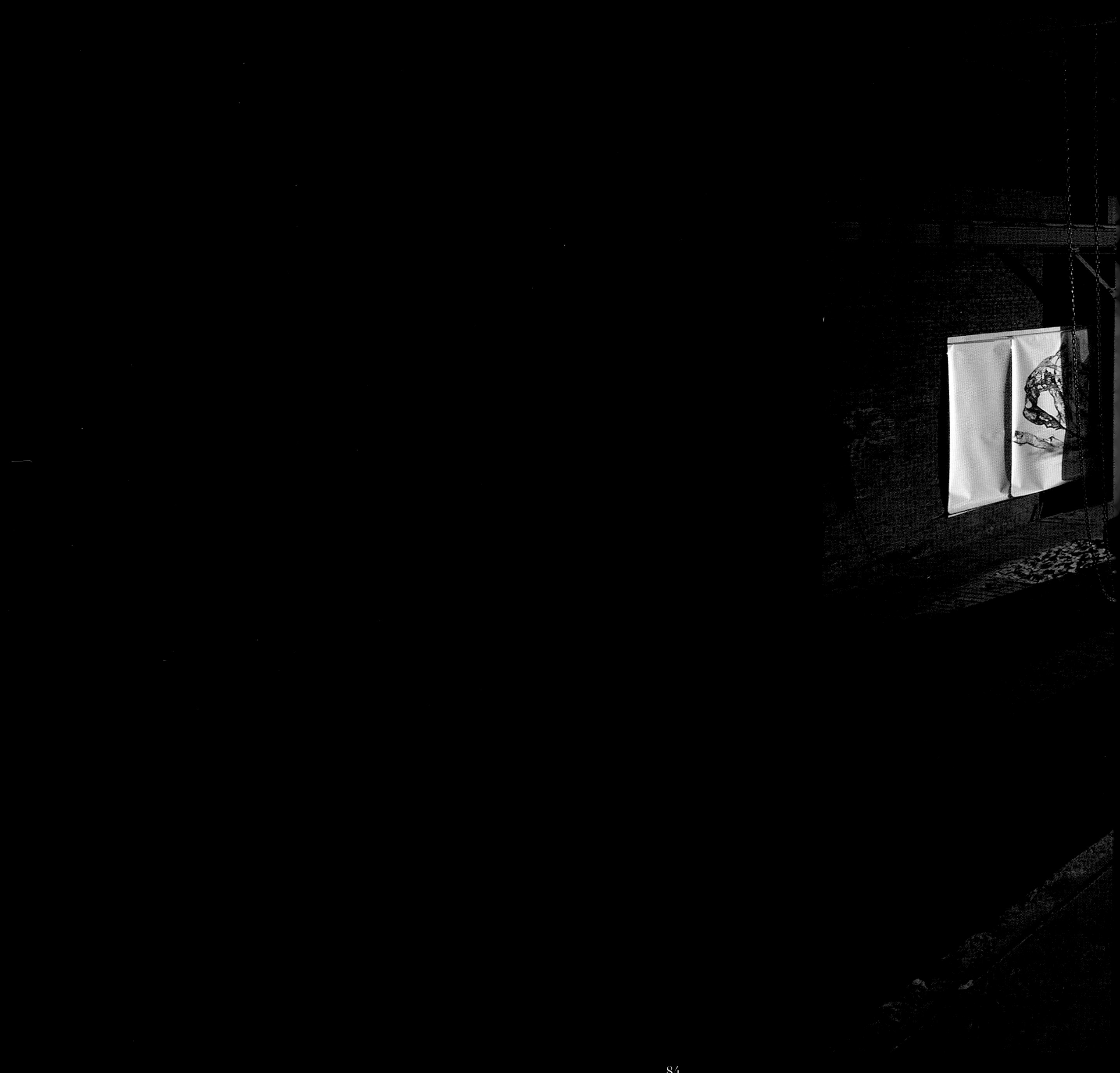

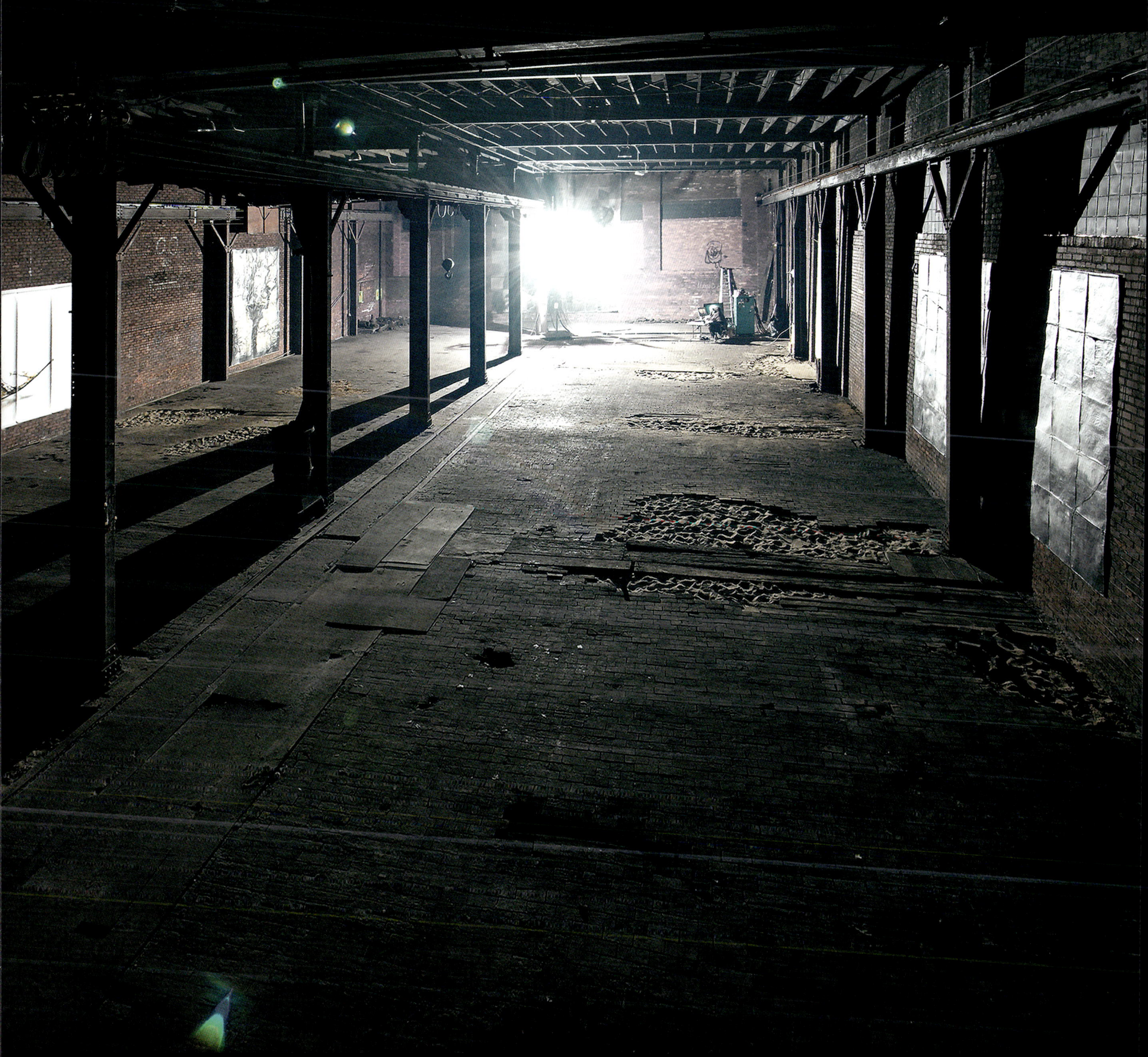

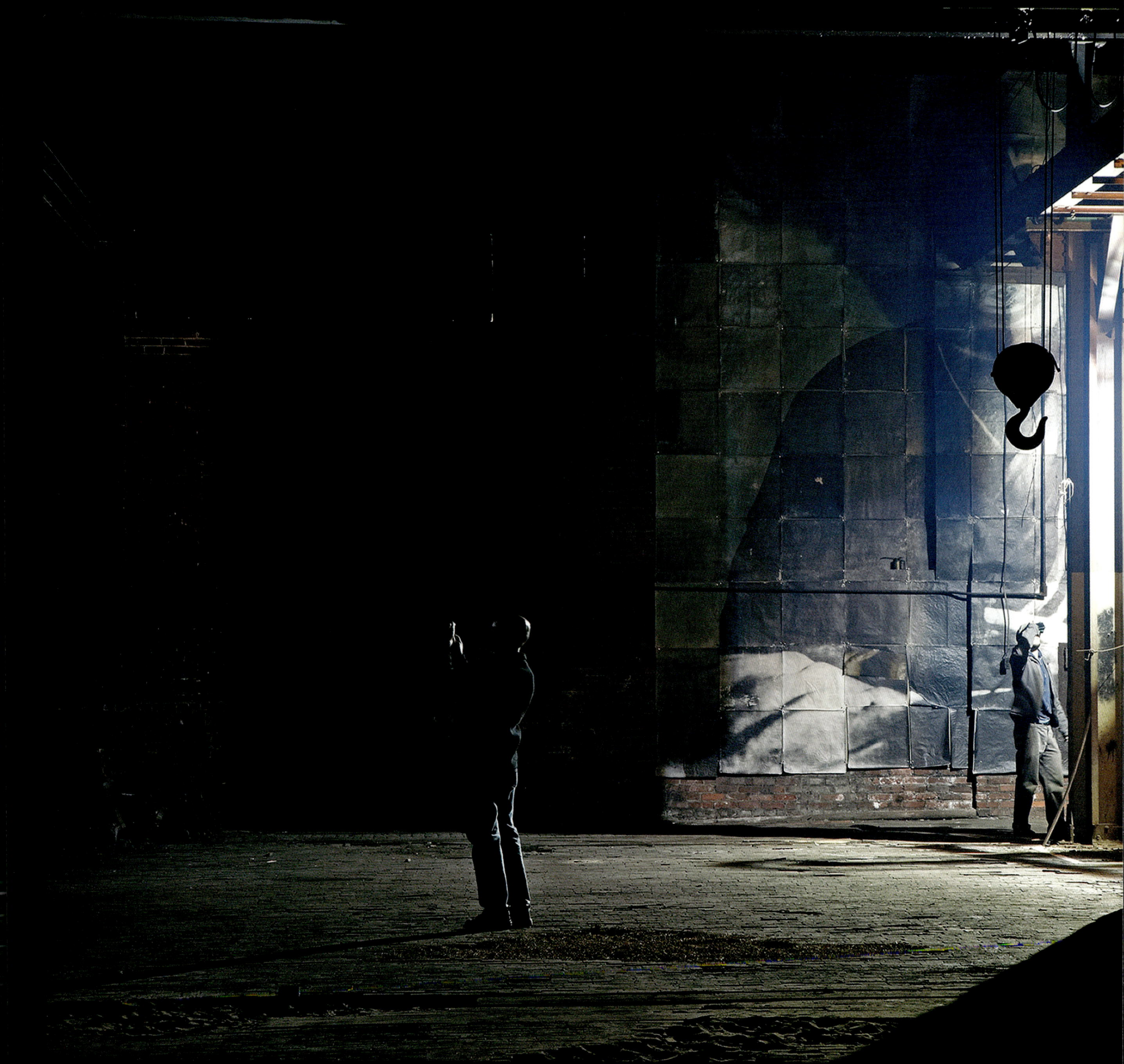

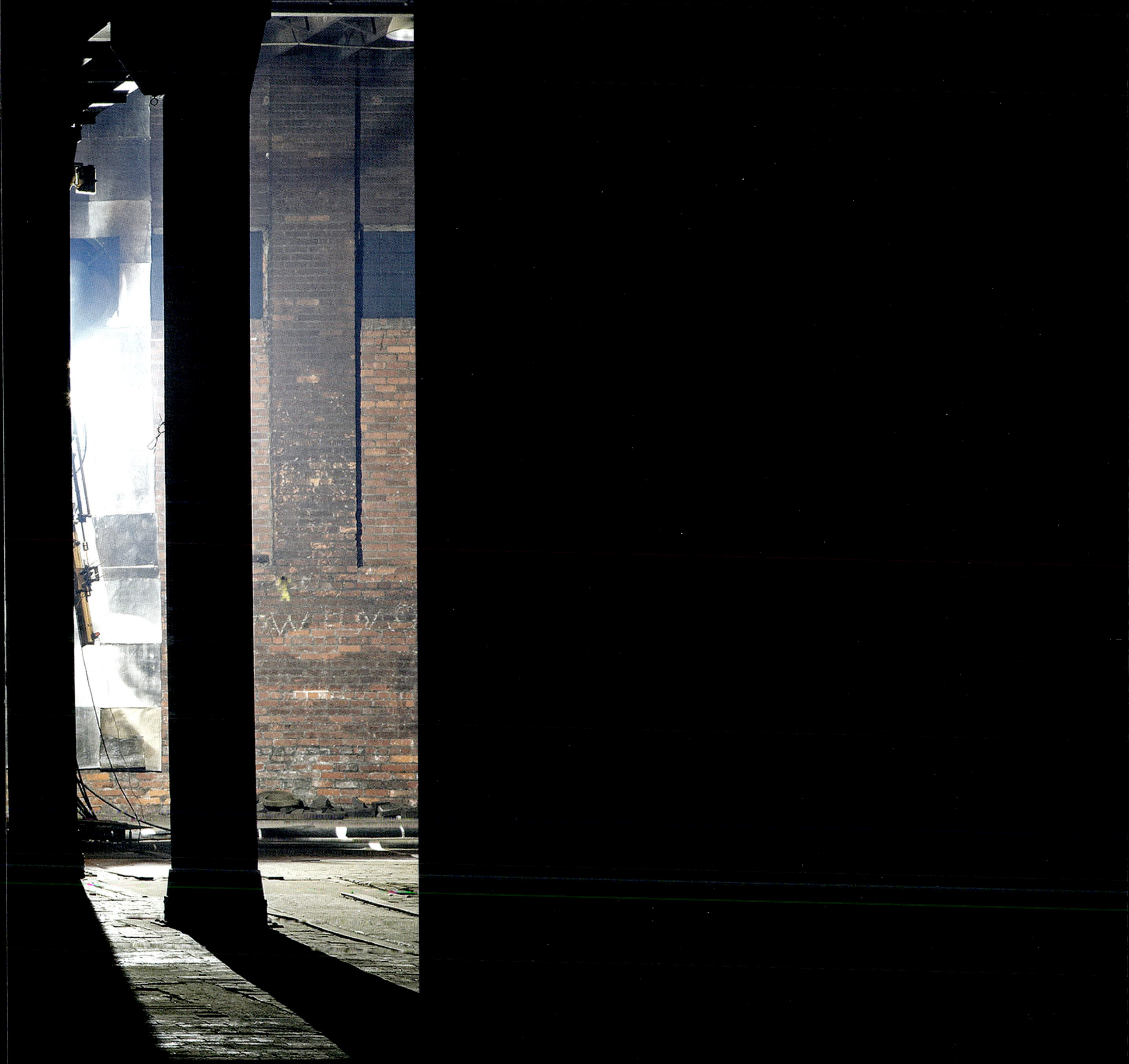

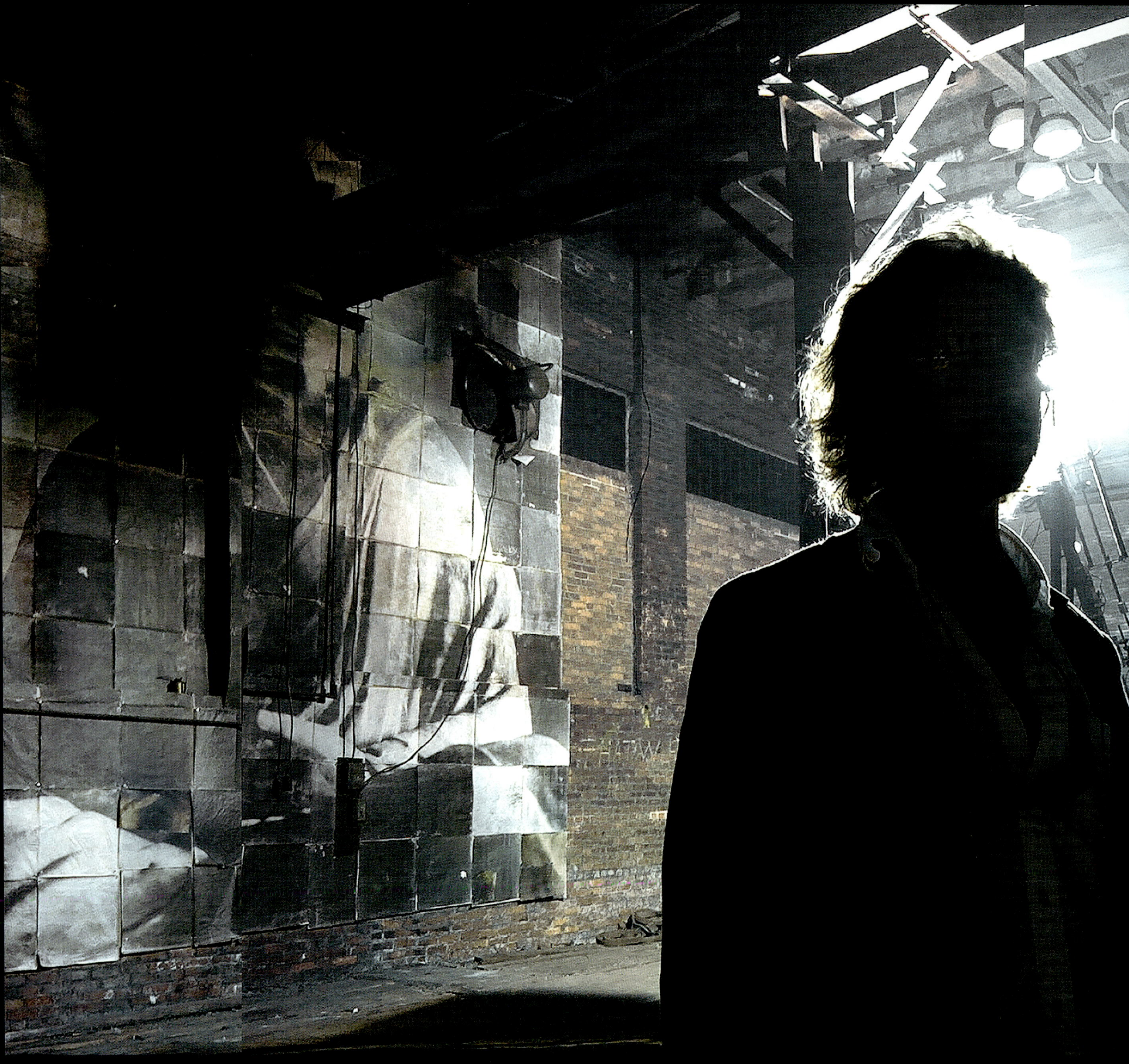

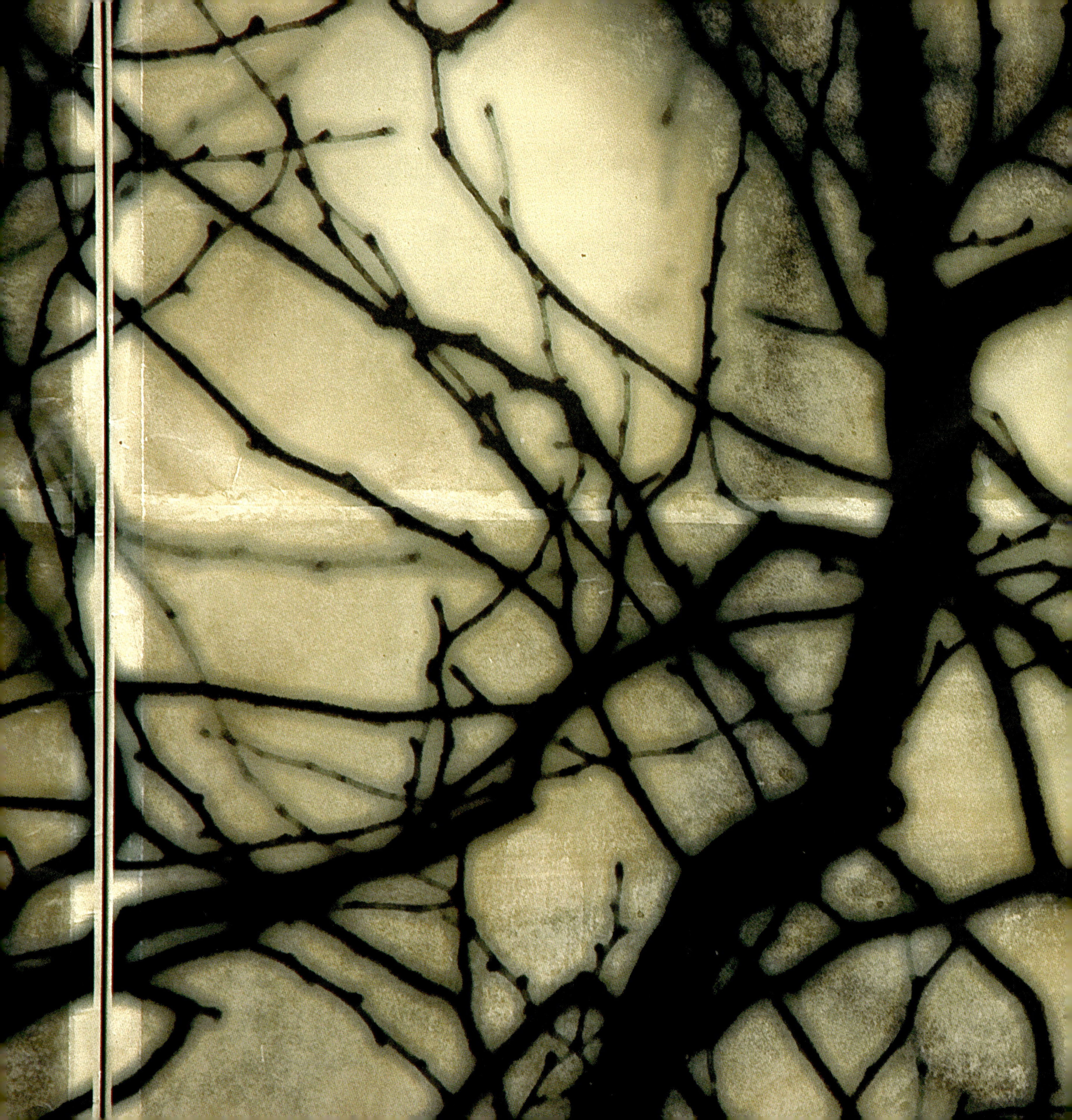

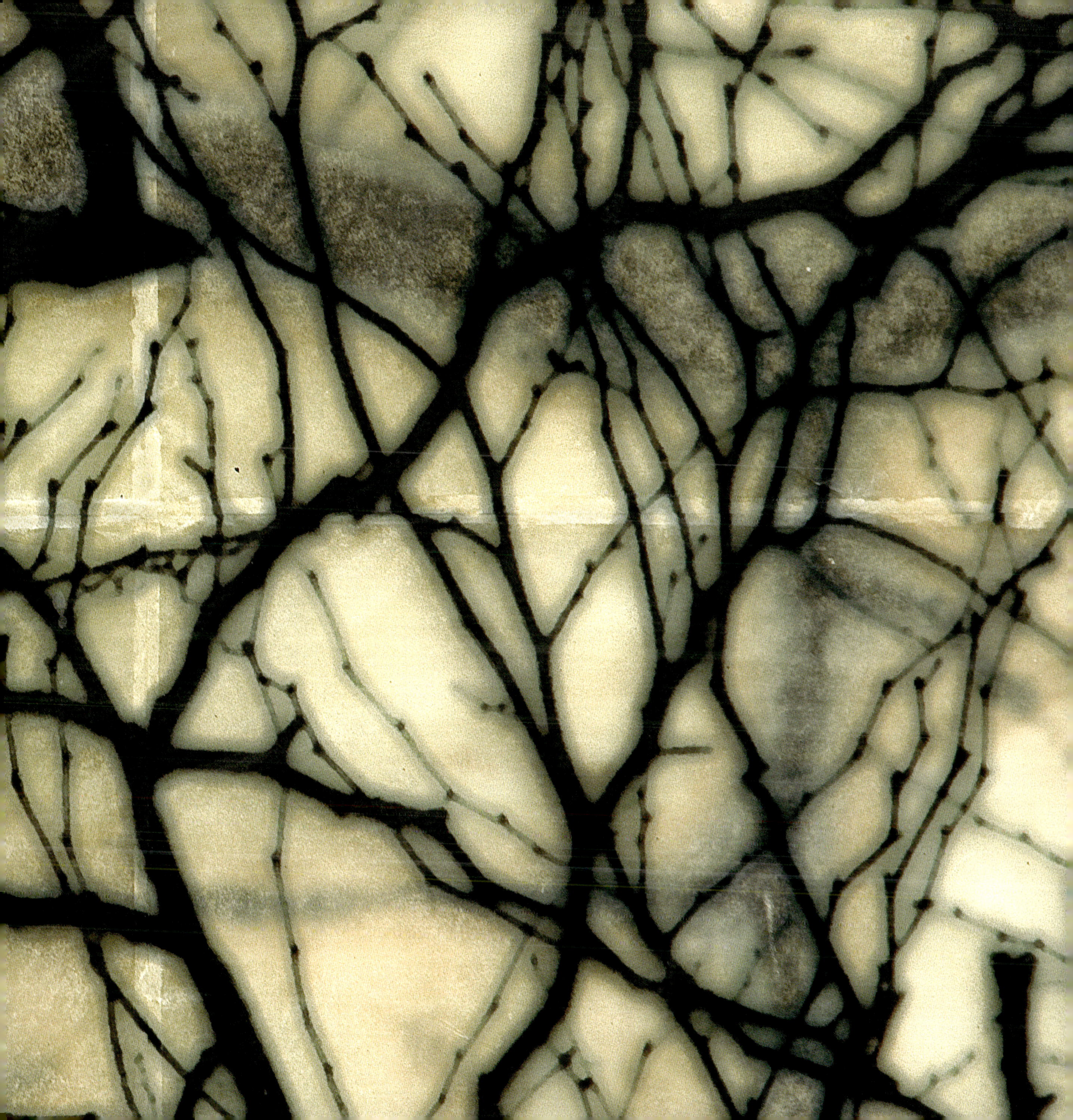

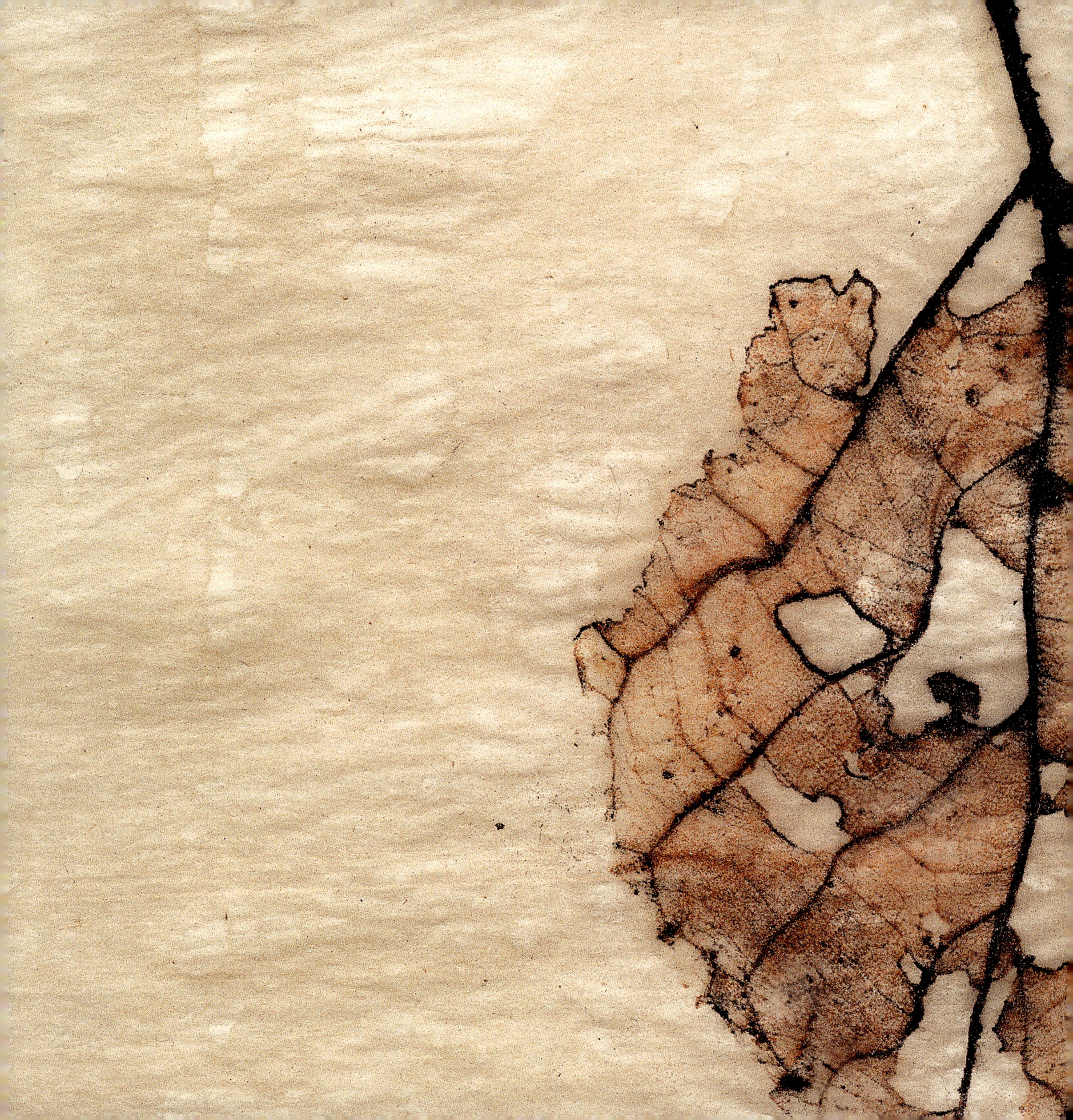

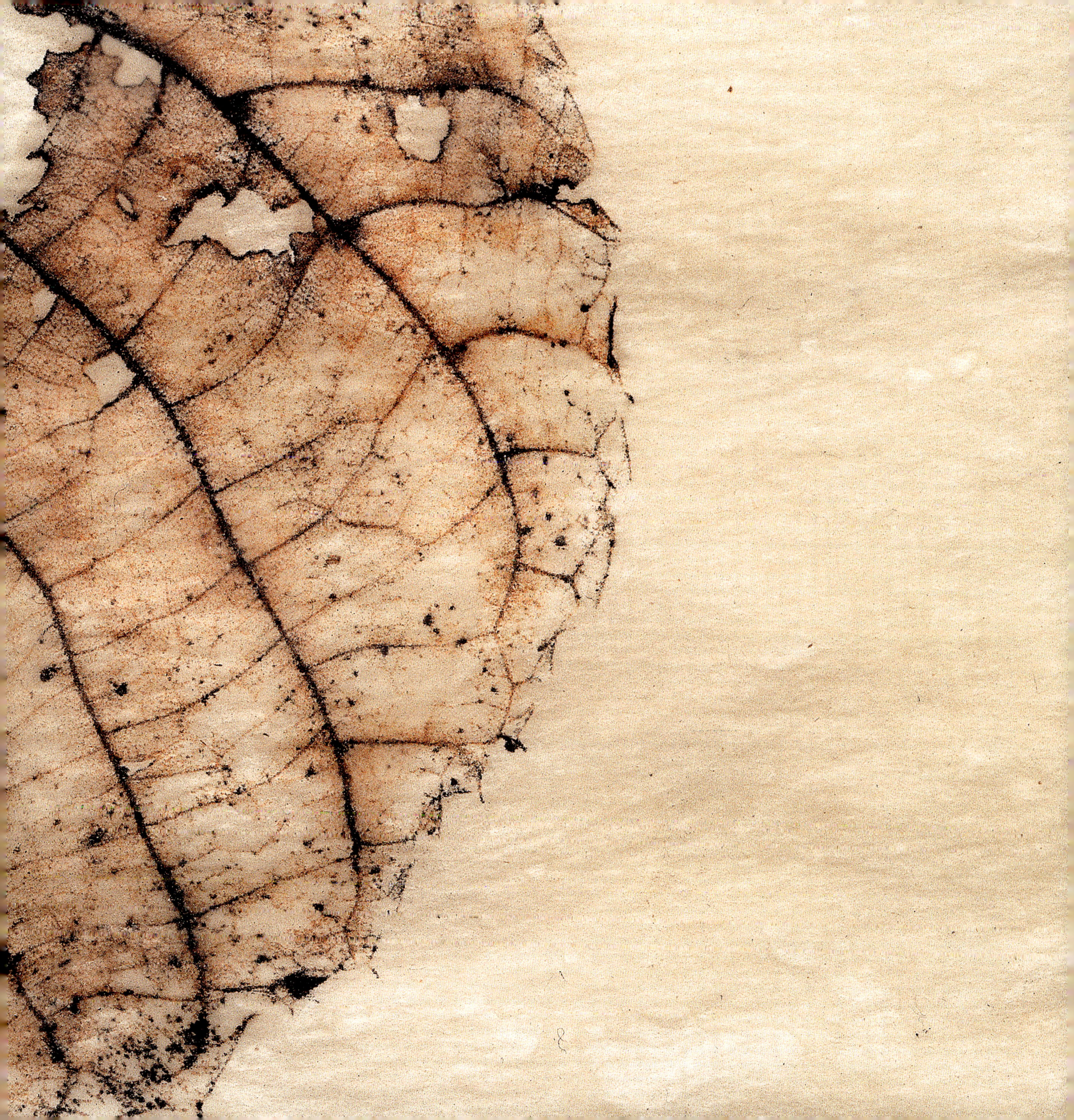

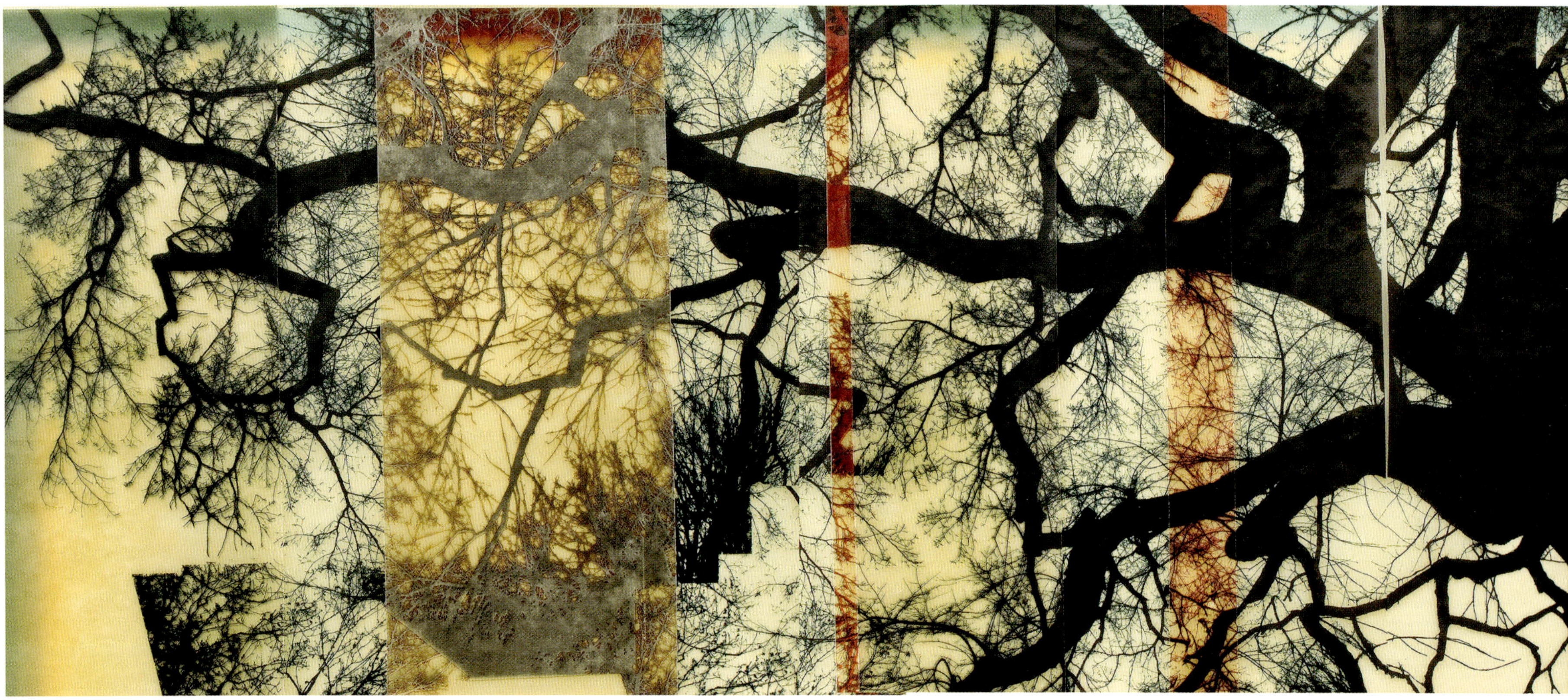

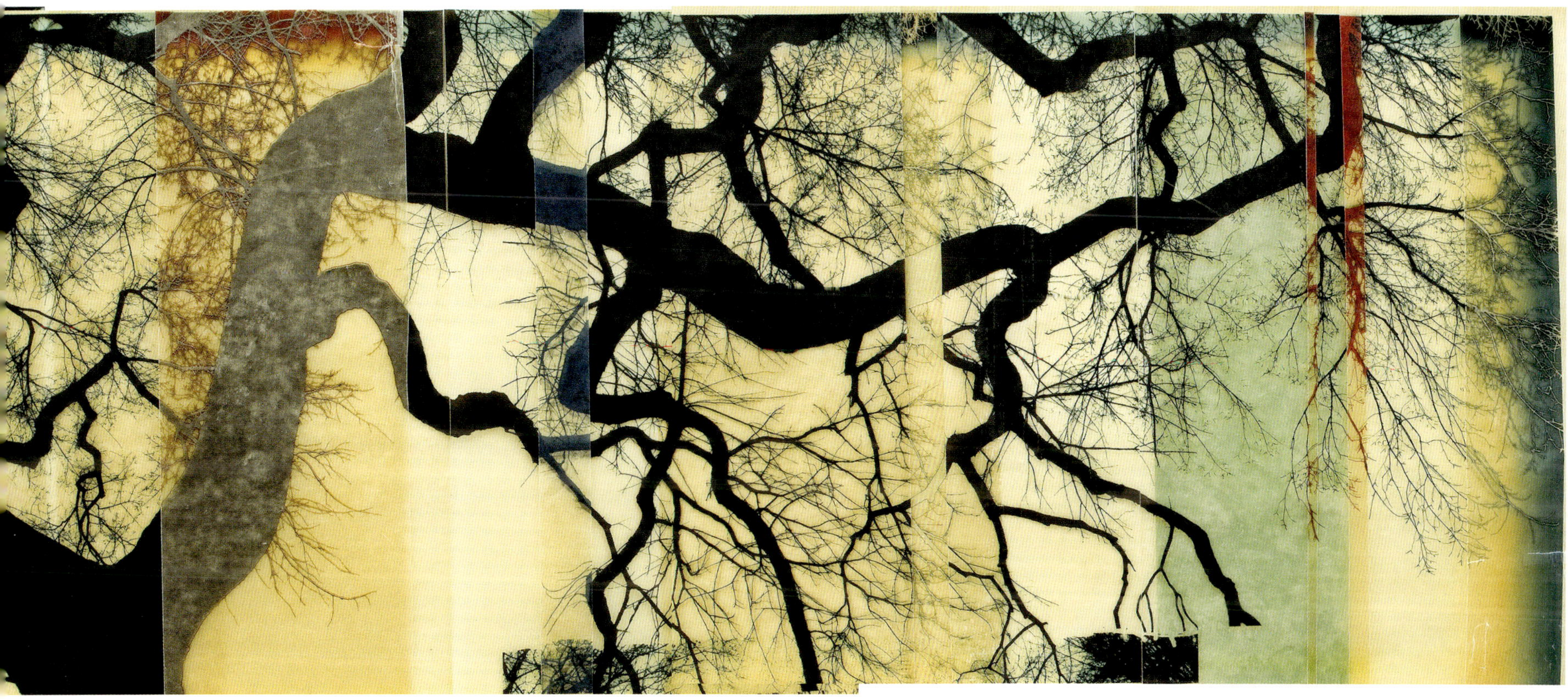

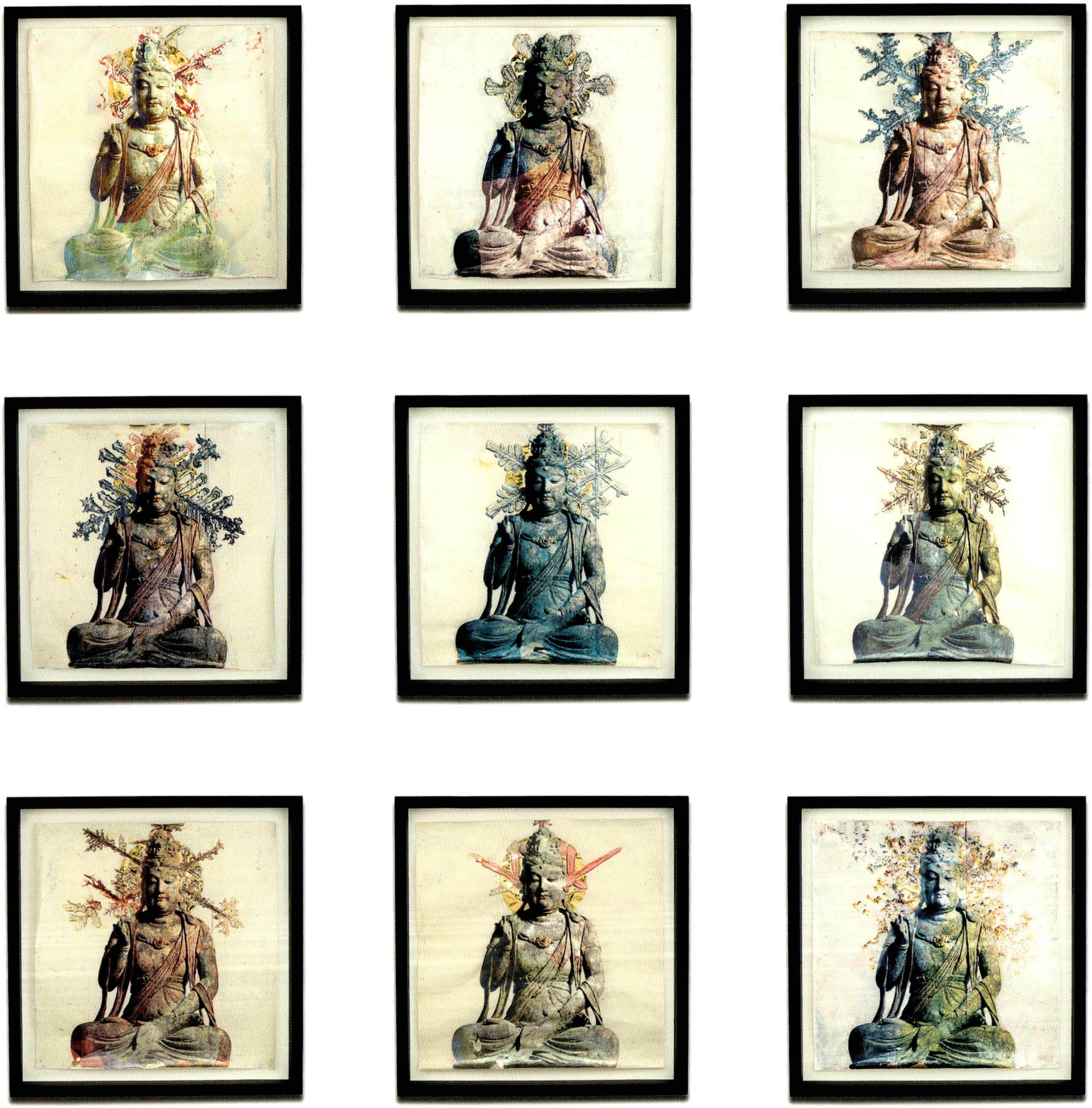

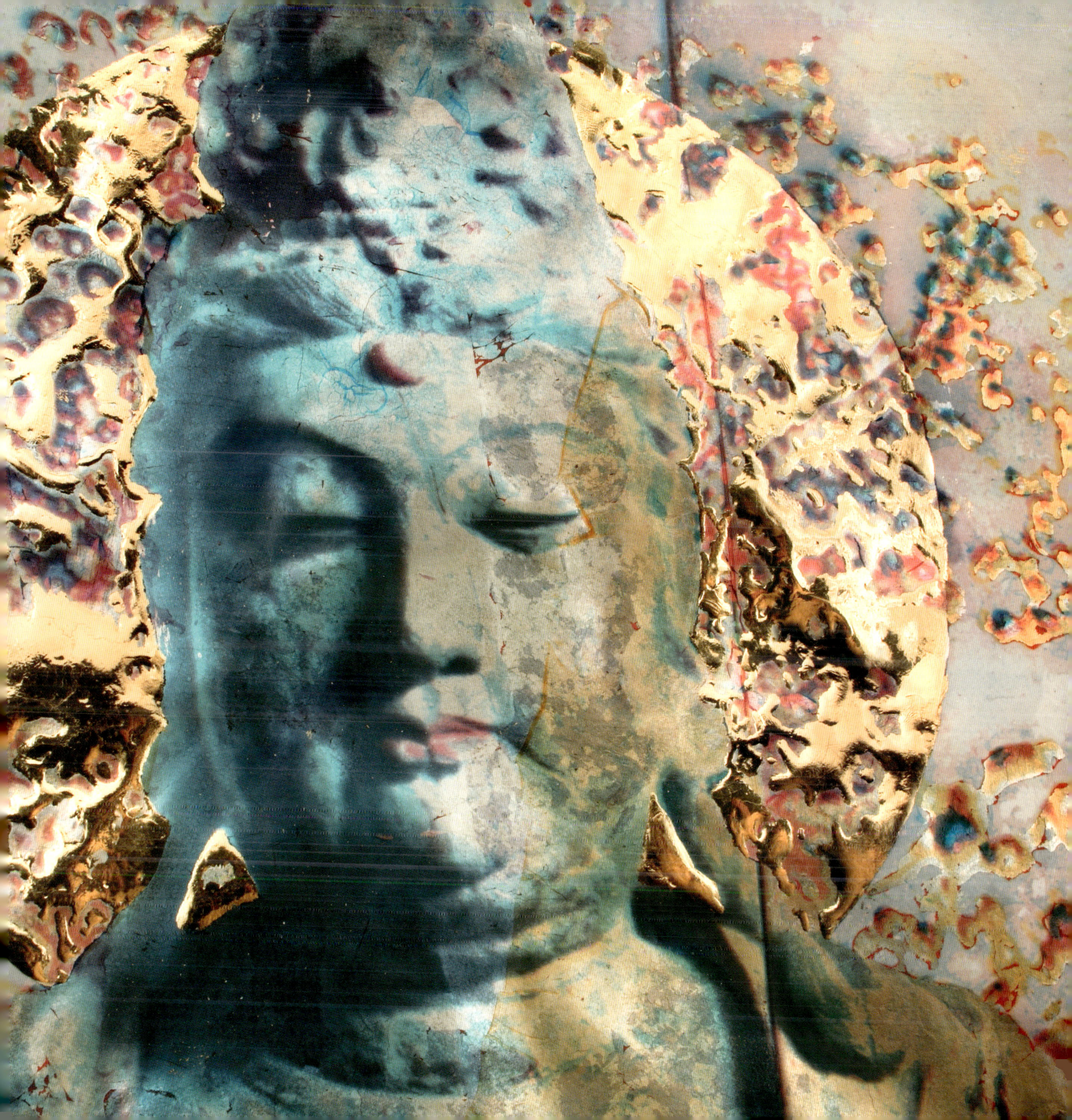

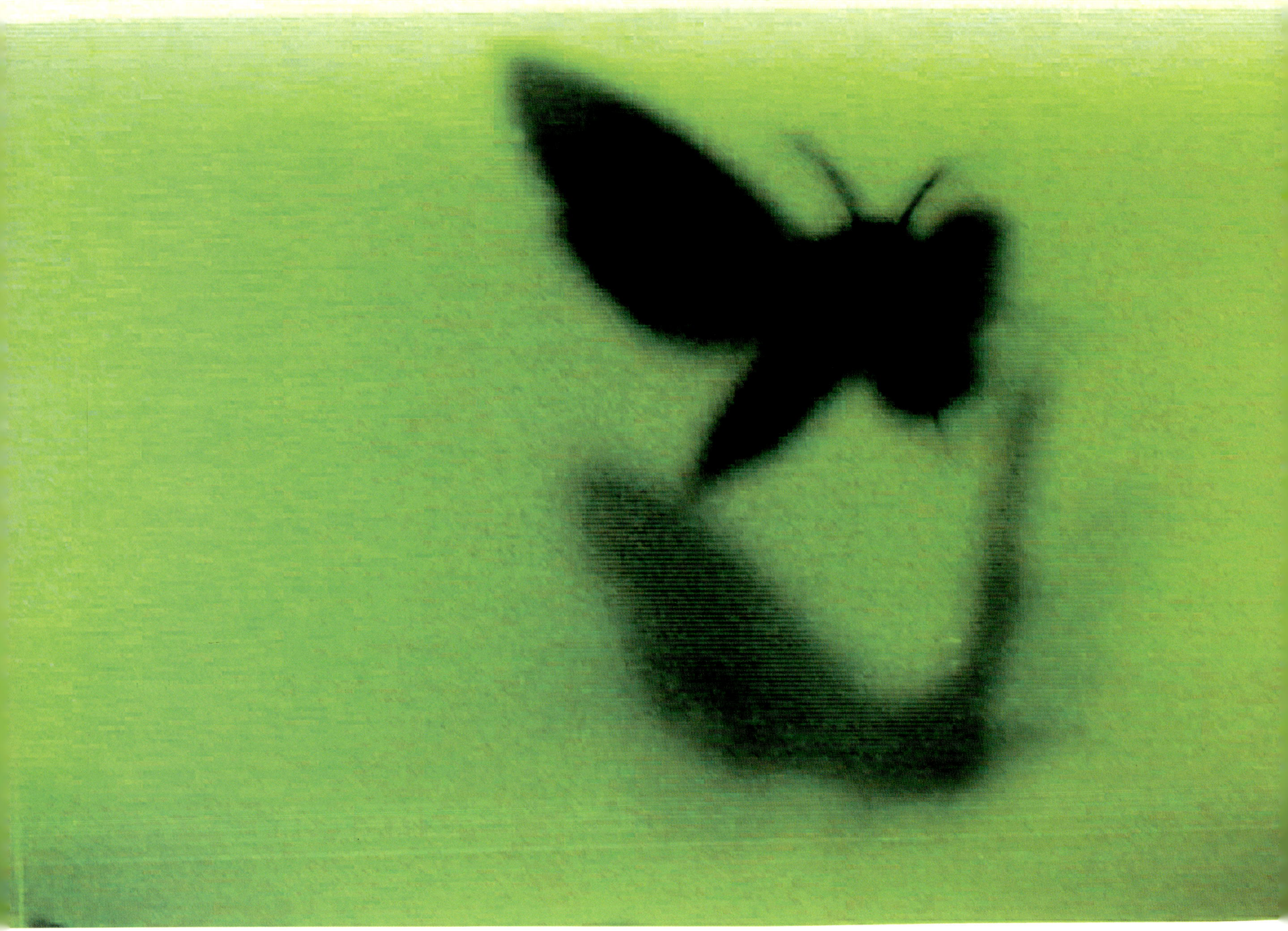

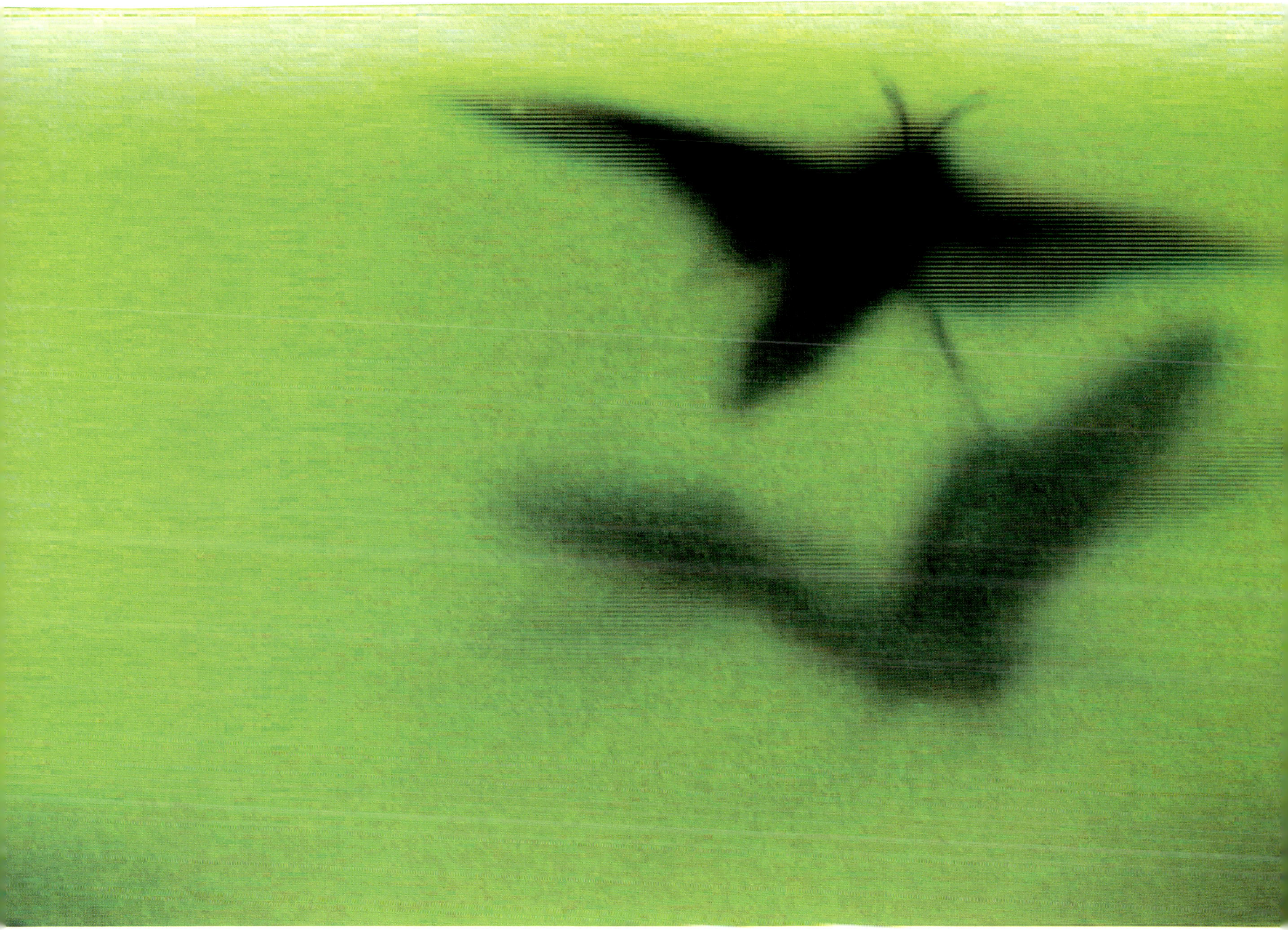

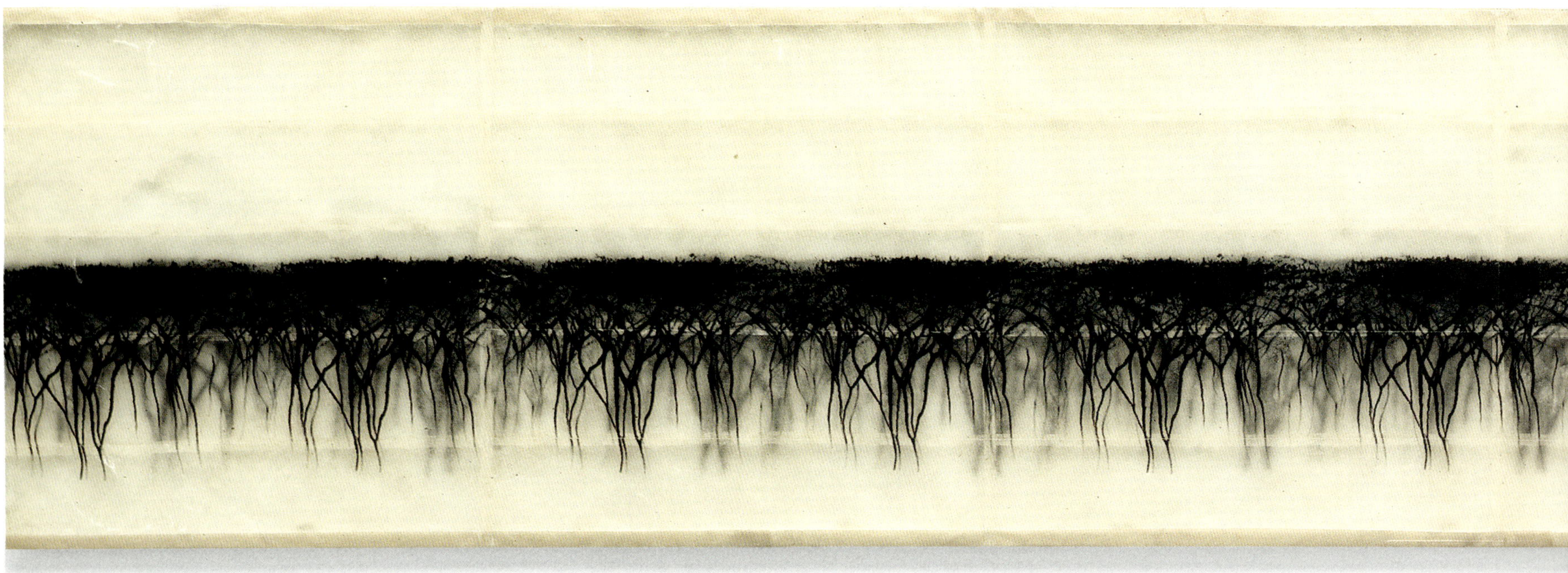

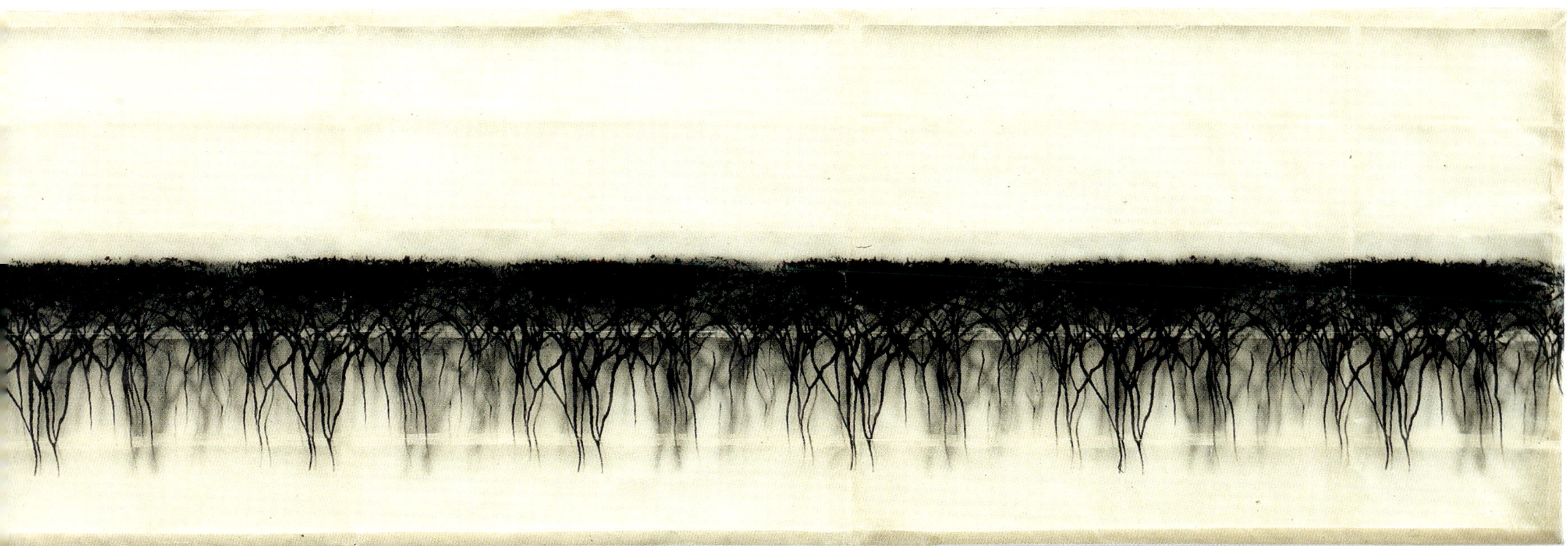

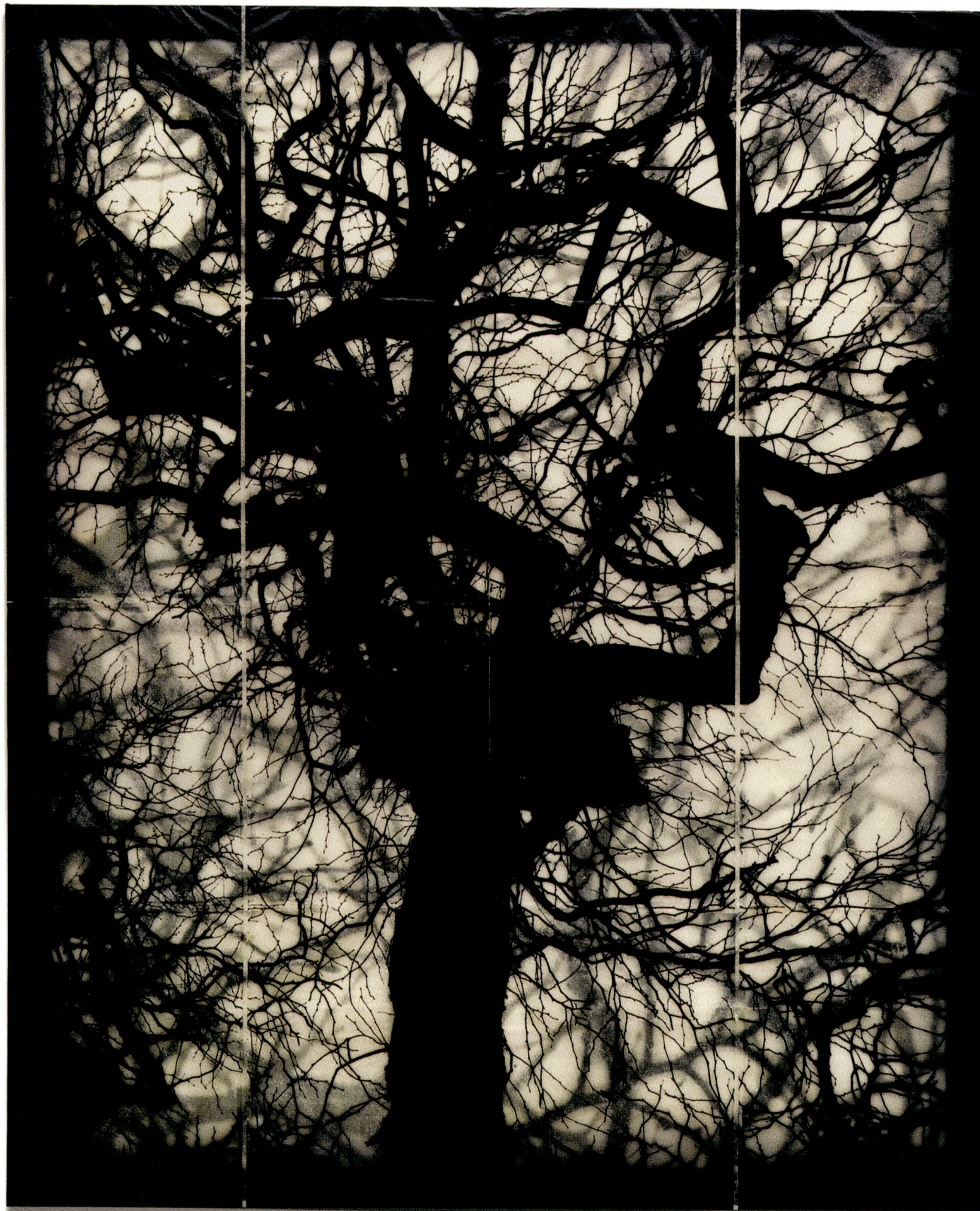

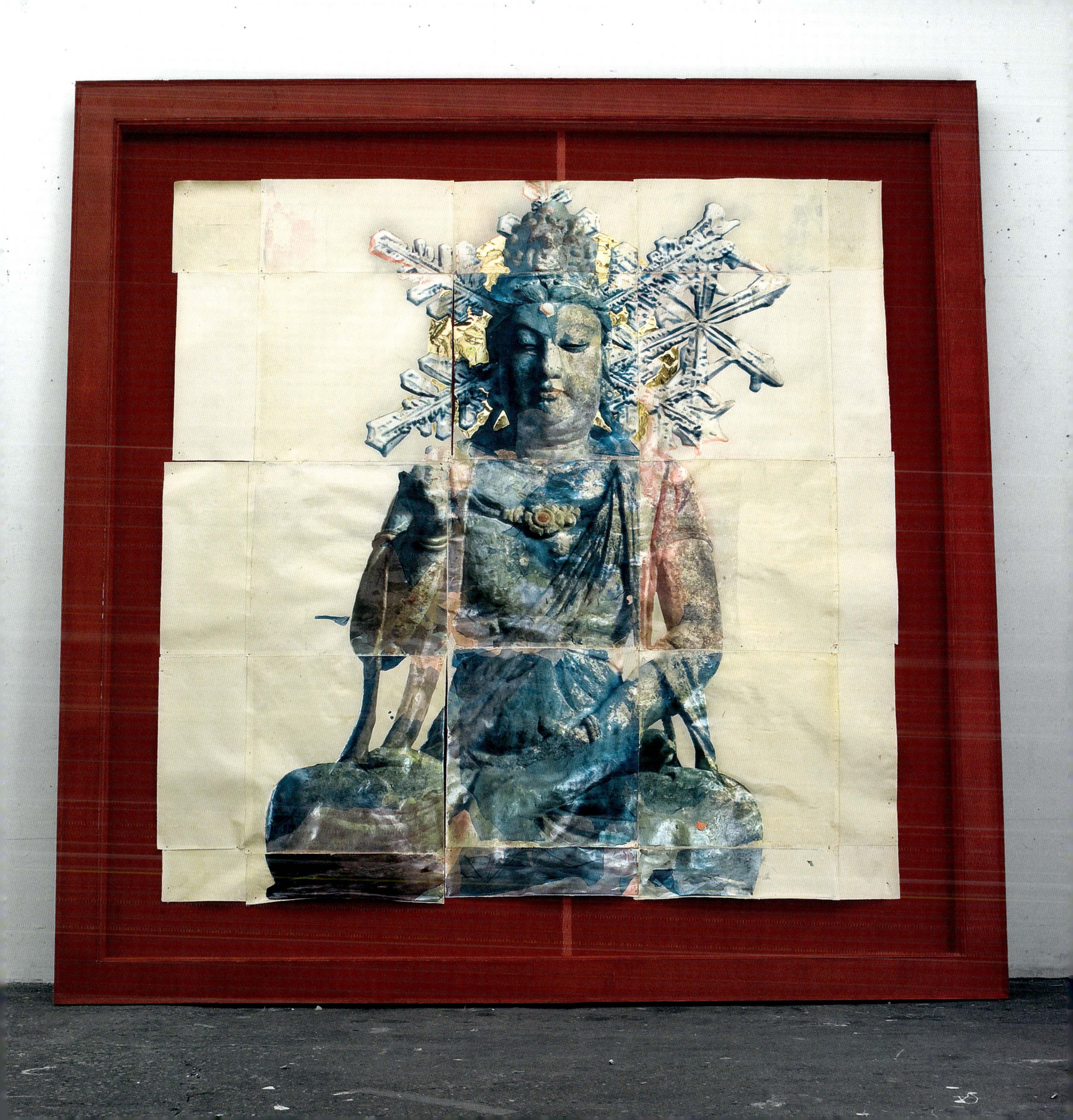

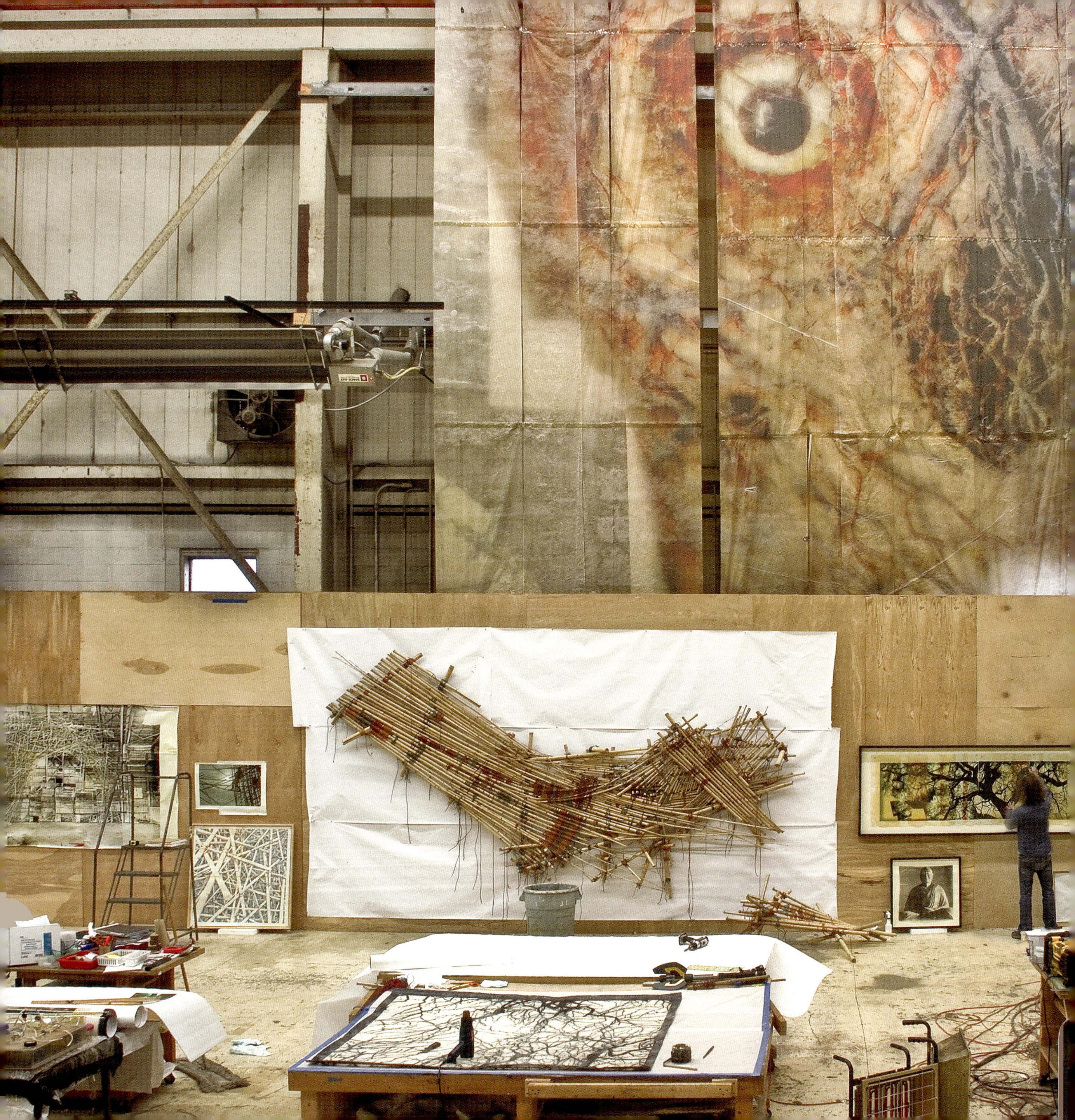

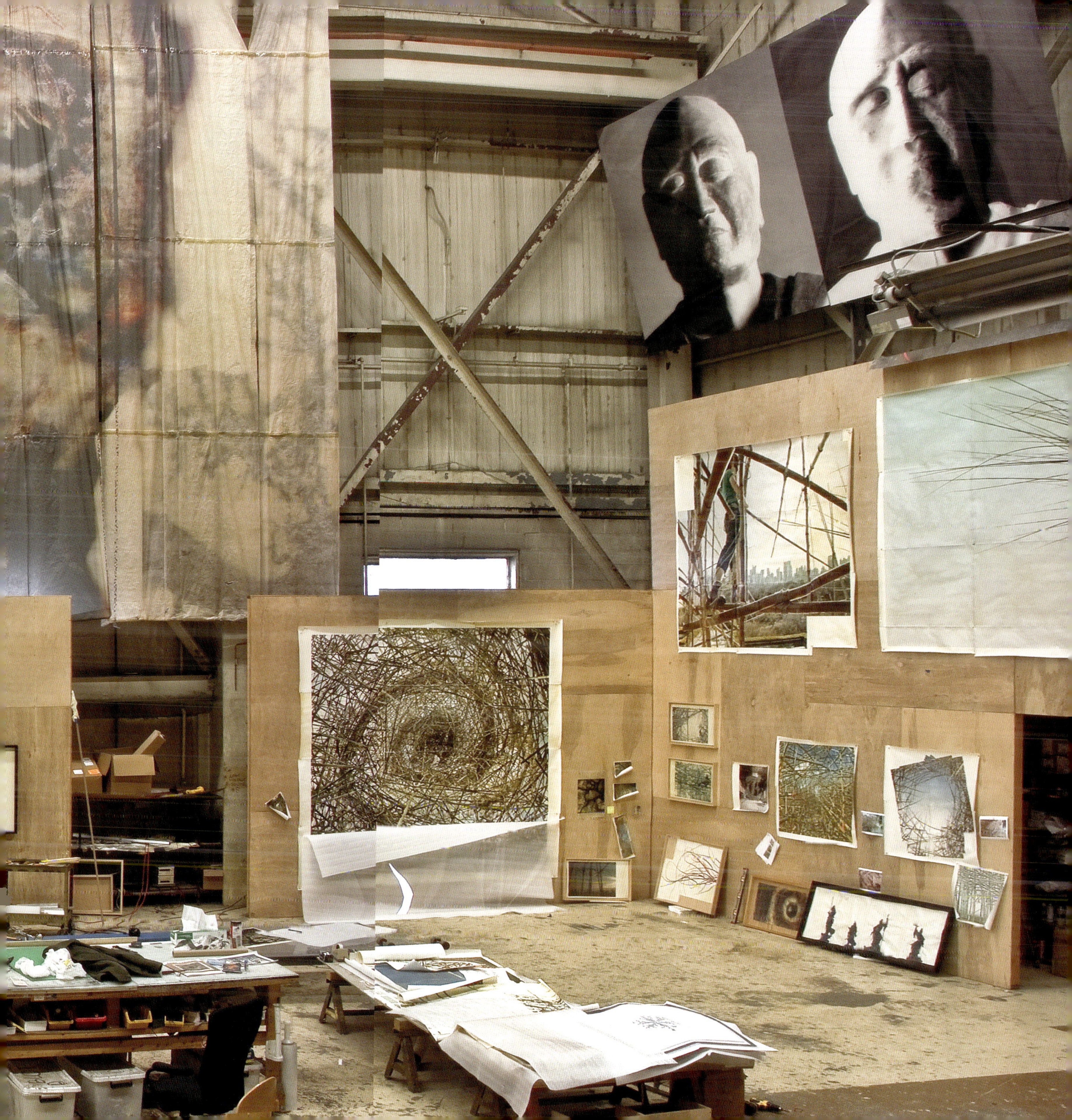

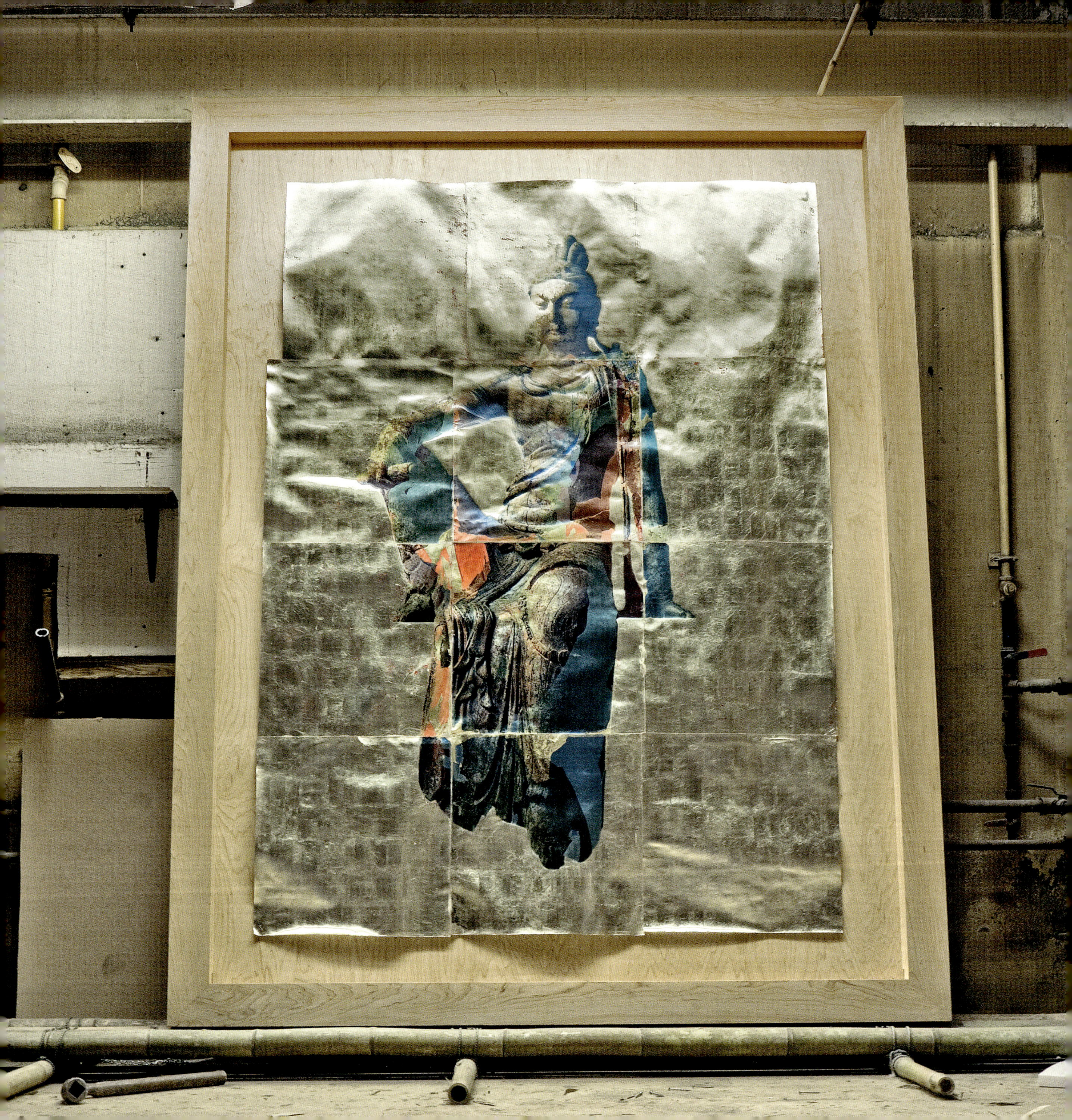

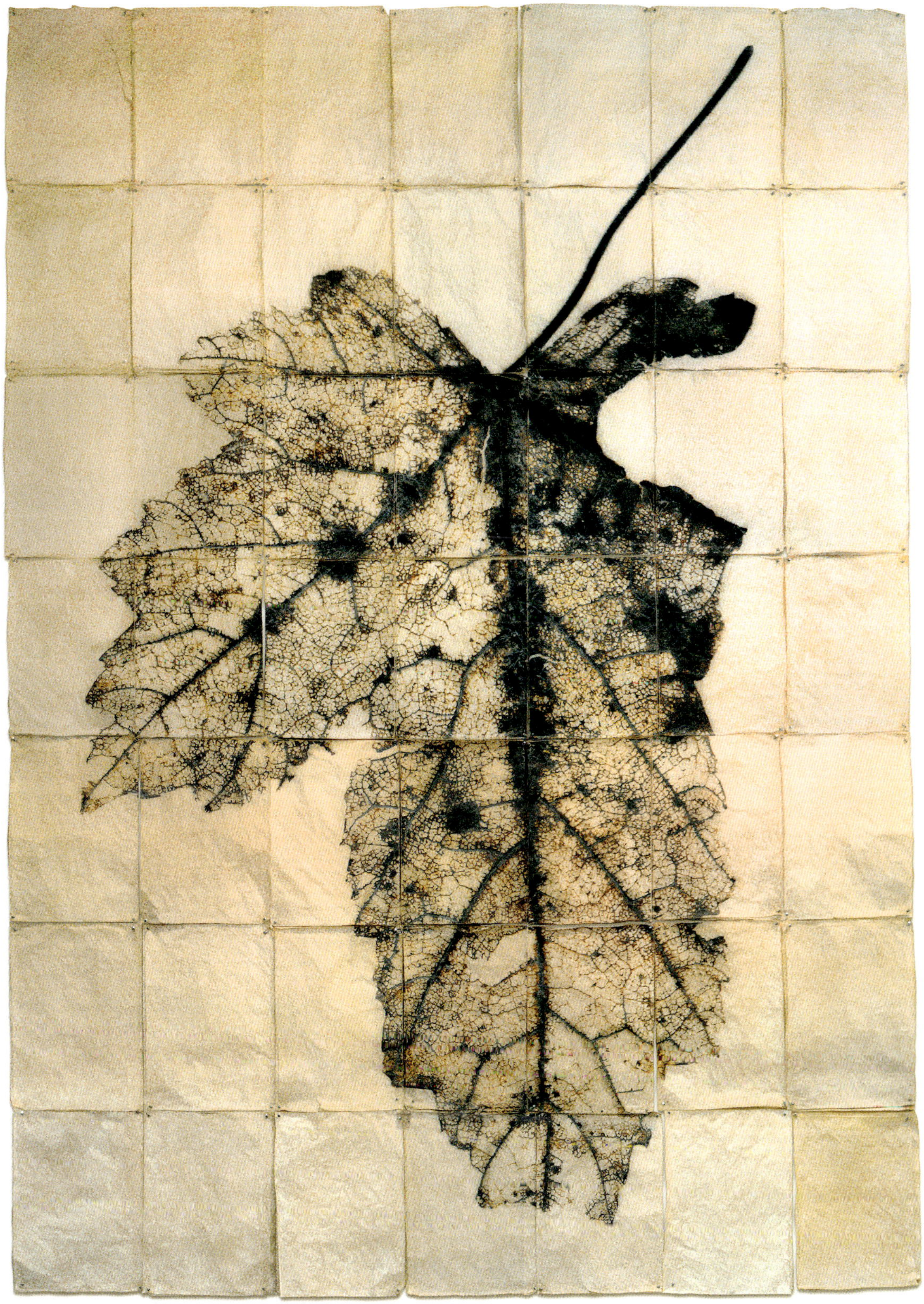

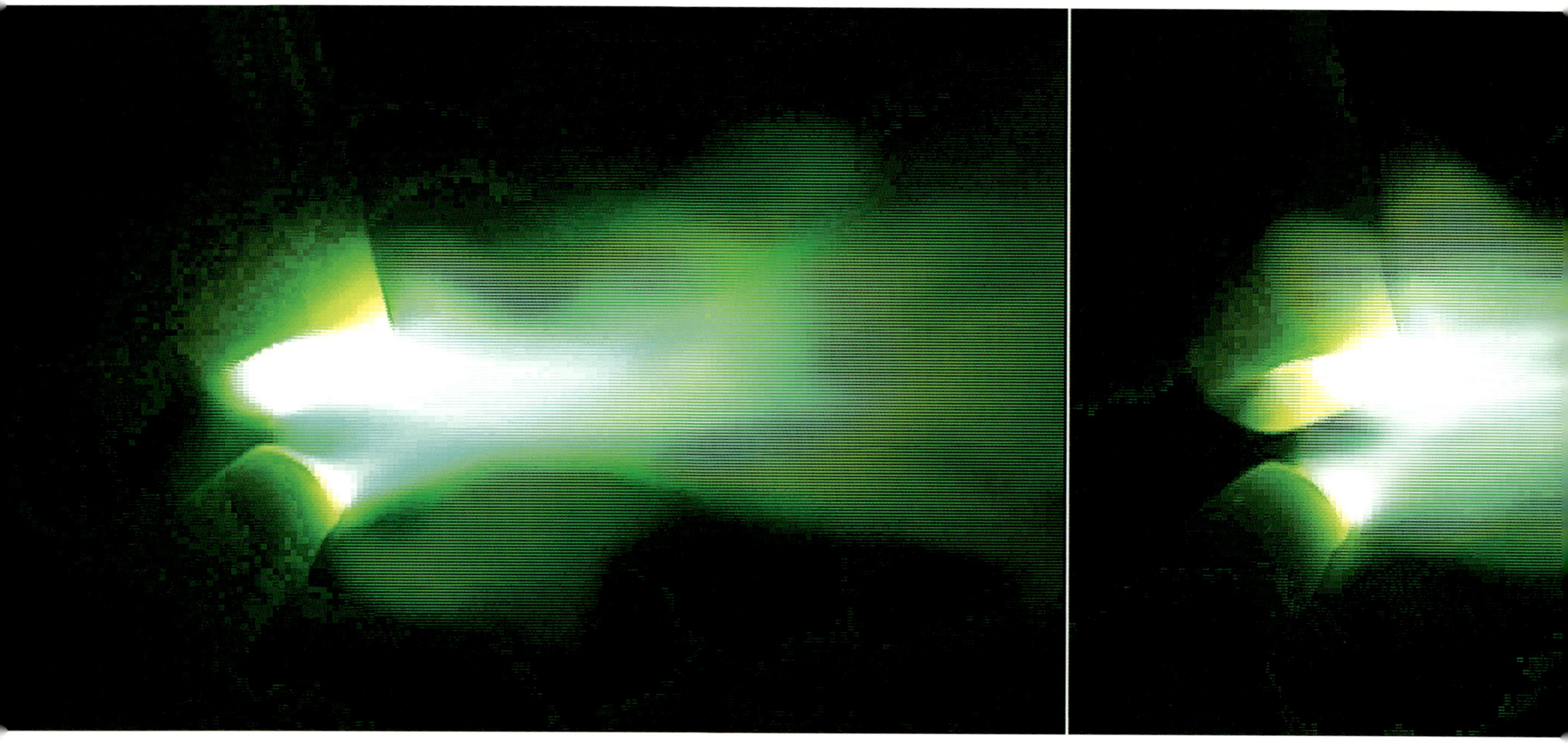

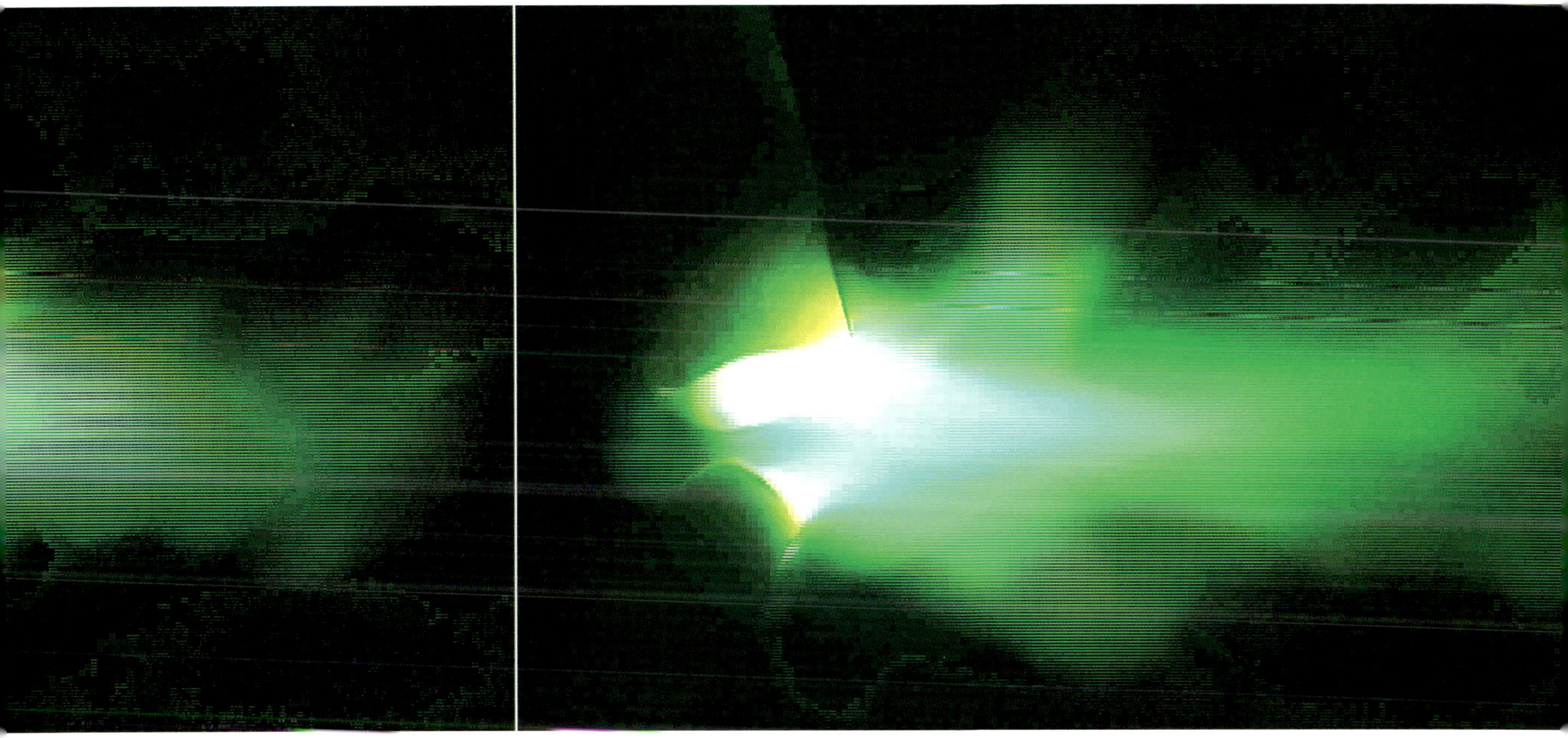

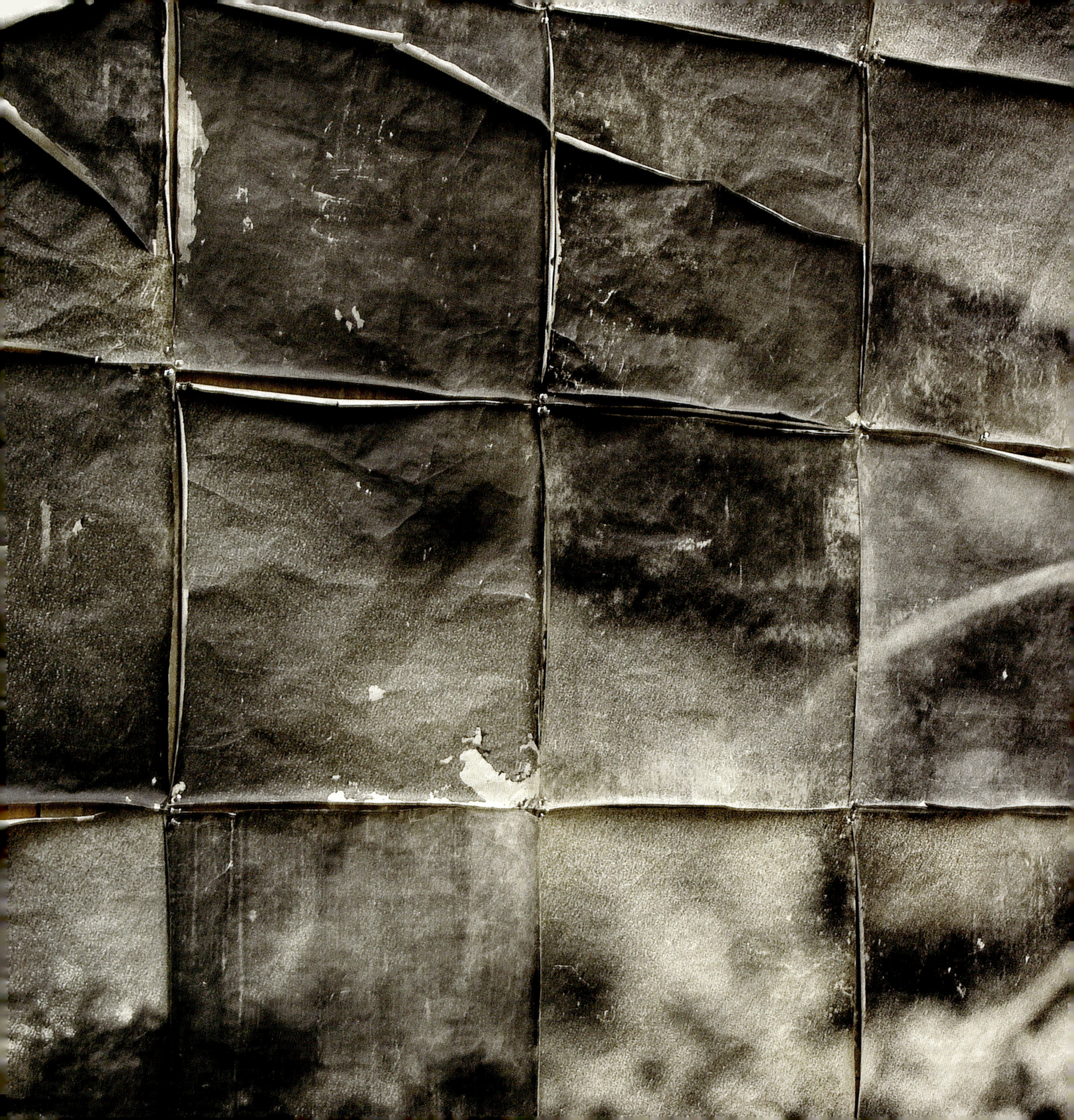

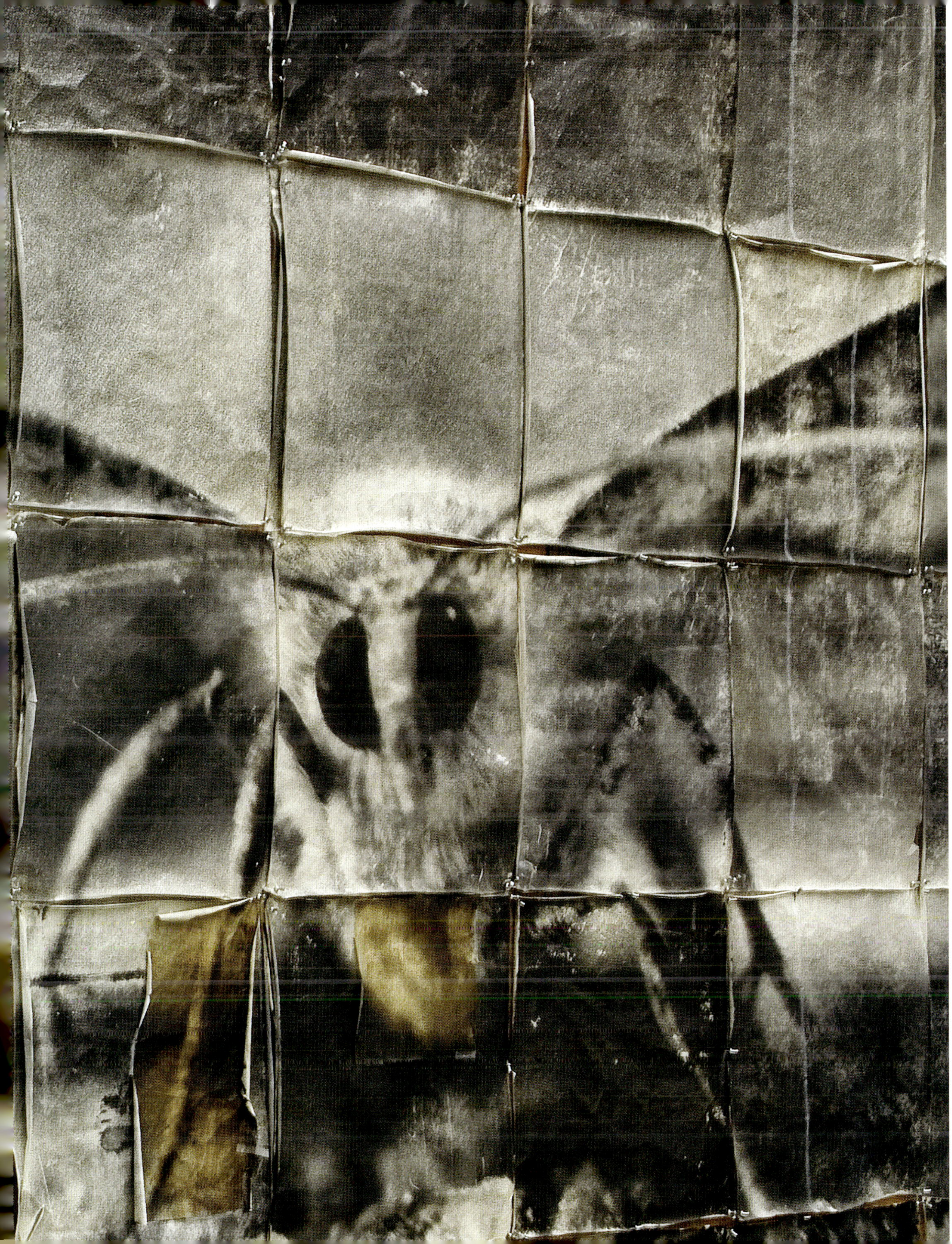

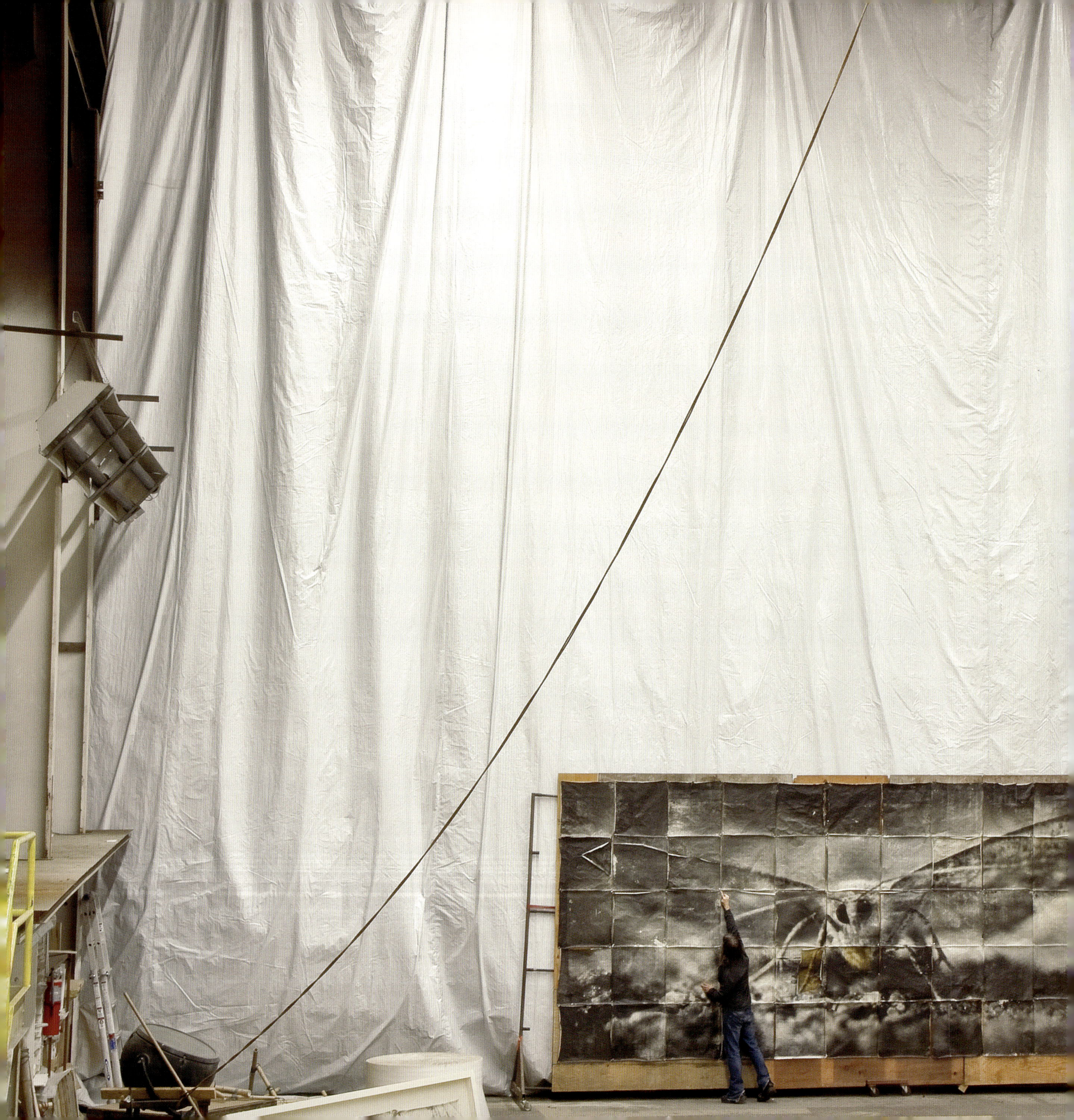

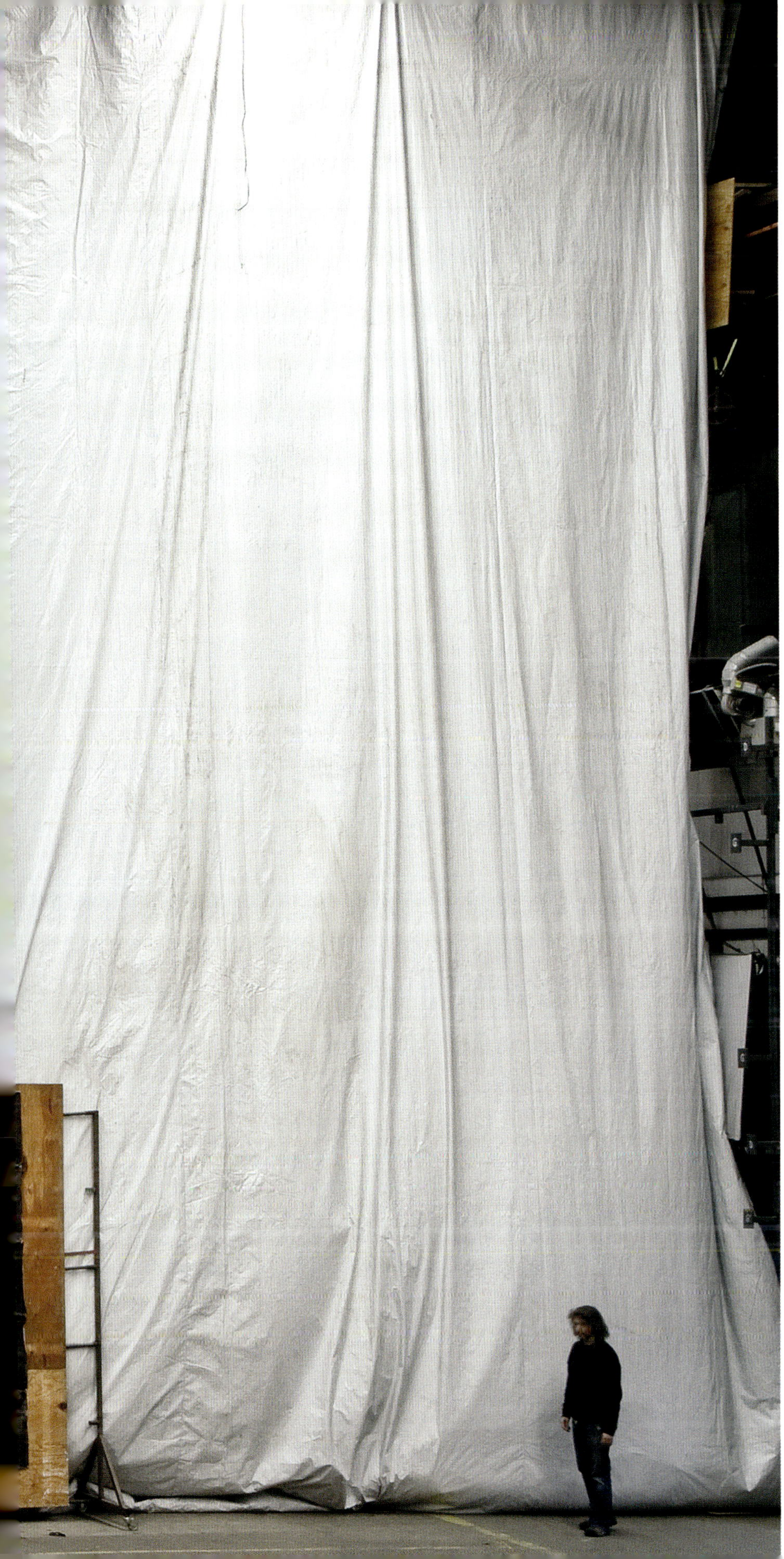

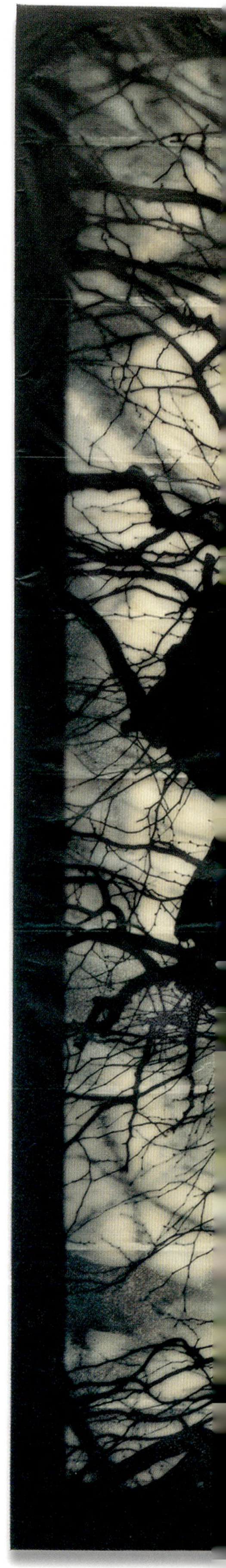

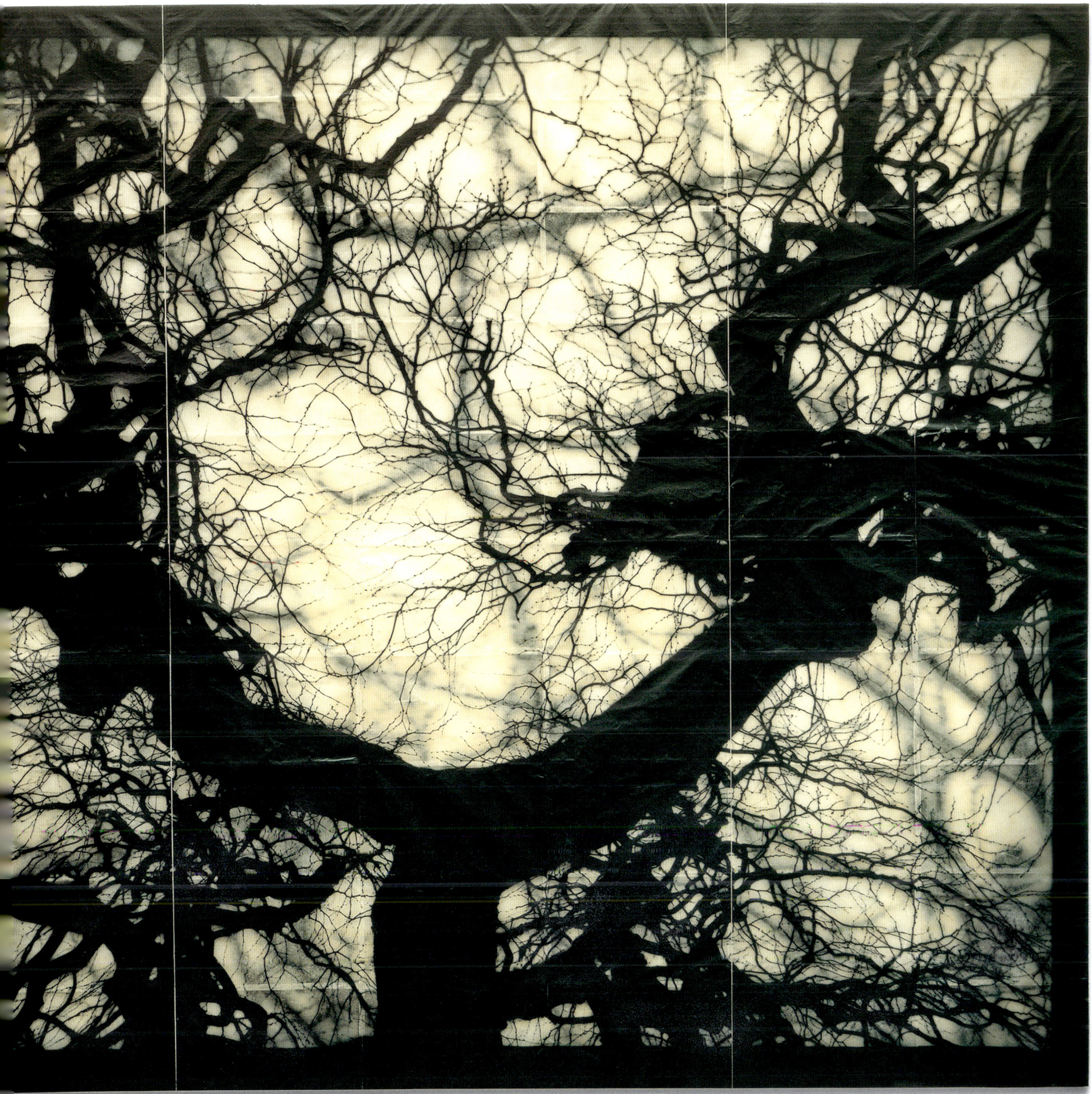

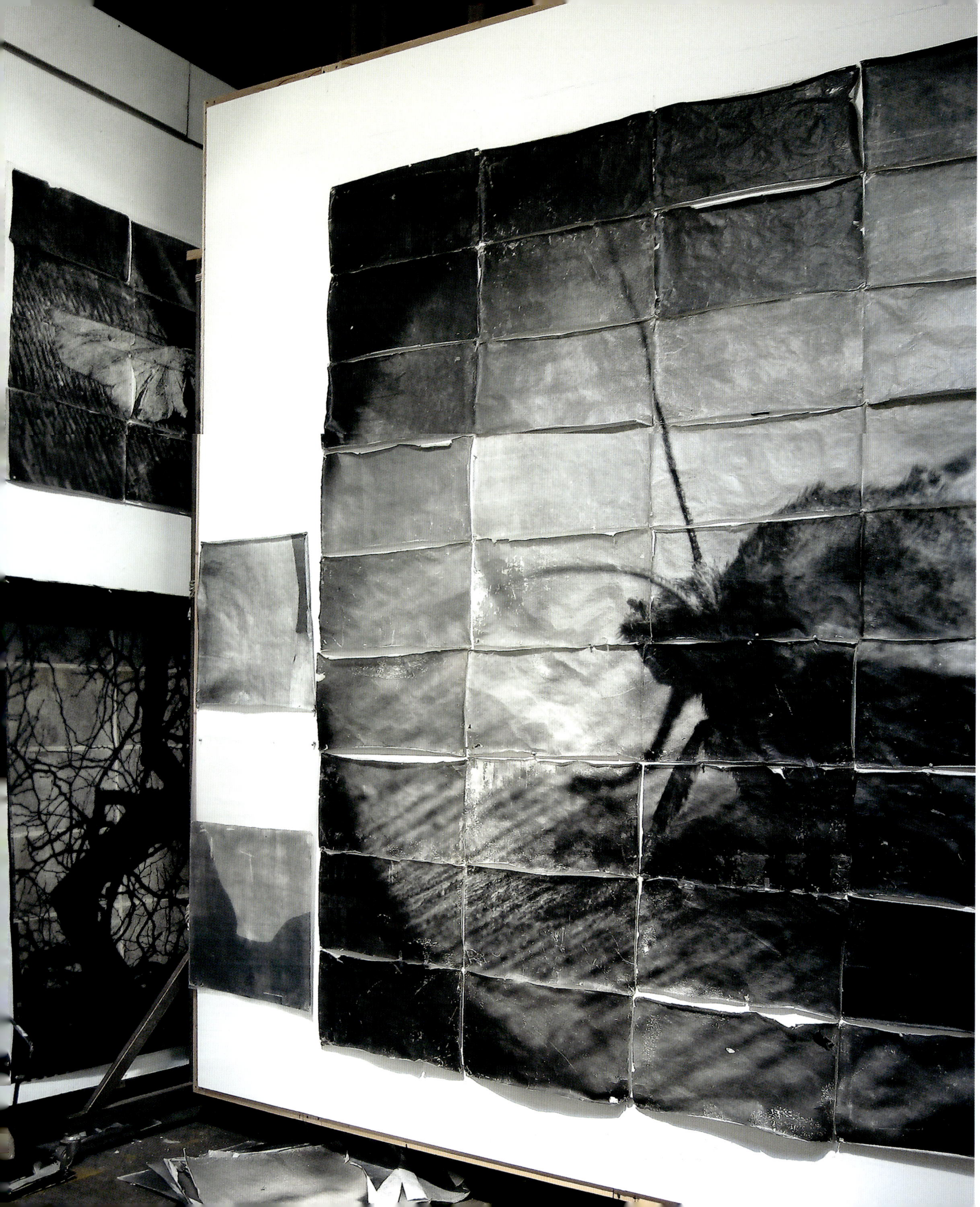

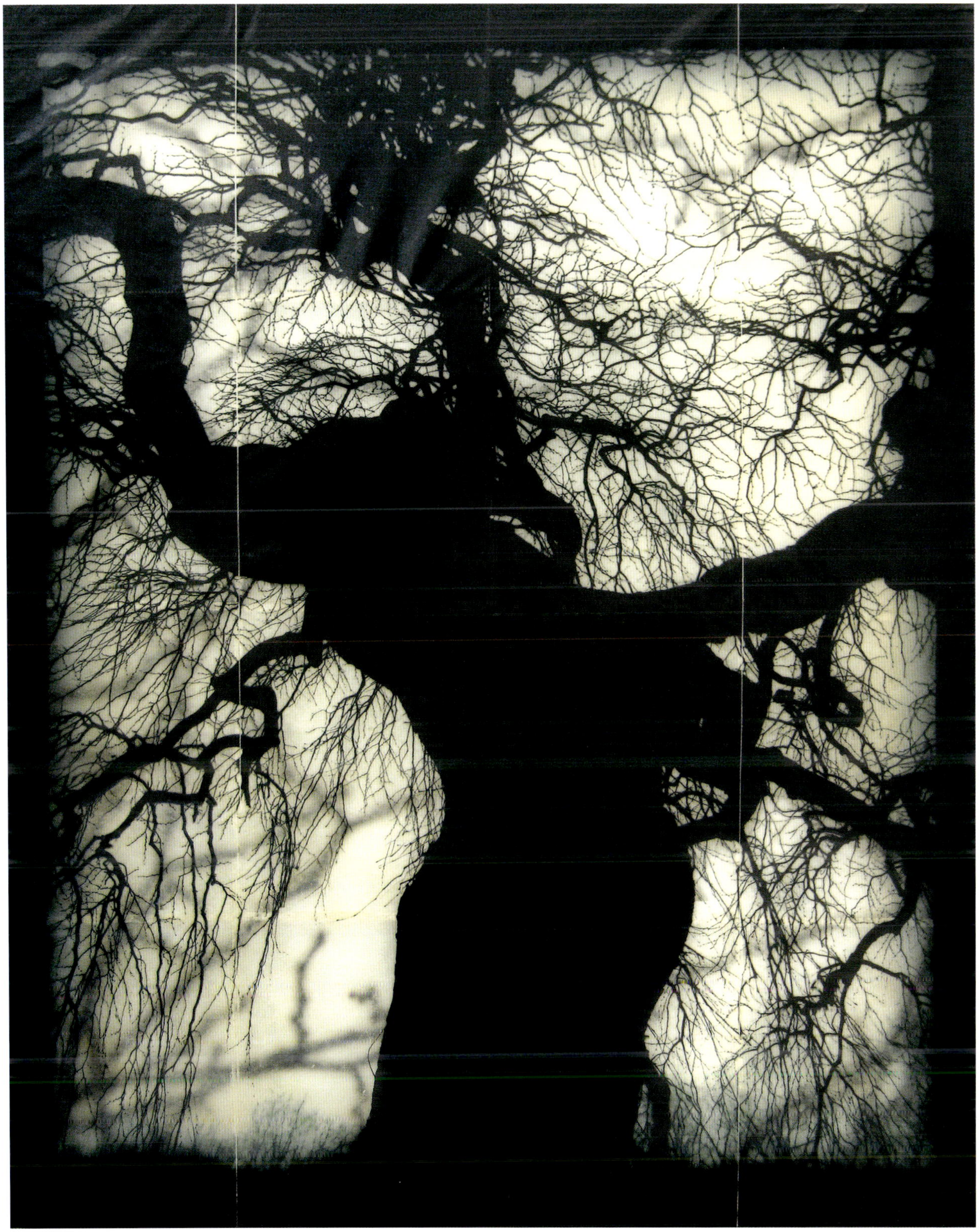

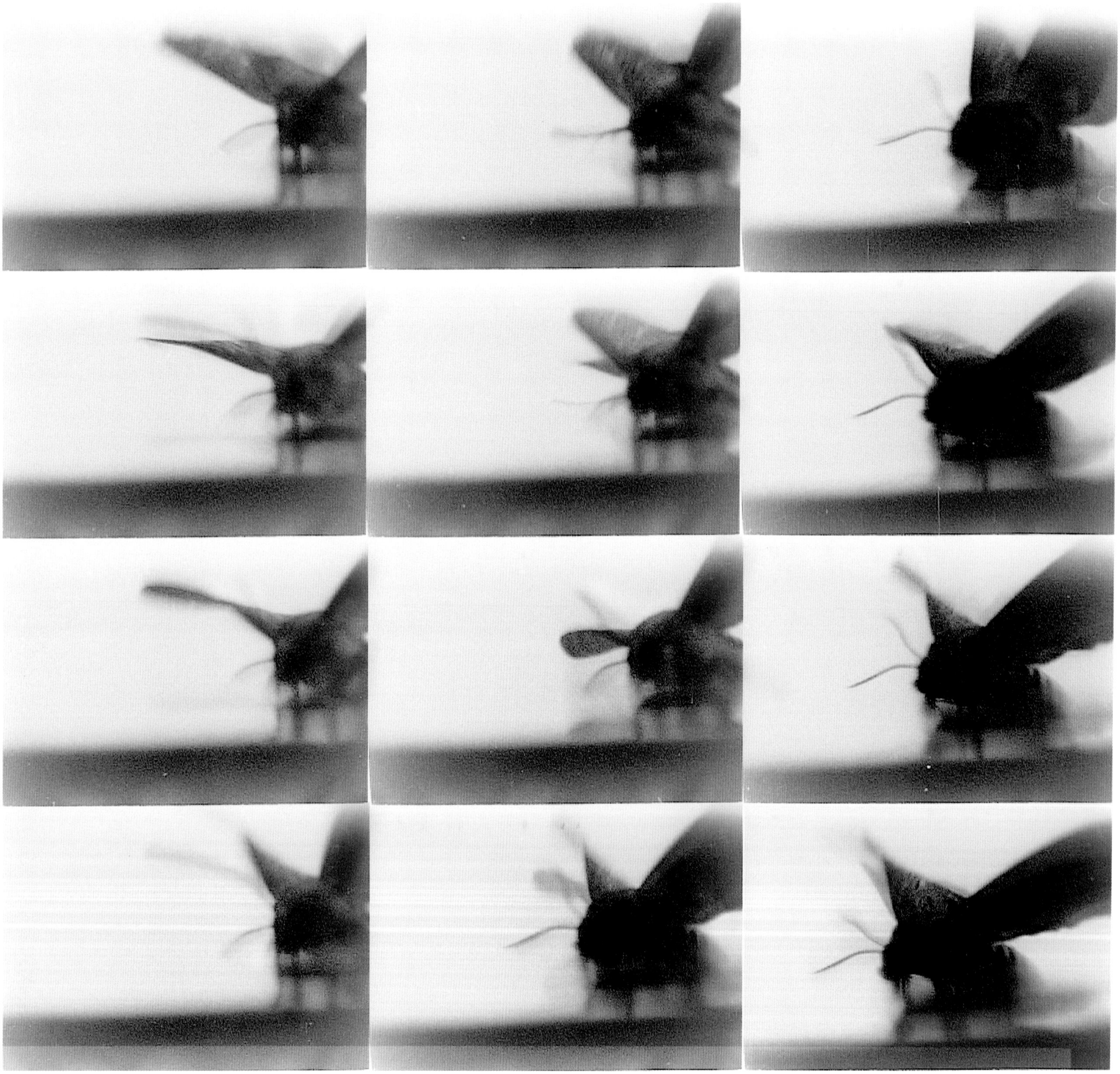

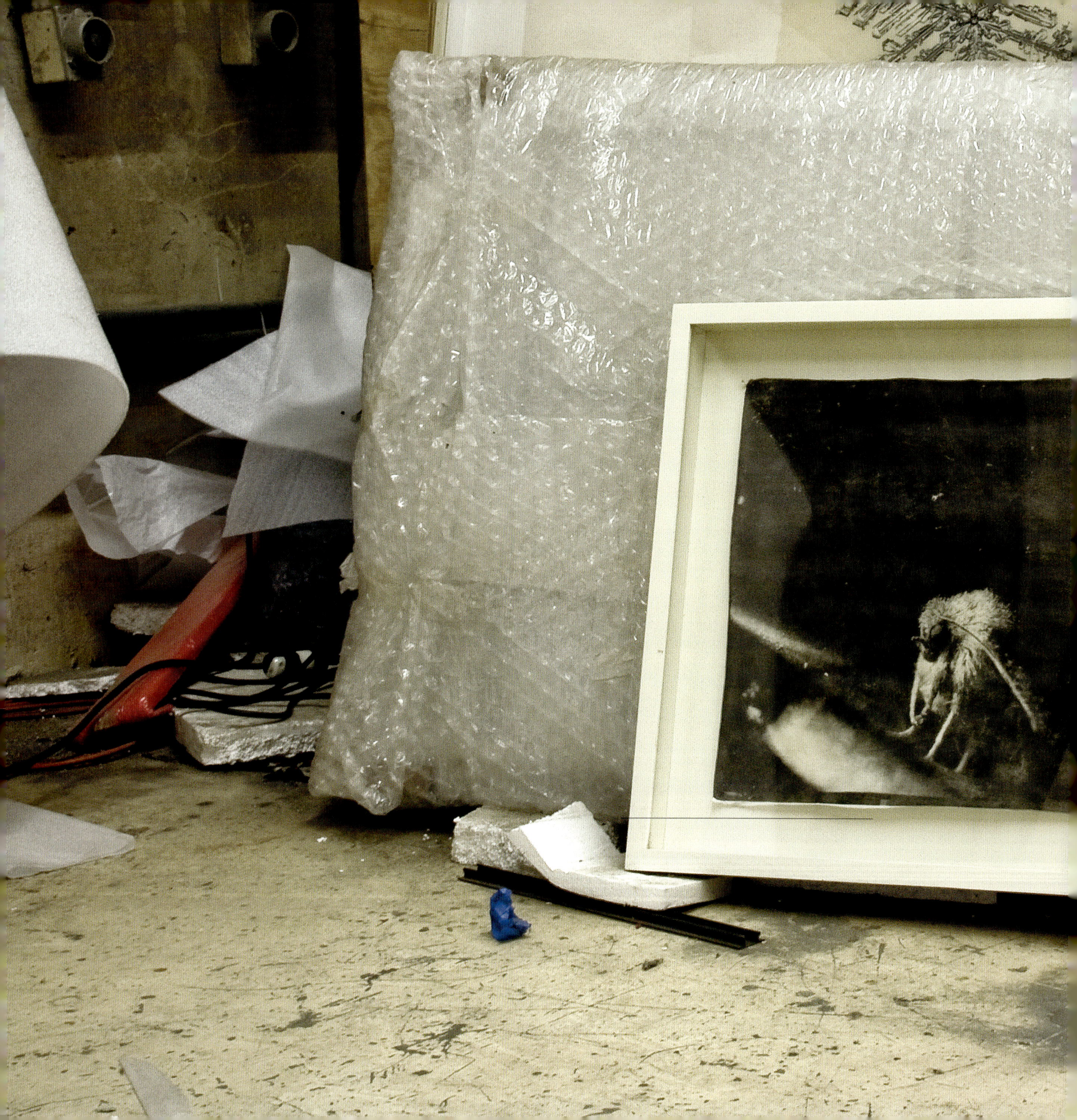

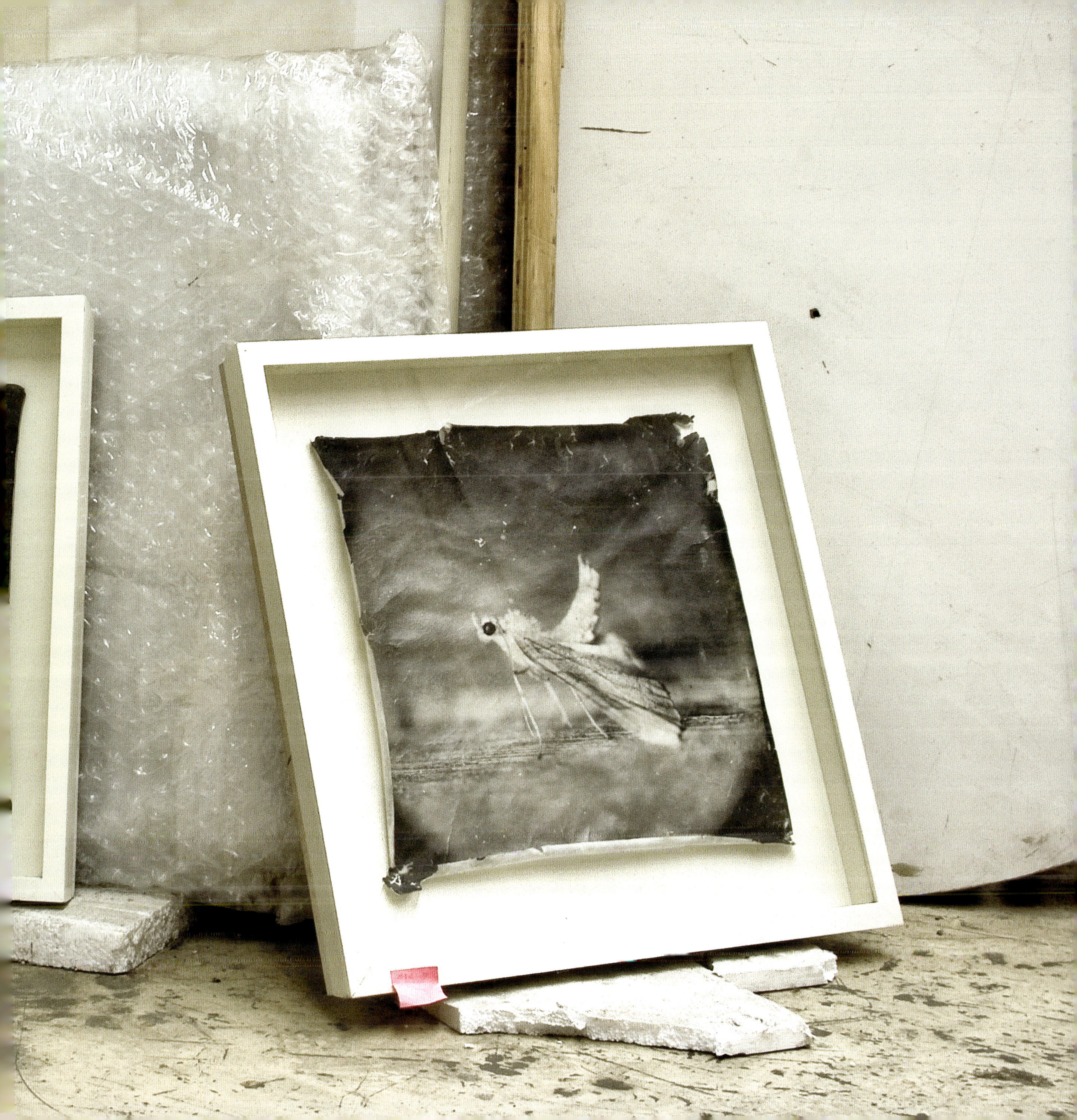

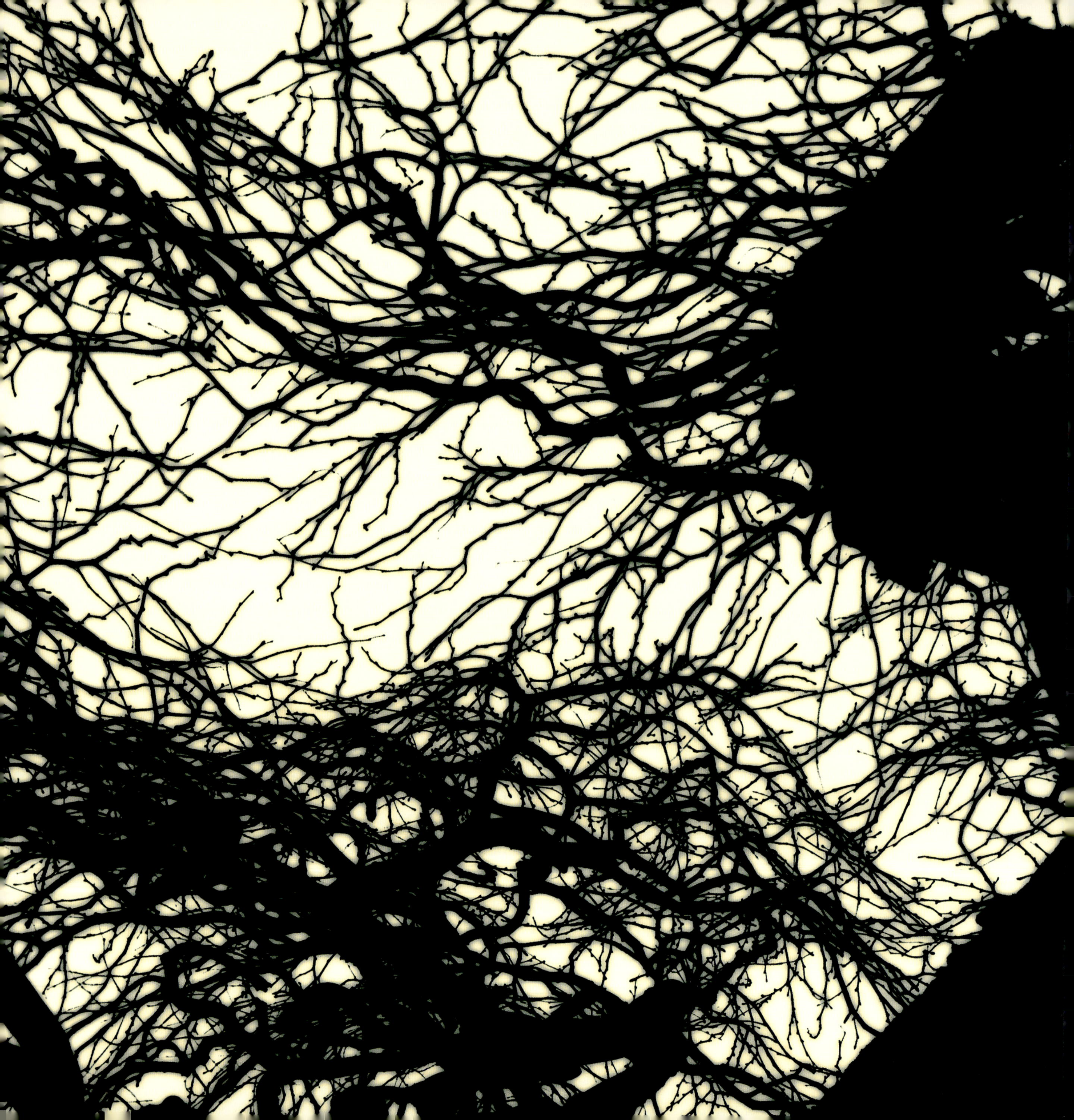

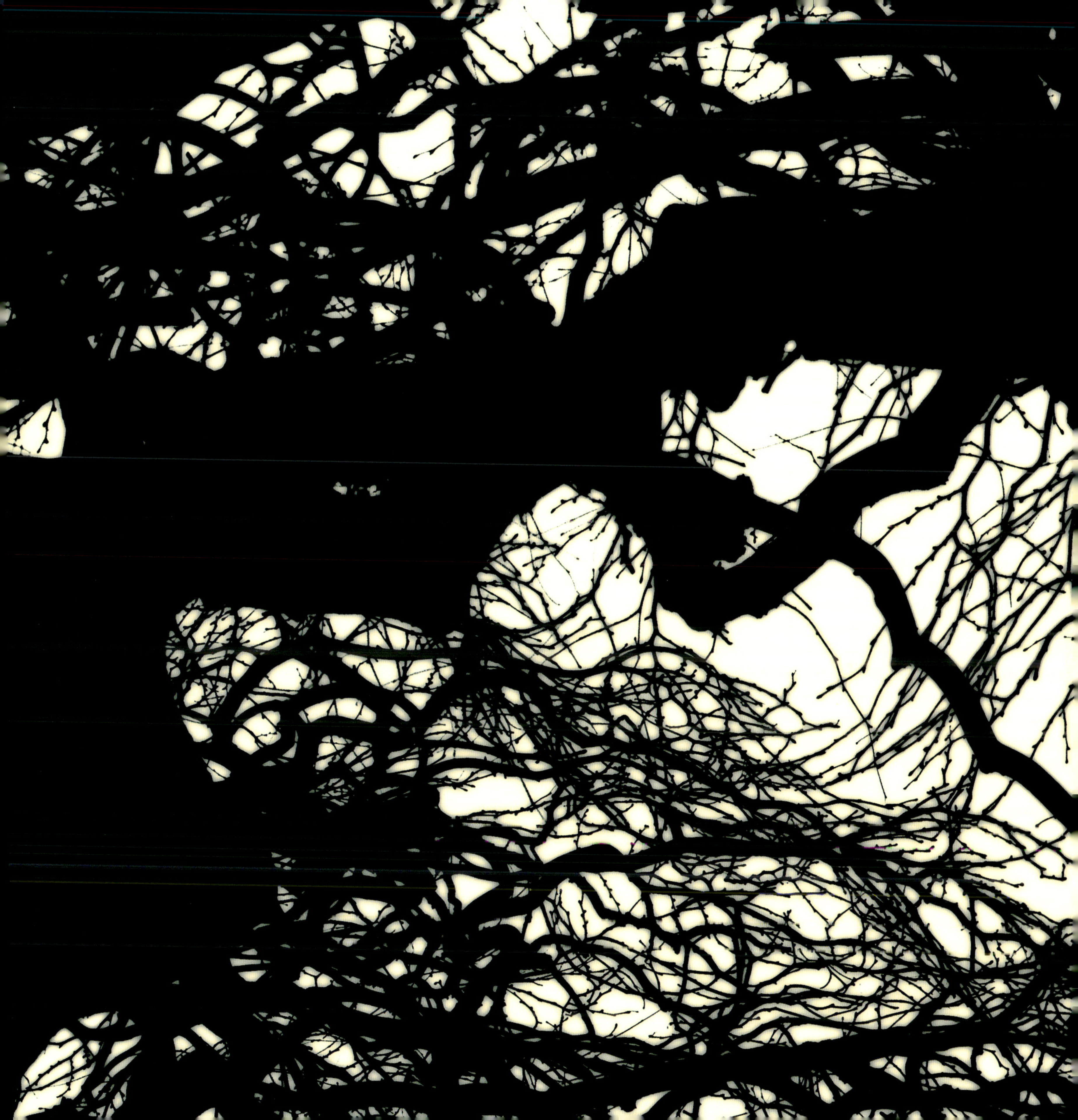

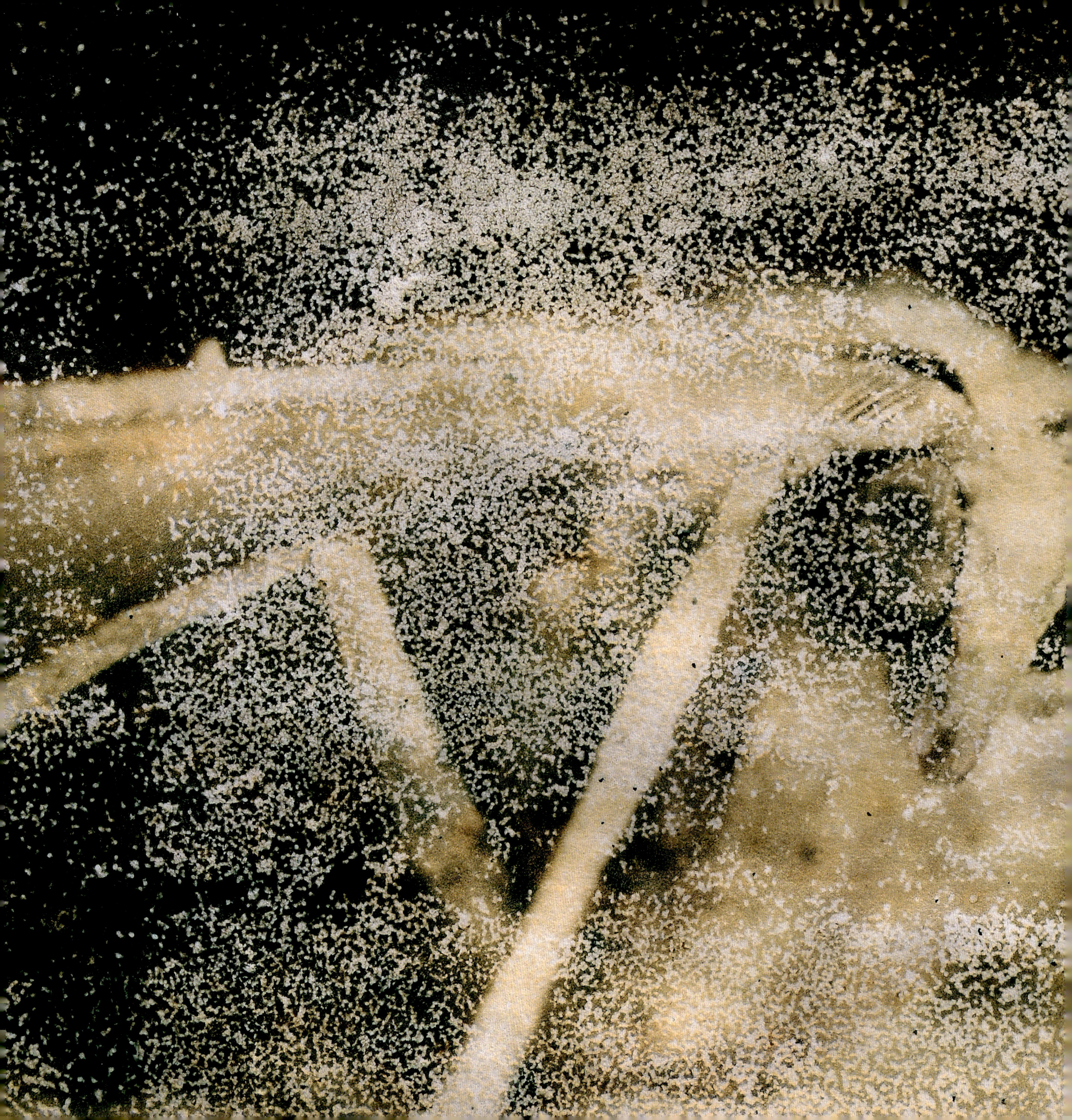

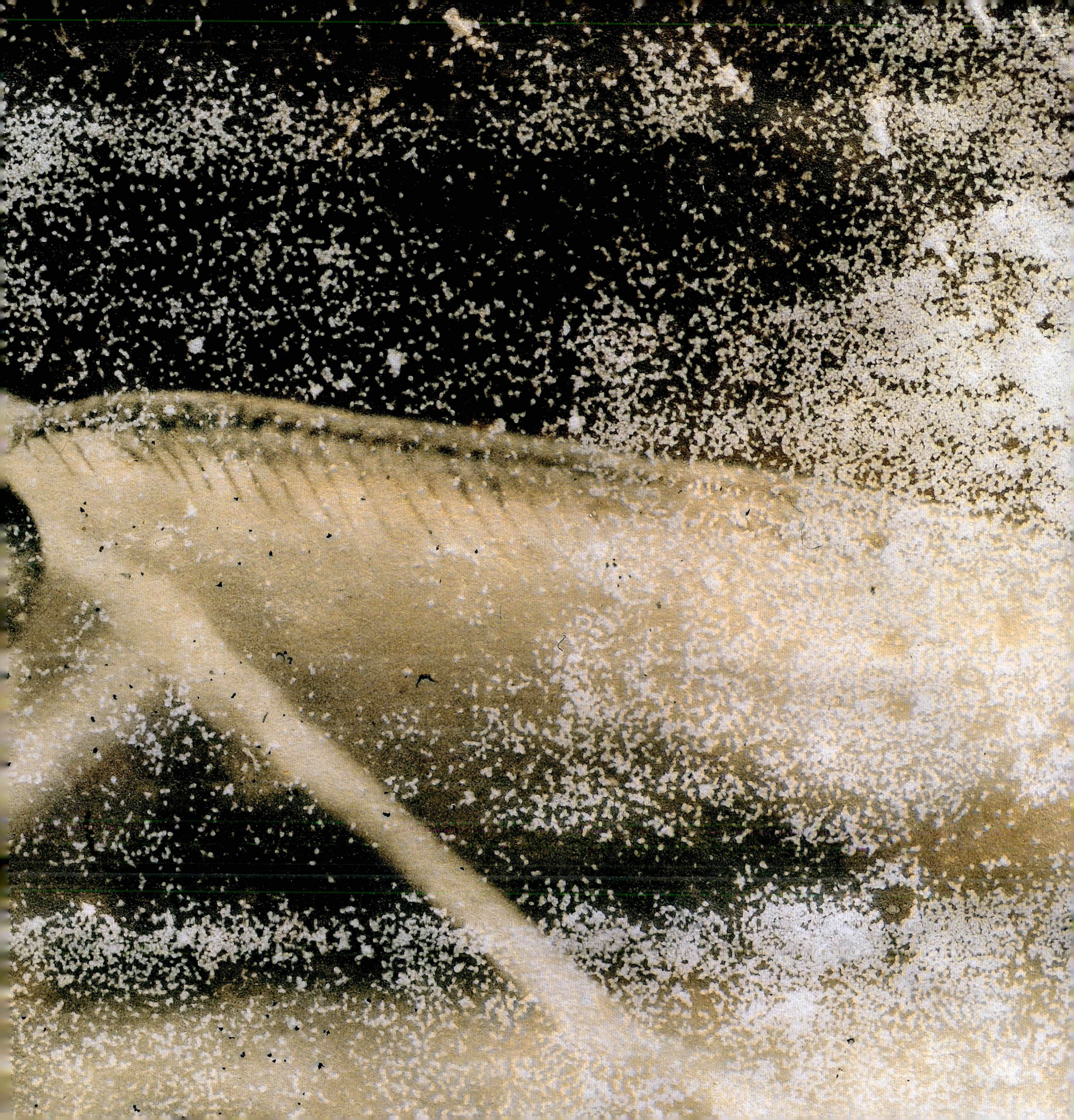

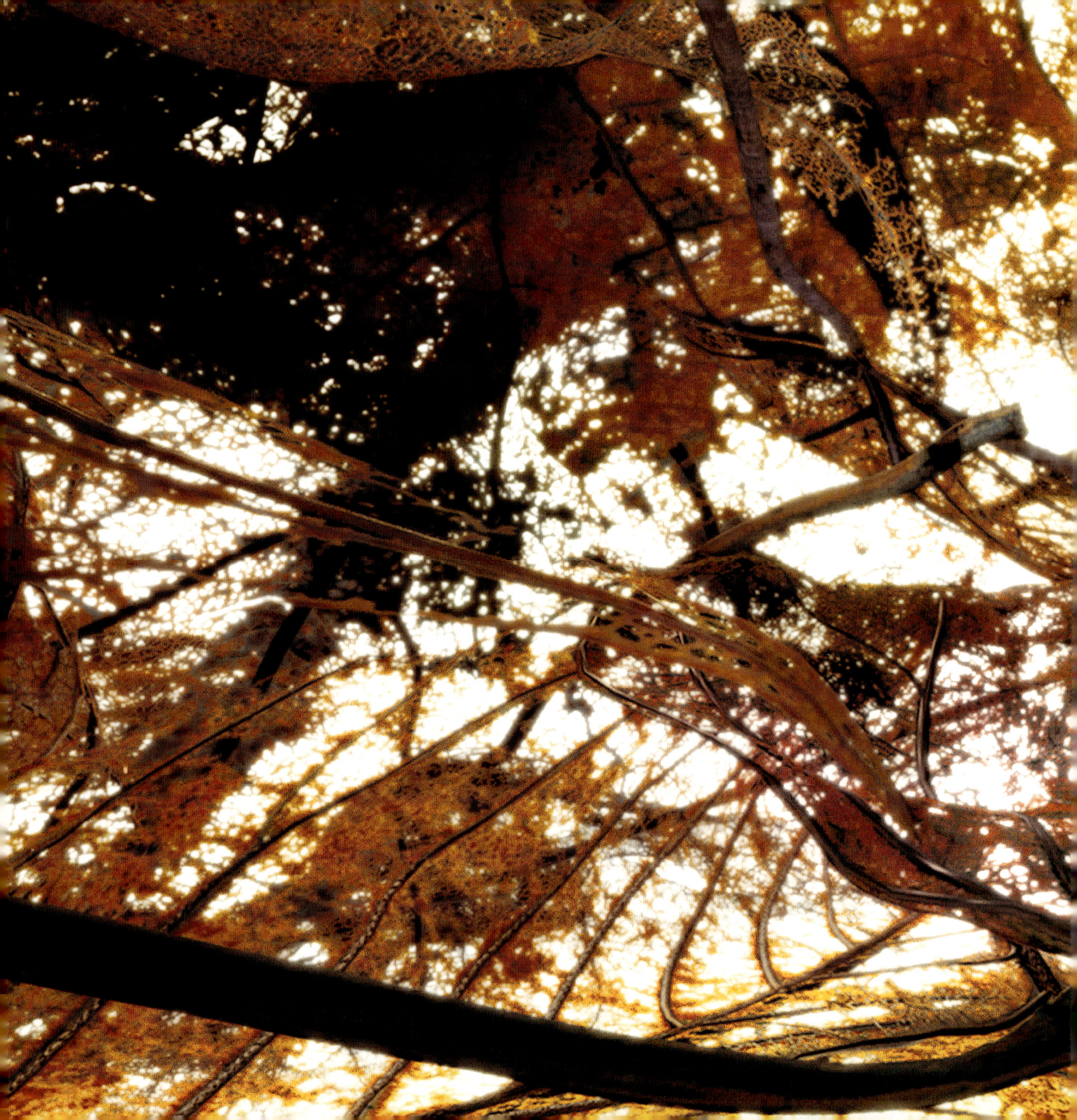

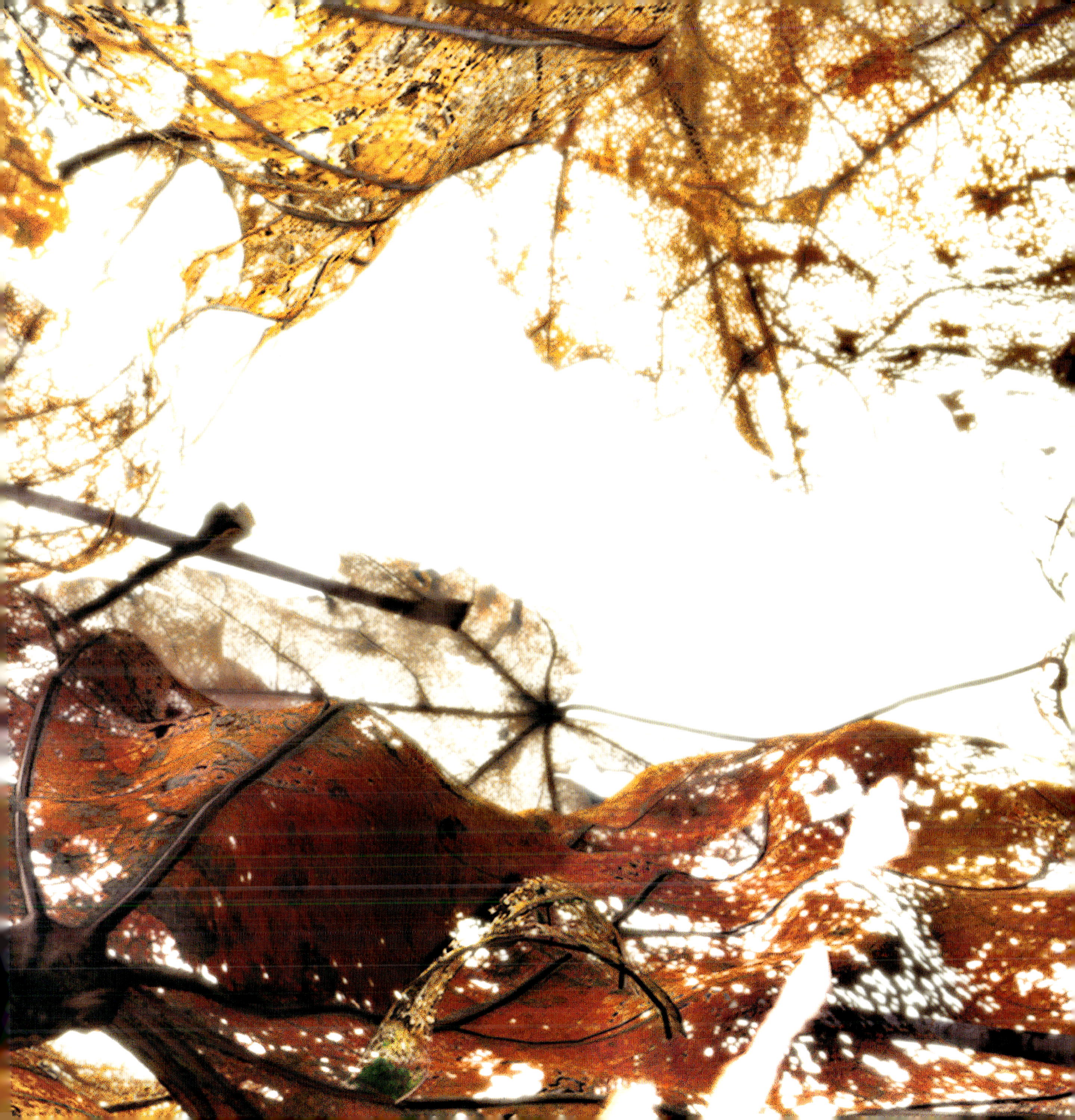

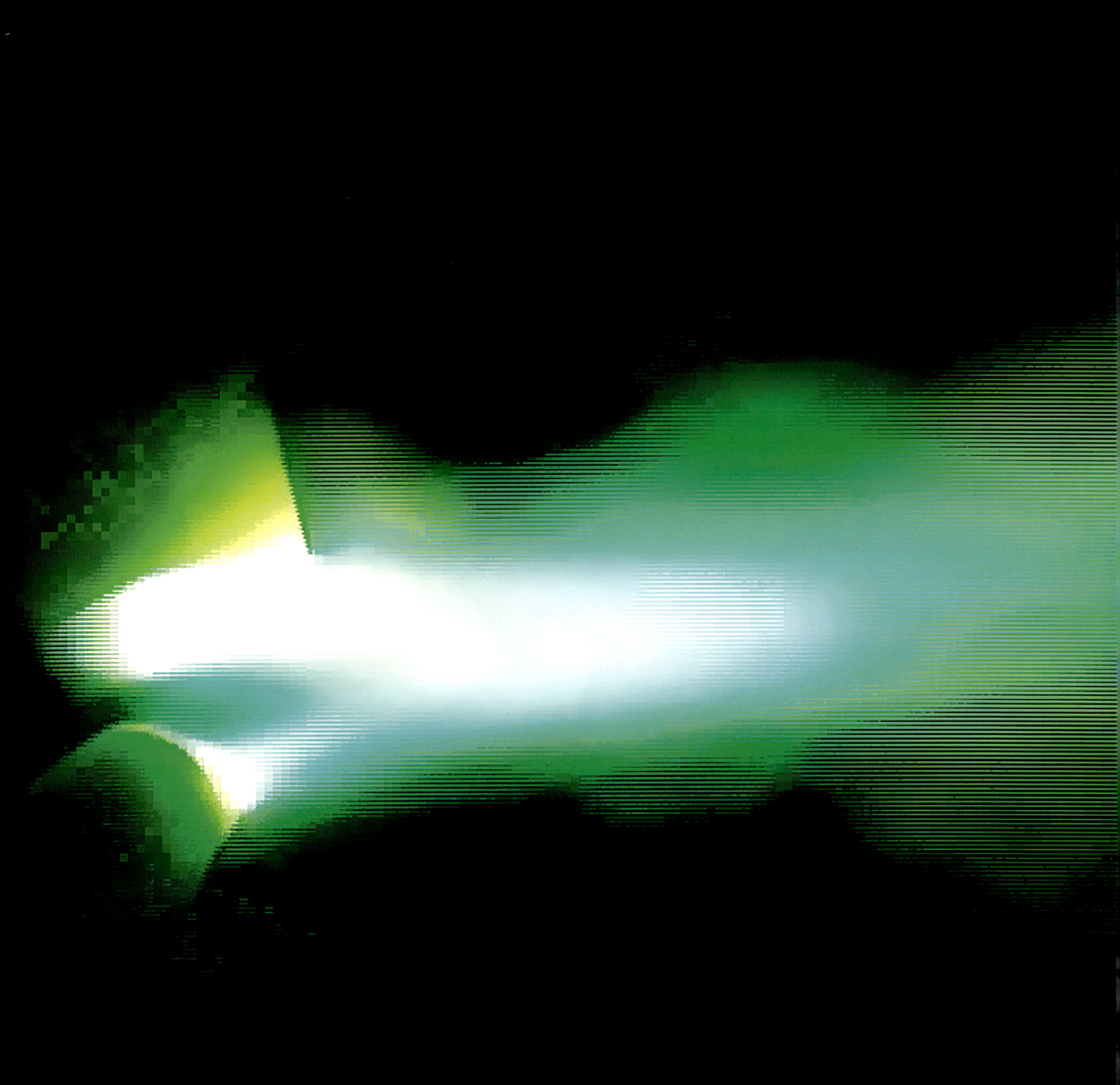

44,000 watt plasma jet, 6,000 degrees F

JAN ÅMAN

Every body in light and shade fills the surrounding air with infinite images of itself; and these, by infinite pyramids diffused in the air, represent this body throughout space and on every side.

—LEONARDO DA VINCI

FIGHTING FIRE WITH FIRE

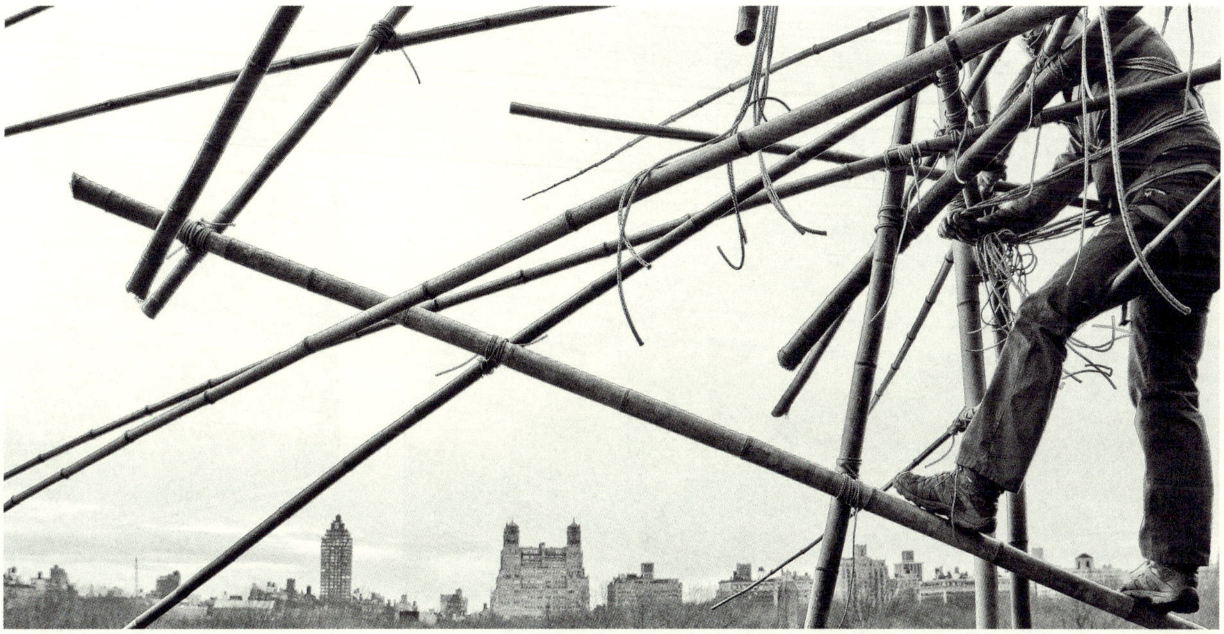

[Fig. 1]
From *Big Bambú: You Can't, You Don't and You Won't Stop*, The Metropolitan Museum of Art, New York, 2010

We clambered around as if in a bird's nest, a house in motion, with Central Park lying quiet around us. We looked out across Manhattan and the skyscrapers looked back at us, as if they were pedestals. [Fig. 1] I thought I caught a glimpse of the famous hawk that lives down by the southwest corner, gliding between the trees near Central Park Zoo. All of this seemed to confirm that we were part of a very specific encounter: one between the most refined, fixed tentacles of urban civilization and organic, transient nature.

I normally suffer terribly from vertigo as soon as I leave the ground, but here I was tranquilly shuffling my way around a rickety, loosely woven bamboo corridor, 65 feet above roof level. The situation called for a heightened presence of mind: I was, after all, in a space diametrically opposed to the monumentality surrounding the park. Calling *Big Bambú* a temporary structure is an understatement. The entire construction was soon to be unlashed, the 33,000 knots on 70 miles of rope untied, the structure dismantled and removed. As if it had never been.

It is no coincidence that the Starns placed their temporary installation on the roof of a very monumental building. That which could never be cemented in place was given its temporary abode right up on top of the institution of institutions, the Metropolitan Museum of Art, symbol of museums' world of ordered culture as well as of New York City's status in the world.

And then it struck me, as I crawled about *Big Bambú*: despite the fact that I have worked with the Starn brothers for a number of years, and have been involved with the *Gravity of Light* project since its incipient spark, it was here among the bamboo poles that I finally realized how everything Doug and Mike Starn have done, and do, really fits together.

The Starns have a special way of expressing themselves, and that expression is wholly the product of an idea about content. And more—an idea about the world and about how we as thinking, civilized beings can act in that world. Like an interplay between a given cultural context and the disappearance from it. It therefore takes a while to get used to the fact that the Starns, when you meet them eye-to-eye, aren't very keen to say very much. Instead they work. Talking to them is about walking around in the middle of ongoing projects and carrying on a dialogue through and about all the works or drafts for works piled around the walls, hanging from the ceiling or sprouting on the floor. The words are filtered through the works. Everything is constantly in progress. Developing organically. The structure of various individual projects is more like a necessary evil. Everything is connected, like the movement in *Big Bambú*. That is

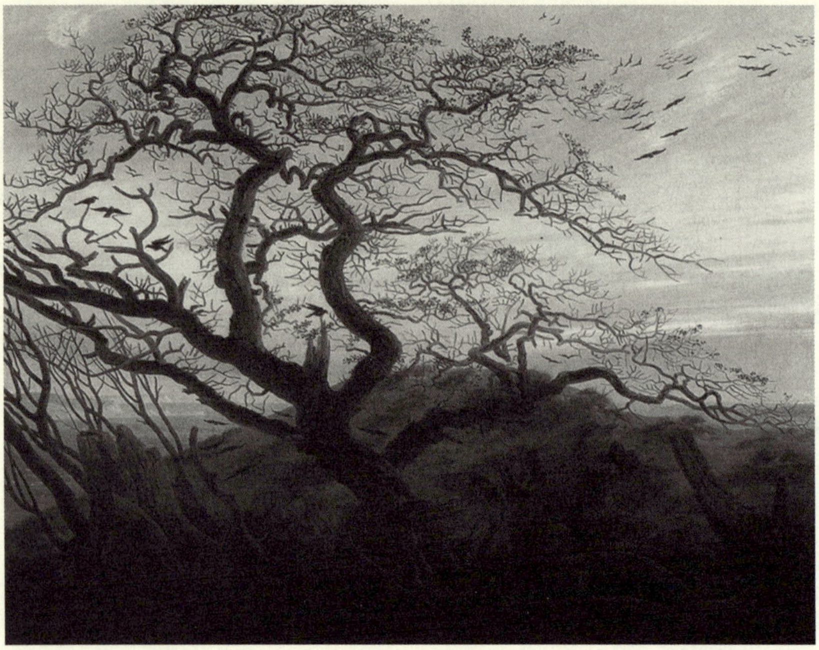

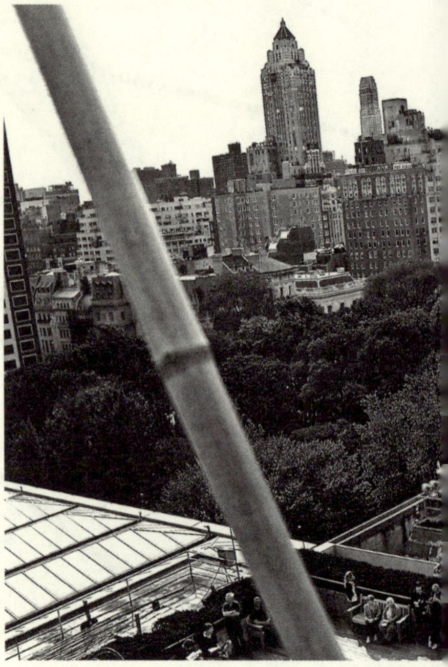

[FIG. 2]
Caspar David Friedrich, *The Tree of Crows*, 1822, oil on canvas, 28.7 x 23.2 in., Musée du Louvre, Paris

why time is their most important artistic element.

The Starn brothers' art calls for its own definition of what a work of art is. Whether they are working with photography, big machines that create light, or bamboo, they always go about it in a manner halfway between that of scientists from a bygone era and contemporary conceptual artists. They explore by doing. Empiricism propels them forward.

The Starns are meticulous. The Starns are never satisfied. Their thoughts on content are forever being processed. But in the same breath as the words are uttered, they become reduced to detail studies, to choices of material, to construction analyses, to molecules and to light moving at the speed of light, in space. That's why they can offer up a staggering institutional critique, almost in passing, in the guise of a sensuous play between light and dark.

Our dialogue in what became *Gravity of Light* began with a conversation about photography. The Starns' photographic work is unlike anyone else's. They go straight to the basic elements of photography: light and darkness. They do so in the theoretical sense, but also in the physical sense. And they do it by means of materials, by means of thin sheets of rice paper, pinned directly to a wall with deceptive simplicity. But they also do it by means of subject matter: the moth approaching the fire and its own death, the leaf decomposing after the sun's rays have stopped giving it life, or the Buddha statue that inverts light and darkness.

Doug and Mike Starns' photography is something more, something other than representation. Which in turn makes it more than photography. It's a process that begins with a shutter opening and momentarily letting in light, just as usual. But as each intermediate step is the logical consequence of the preceding one, elements are added that turn the result into a physical encounter with the essence of darkness and light, which is quite distinct from what photography normally allows.

What began as an innocent conversation about representation, light, and darkness led to Doug and Mike donning their lab coats. They decided to use carbon electrodes and electricity to actually create light—physical, living, burning, consuming, and illuminating light: *Gravity of Light*.

Their work brings to mind the German Romantic tradition in which science, light, and death always appeared in a trinity that was as logical as it was dangerous. German Romanticism was about the archeology of the heart, of life and death—but as a way of understanding the world scientifically. The decomposing leaf carried a confirmation of a divine mathematical order—as it actually does. In a poetic sense that is tantamount to

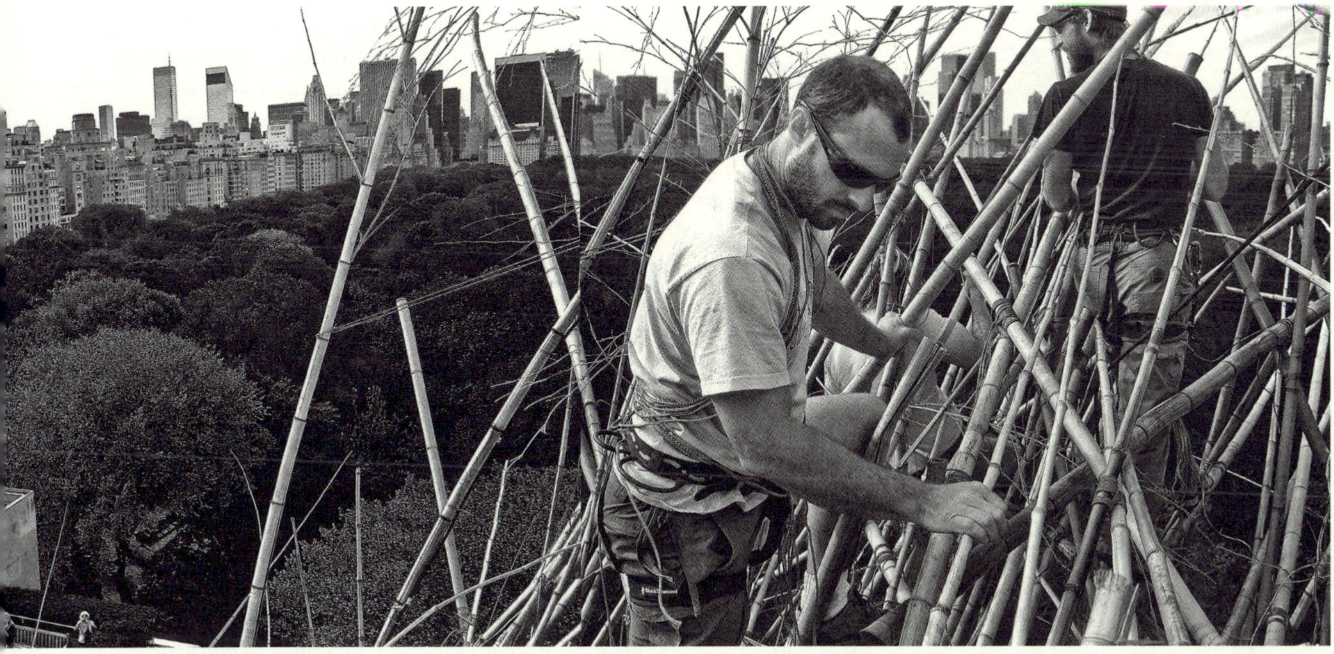

[Fig. 3]
From *Big Bambú: You Can't, You Don't and You Won't Stop*, The Metropolitan Museum of Art, New York, 2010

something that can never reach its completion. And that in turn means embarking on—as Caspar David Friedrich did [Fig. 2]—the pursuit of culture, while simultaneously turning one's back on civilization. It comes as no surprise that eighteenth-century philosopher Novalis stated in one of his "Fragments": "Only the incomplete can be understood, can lead us further."

That was what I thought I caught a glimpse of up there on the roof of the Metropolitan Museum of Art [Fig. 3]. Being artists, the Starns' obvious context is the art world. It's their stage, a stage of institutional weight and economic might. And now they stood on the very acme of institutions. But they had made a radical choice: they were there as a kind of scientific explorer of nomadism. They chose movement and transience where others would only have seen stability.

The Starns' art centers precisely on this paradox: the transient in the institutional. And of course it is precisely this that is exceptional about *Gravity of Light*. The whole project is about something crazy: to actually create light—to play God, to transform space. And the thing is: it is a logical step. Their photographic work was never really about representation. Now they could go all the way: to produce light.

They create a light so bright, so white that the imprudent viewer can actually get sunburned. The light—or rather the source of light, the carbon arc lamp—has its basis in a society of inventions that still believed in progress. The carbon arc lamp eventually led to the invention of the light bulb—which led to light in every person's home. The construction is nothing less than a second fundamental milestone on the road of light toward everyday human existence. The first was making fire by striking stones against each other. Thousands of years earlier.

Gravity of Light creates and recreates a light that brings order. It is a light that creates civilization. A light that would later be adapted, designed, and made quotidian. The Starns show us the same light, our everyday light, in its original form—when it is still chaotic, wild, and even dangerous. When we were installing the carbon arc lamp for the first time, we soon realized that we'd have to open up a hole in the ceiling and install additional ventilation systems to make sure that the gases produced didn't jeopardize visitors' health.

The Starns play with fire, in all senses of the verb. The lamp runs at 6000° Fahrenheit and the light is an open-air plasma, not an ordinary light—or even fire. They play with the original—just at the moment when it is about to become cultural order. They investigate the moment when the invention is still innovation, when it is still wild and uncanny, before it is standardized, labeled,

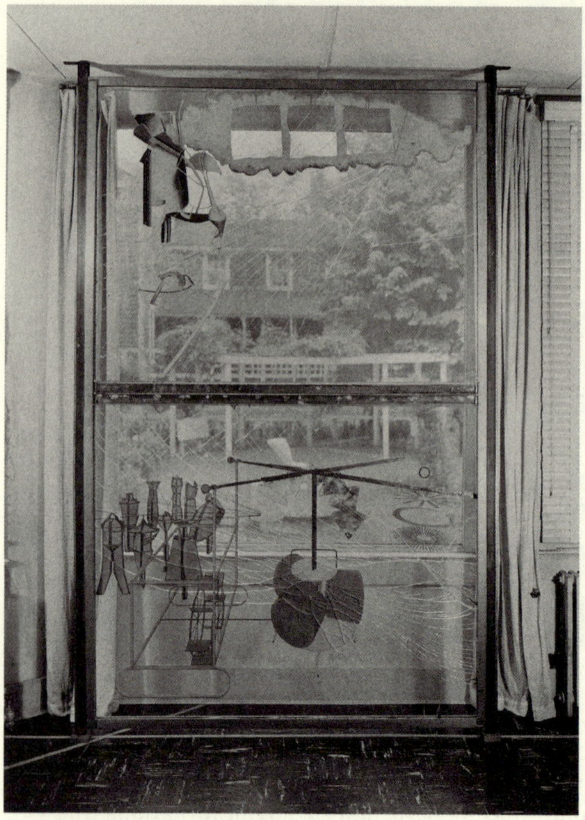

[FIG. 4]
Marcel Duchamp, *The Bride Stripped Bare by Her Bachelors, Even (The Large Glass)*, 1915–23, Oil, varnish, lead foil, lead wire, and dust on two glass panels, 109.25 x 70 x 3.375 in., © Artists Rights Society (ARS), New York / ADAGP, Paris / Estate of Marcel Duchamp
Photo courtesy Philadelphia Museum of Art

and domesticated. It is the light bulb as raw force, at the moment before we, as a culture, learned to harness it.

It is therefore no coincidence that the Starns like to refer to Leonardo da Vinci's painting of John the Baptist. The painting is unusual, even for Leonardo. The saint is depicted alone, smiling in androgynous fashion, against a dark background—very unlike the artist's *Mona Lisa*, who is shown against an inexplicable yet clearly visible landscape. The contrast is usually interpreted as a biblical allusion to John the Baptist's position as "the light [that] shineth in darkness."

Opinions diverge as to the meaning of John's pointing to the sky with his right forefinger. The most common interpretation is that it is a literal description of salvation through baptism. Others, however, argue that the message is more intricate. In this period, the left hand represented chaos, the right hand order. John isn't just pointing towards God but towards fire—the Divine fire. It is a fire that rages every bit as much as the fire in Hades. But it is a fire that burns to create order, an inexplicable order. It is a fire that is the Word in its pure sense.

Leonardo and the Renaissance shifted the perspective: from the flat surface to the illusion of depth. The order of fire was therefore directly connected with that of mathematics. Seeing the world was synonymous to calculating it. In Leonardo's own words from Volume 1 of his collected notebooks:

> *Among all the studies of natural causes and reasons Light chiefly delights the beholder; and among the great features of Mathematics the certainty of its demonstrations is what pre-eminently [tends to] elevate the mind of the investigator. Perspective, therefore, must be preferred to all the discourses and systems of human learning. In this branch [of science] the beam of light is explained on those methods of demonstration that form the glory not so much of Mathematics as of Physics and are graced with the flowers of both.*

Perhaps *Gravity of Light* is about precisely this. As moths are drawn to the flame, so our eyes are drawn to the source of light, the one we neither can nor may look at—as at God—once the carbon arc lamp is switched on. The light is so white that we have no possibility of looking at it without being blinded. And still the fire seeks our gaze. At first glance it extinguishes interest in the rest of the space: it eats up all the energy.

But once the eye becomes accustomed to the light, something else happens, something that would have made Leonardo's jaw drop if he'd been allowed to experience what the Starns have succeeded in doing. When the eye begins to see again, the room slowly re-emerges. We glimpse the photographs pinned to the walls—and we start at the walls and the room itself again. But it is no longer the same room. Everything is changed.

For the fire, the white light, has changed reality, changed the space. We are no longer in the room we thought we were in. The burning light transforms it. The proportions are altered. Distances are pushed all out of joint by a light so white as only the Starns' carbon arc lamp—or a Divine fire—can create. Science enters into an alliance with the Divine.

A new mathematical space, a new perspectival

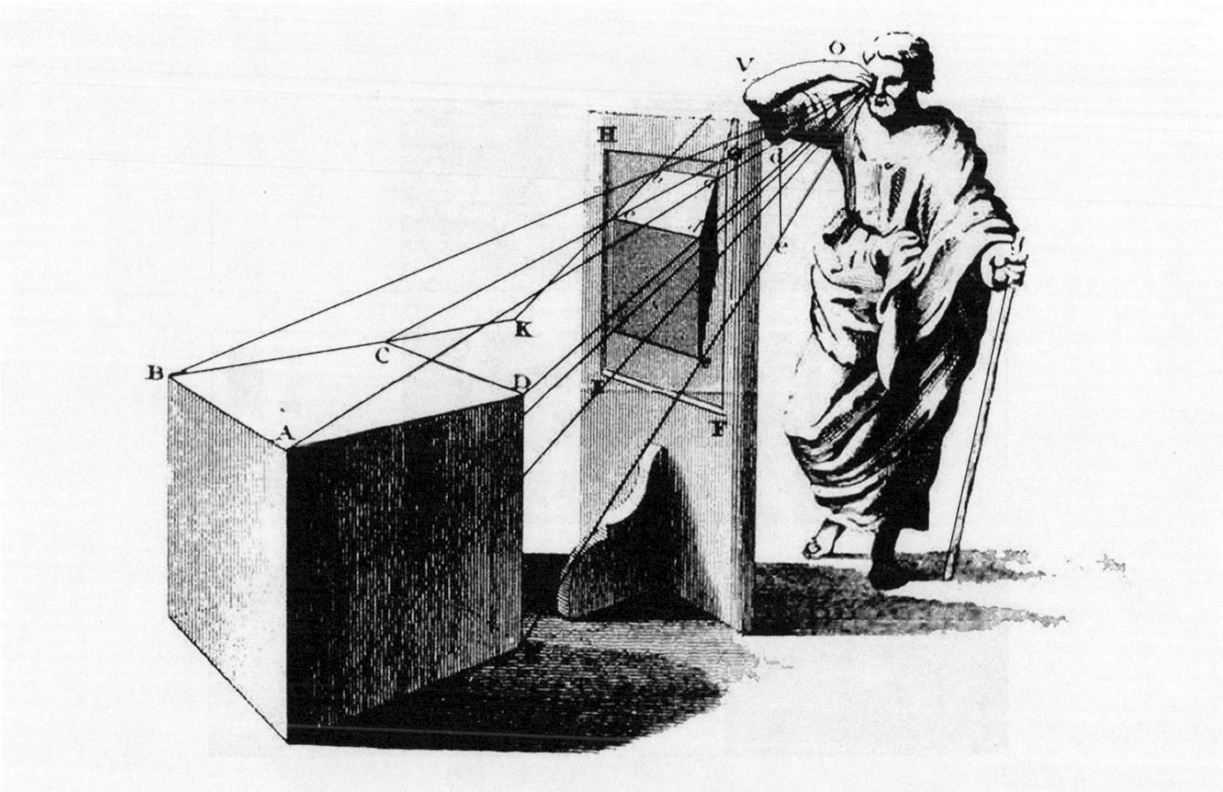

The visual cone, from B. Taylor, *New Principles of Linear Perspective* (1715).

[Fig. 5]
The Visual Cone, from Brook Taylor, *New Principles of Linear Perspective*, 1719

space arises which—due to the living, burning light—behaves as if it were moving rather than static.

Over the past five years I have dug ever deeper into the oeuvre of Marcel Duchamp. And I realize now that a specific side of Duchamp has a direct connection with the Starn brothers' way of relating to art and to the world.

Leonardo da Vinci was one of the few artists who interested the discriminating Duchamp. *The Bride Stripped Bare by Her Bachelors, Even (The Large Glass)* [Fig. 4] is, formally speaking, a play on Renaissance perspective painting. Where Leonardo and his contemporaries learned to work with a matrix that placed the reality/subject to be depicted in perspective [Fig. 5], Duchamp in *The Large Glass* sticks to the matrix itself, to what exists halfway between subject and spectator: the glass. The matrix is the pure mathematics, the purely formal, but at the same time an in-between—where our normal spatial perceptions no longer apply. Duchamp was not content with turning objects inside out as the cubists were. Duchamp wanted an art that matched what happens in our heads when we perceive. He therefore thought the matrix better matched how we see than either subject or reality do. Duchamp sought the movement that is in our heads.

With *Gravity of Light*, Doug and Mike Starn have brought the matrix out into the space. The burning white fire creates another order, an order that dislocates our mechanisms of perception, an order that dislocates distances and proportions. The Starn brothers create a living space so far beyond representation that it leads our brains and our eyes right out into the common space.

According to Leonardo, purifying fire was transforming fire. That which alters spatial proportions. That which makes civilization's institutions levitate. That which sets houses in motion.

Translated by Tomas Tranaeus

IMAGE INDEX

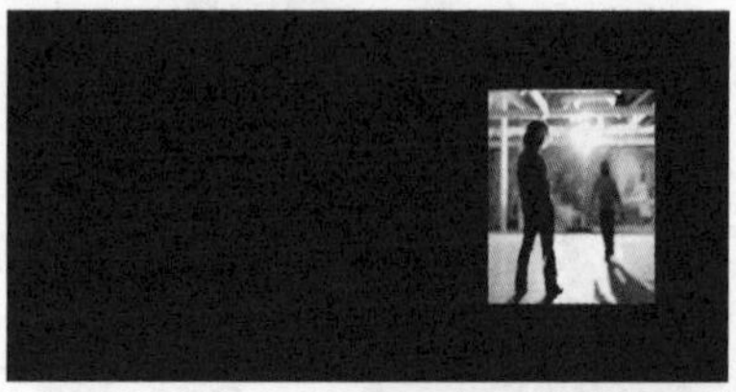

i ii

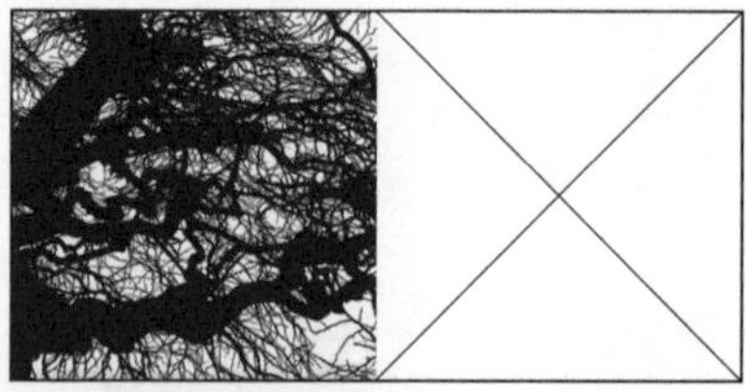

iii

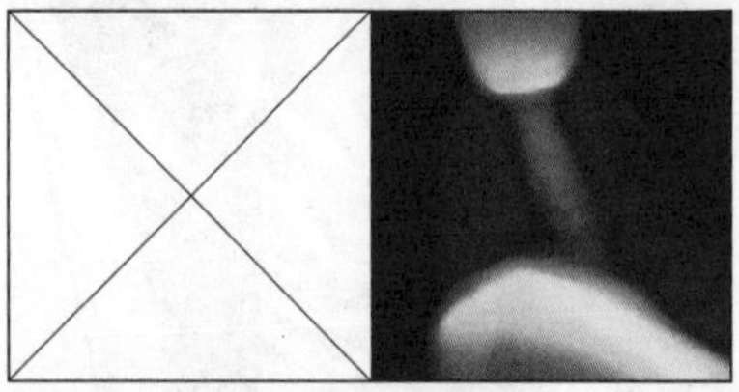

17

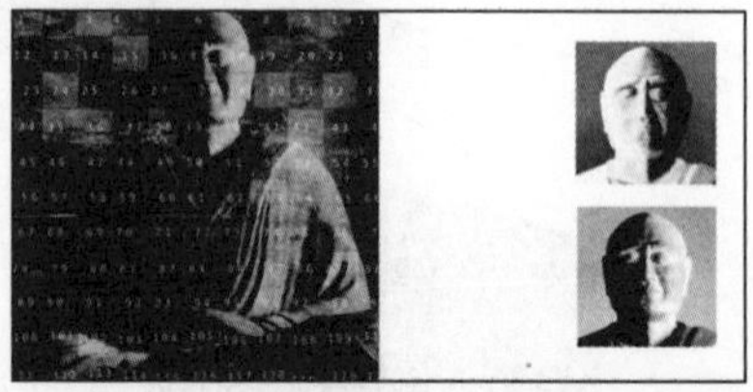

18 19

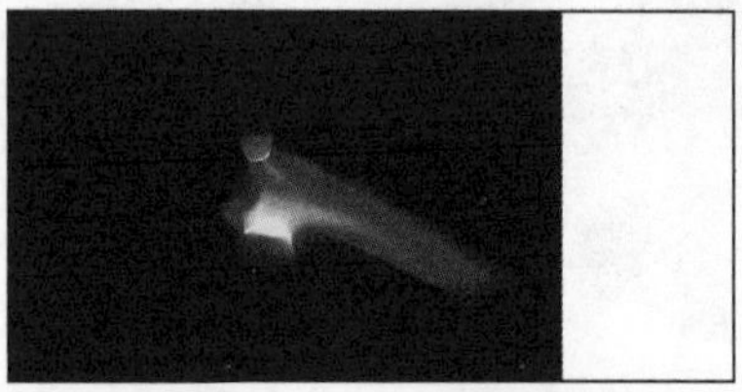

20 21

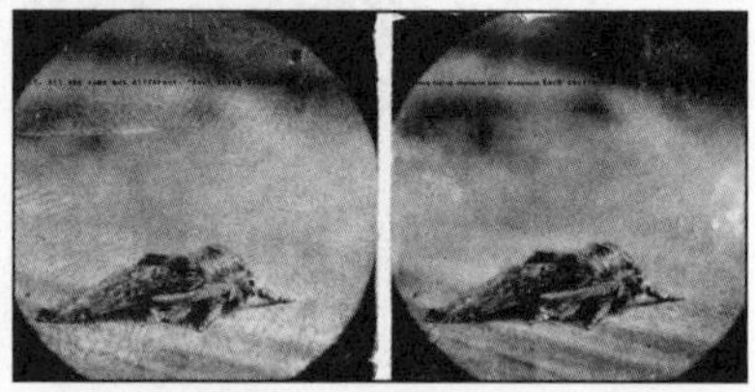

22 23

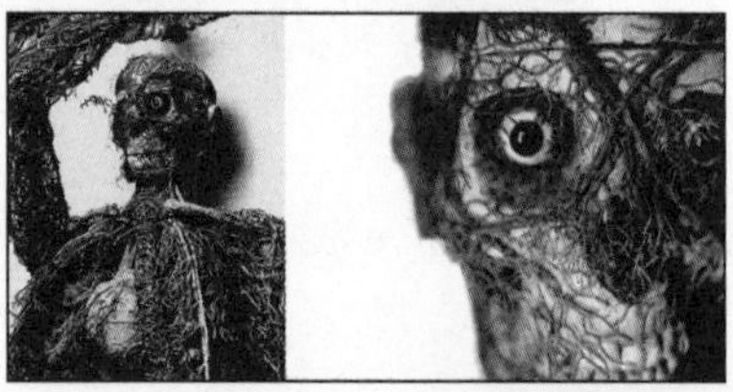

24 25

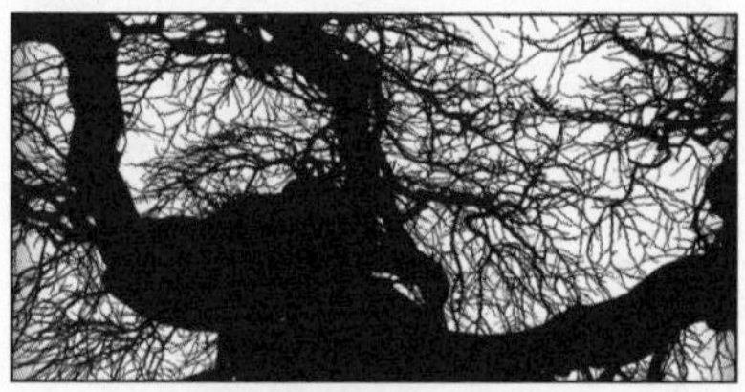

26 27

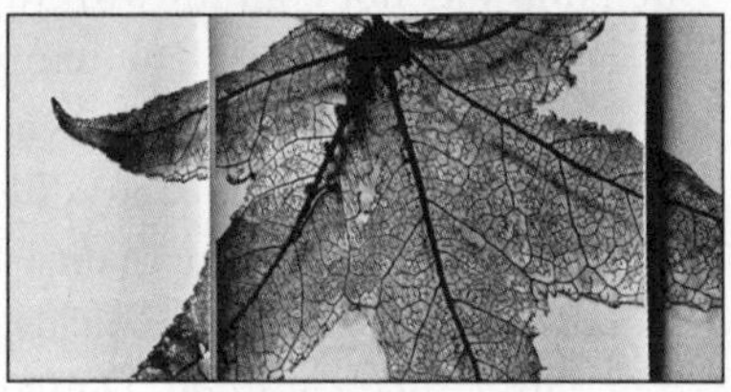

28 29

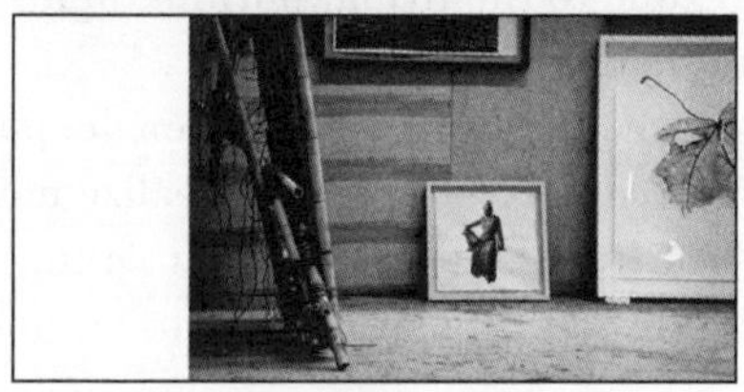

30 31

ii *Gravity of Light*, Curated by Jan Åman 2004–05, Färgfabriken Kunsthalle, Stockholm, Sweden

iii *Structure of Thought 14* (detail), 2005, digital file of Gampi layer

17 *Leonardo's St. John or this is my middle finger*, 2004, digital film still of plasma jet

18 *Coincidence of Opposites*, artist book, index page, from a five-volume series on *Gravity of Light*

19 *Ganjin* (negative) (detail) / *Ganjin* (positive) (detail), 2000–05, lambda digital C-prints mounted on aluminum, 120 x 120 in. each

20–21 *Leonardo's St. John or this is my middle finger*, 2004, digital film still of plasma jet

22–23 *The Same But Different*, artist book, from a five-volume series on *Gravity of Light*

24 Macchine Anatomiche, Napoli, Italy

25 *Take Off Your Skin, It Ain't No Sin* (detail), 2005, digital stereoscopy file

26–27 *Structure of Thought 21* (detail), 2008, digital file of Gampi layer

28–29 *Black Pulse 4 (lambda)* (detail), 2000, lambda digital C-print, 111 x 144 in.

30–31 Studio view, 2012, Beacon, New York

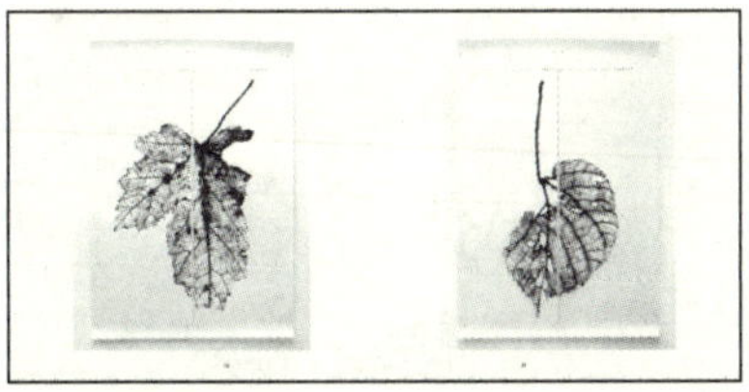

32 33

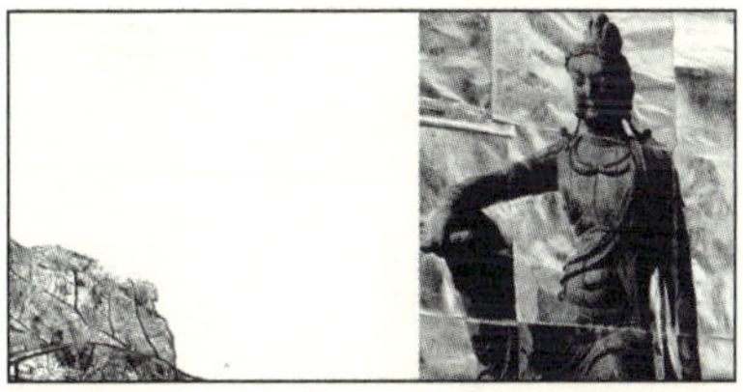

34 35

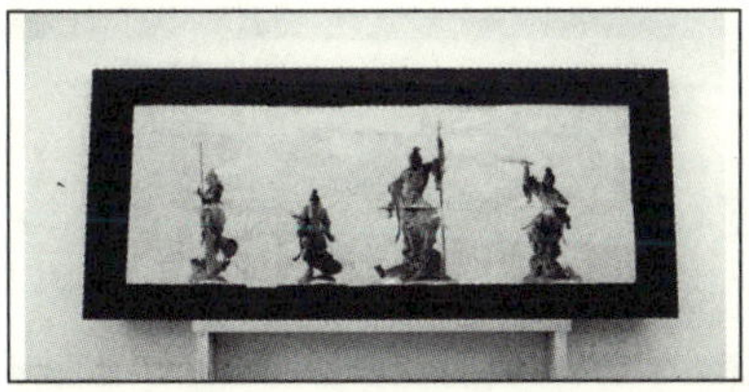

36 37

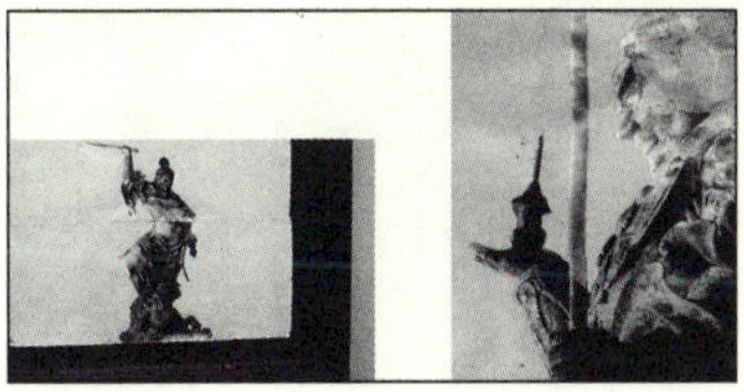

38 39

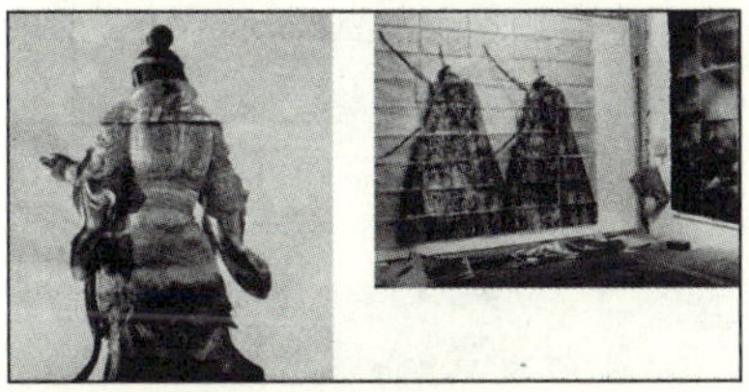

40 41

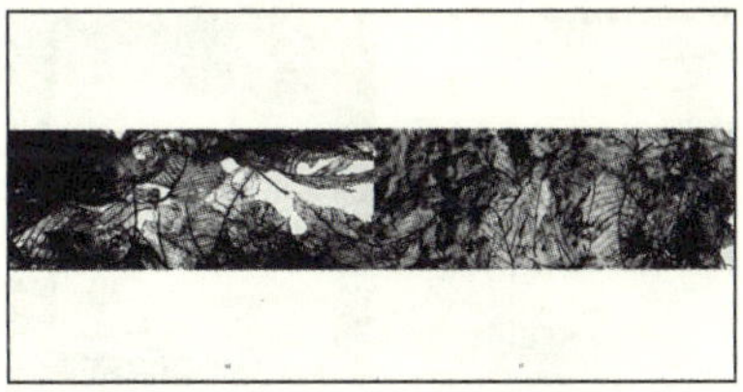

42 43

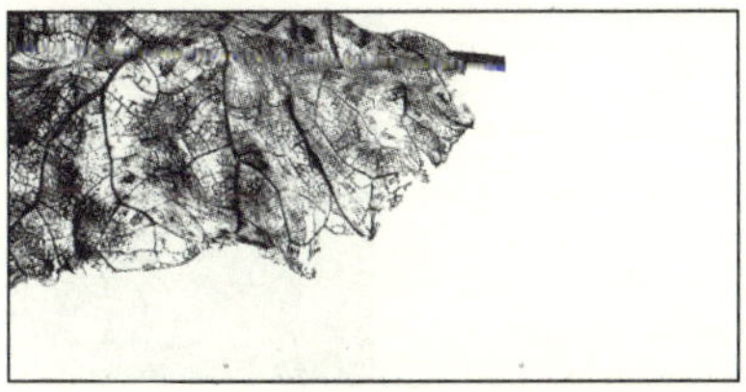

44 45

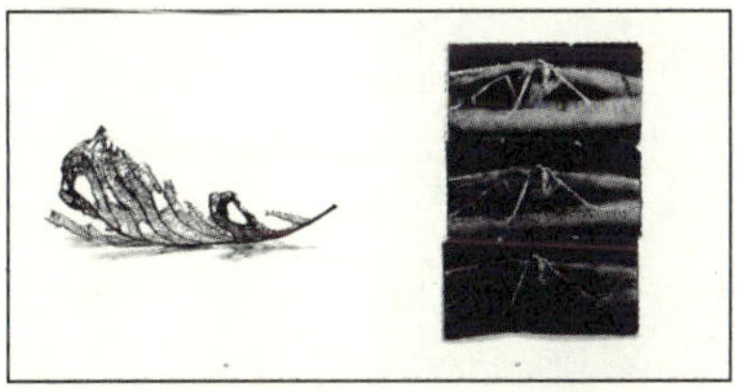

46 47

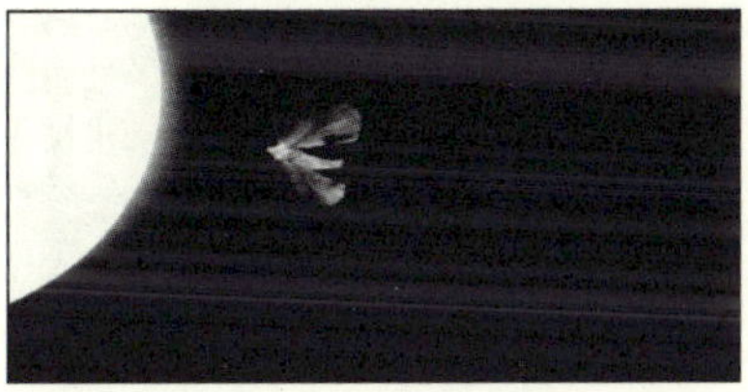

48 49

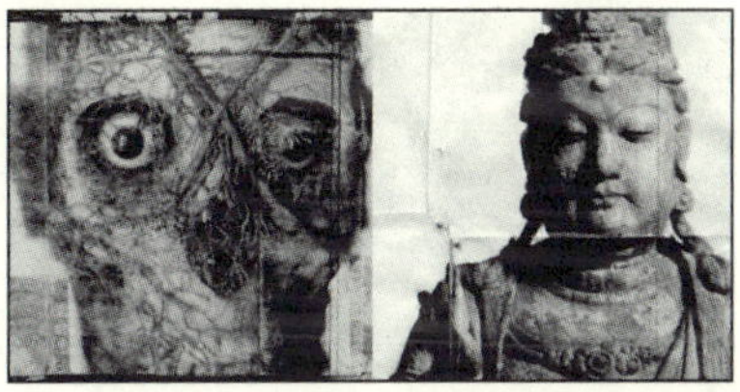

50 51

32 *Black Pulse 3 (lambda)*, 2000, lambda digital C-print, 70 x 47 in.

33 *Black Pulse 6 (lambda)*, 2000, lambda digital C-print, 70 x 47 in.

34 *Black Pulse 11 (lambda)* (detail), 2000, digital file

35 *Manjushri* (detail), 2005–08, unique color carbon print (watercolor pigments and gelatin) on Zerkall paper with 16k gold and palladium leaf water gilding, 94 x 75 in.

36–37 *The light in there was blinding, full of God and hate and truth*, 2005–07, unique color carbon print (watercolor pigments and gelatin) on Zerkall paper with 16k gold and palladium leaf water gilding, 65 x 152 in.

38–40 *The light in there was blinding, full of God and hate and truth* (details), 2005–07

41 Studio view, 2003, Brooklyn, New York

42–43 *Black Pulse*, video animation stills

44–45 *Black Pulse 11 (lambda)* (detail), 2000, digital file

46 *Black Pulse 17 (lambda)*, 2000, digital file

47 *ATL 19 (triple) Ephemera*, 1996–2003, sulfur toned hand-coated silver emulsion on tea-stained Thai mulberry paper with Scotch tape, 30 x 20 in.

48–49 *ATL Film Still 5* (detail), 1996–2003, digital file

50 *Flay Me* (detail), 2007, ink-jet prints on Thai mulberry and Gampi papers with varnish, encaustic, 16k gold water gilding, and velvet

51 *Guanyin* (detail), 2005, unique four-color carbon print (watercolor pigments and gelatin) on Zerkall paper

IMAGE INDEX

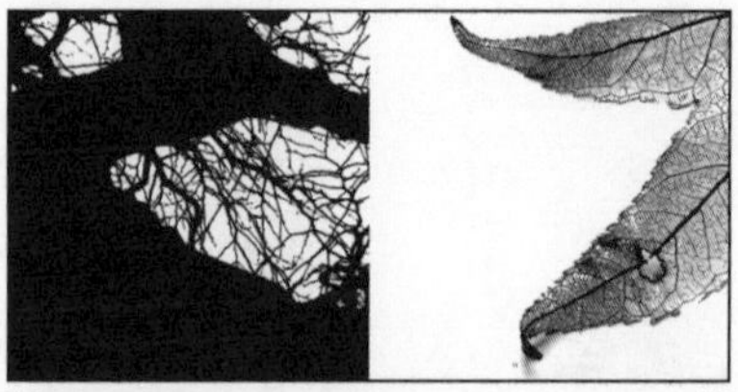

52 53

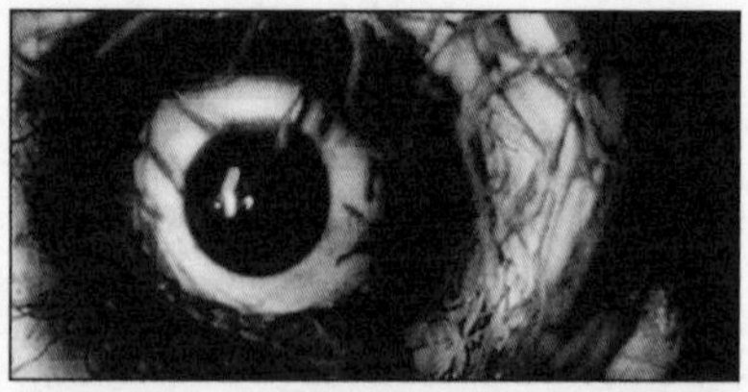

54 55

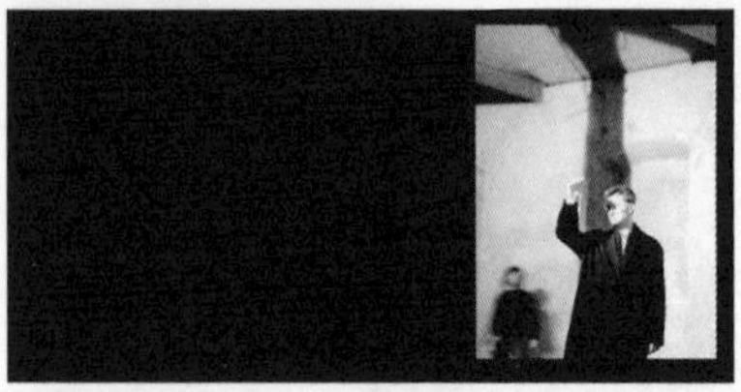

56 57

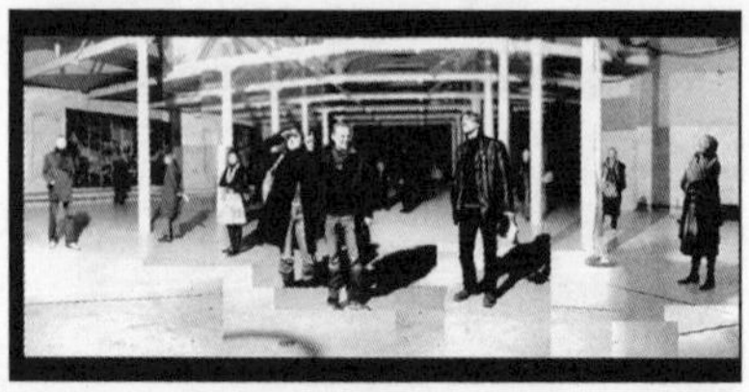

58 59

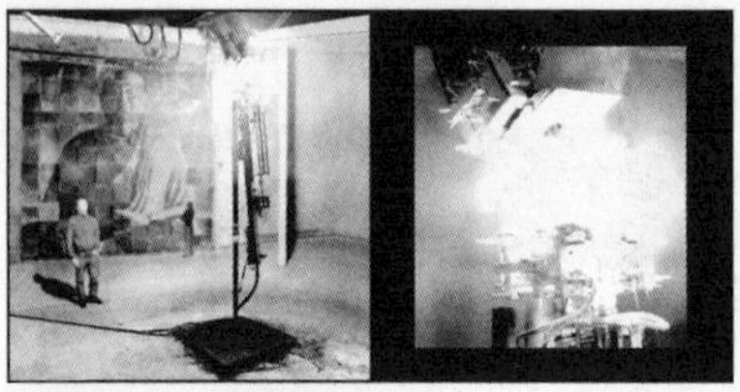

60 61

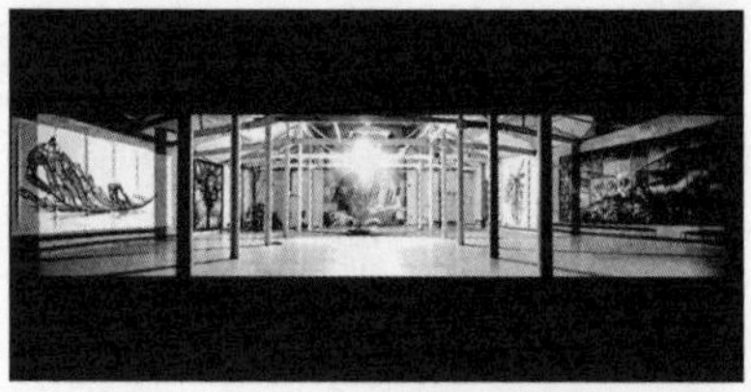

62 63

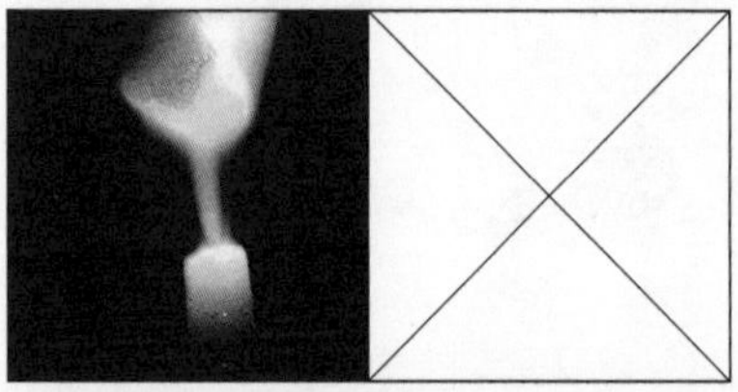

64

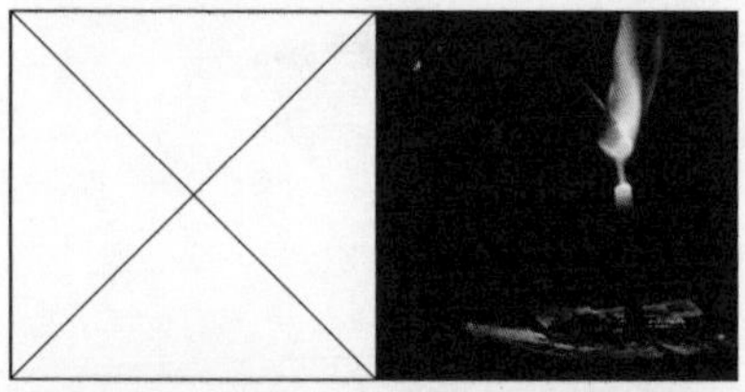

81

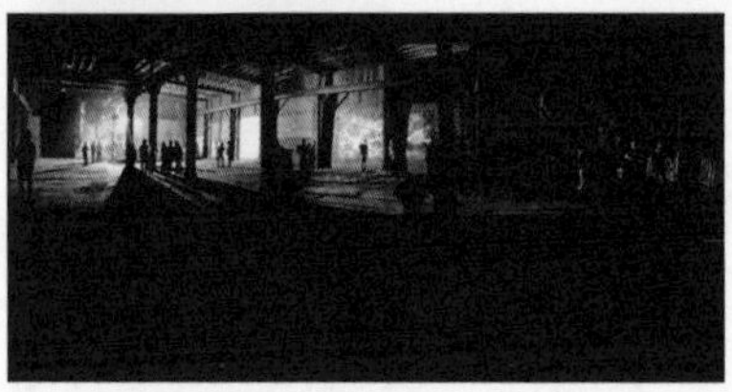

82 83

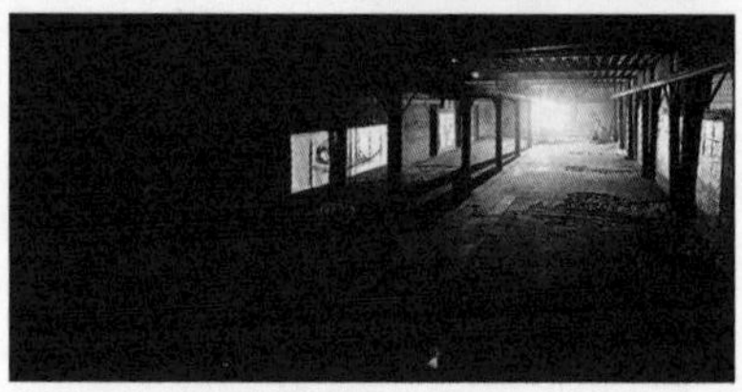

84 85

52 *Structure of Thought 10* (detail), 2003, digital file of Gampi layer

53 *Black Pulse 4 (lambda)* (detail), 2000, digital file

54–55 *Daruma's immodest eye* (detail), 2005, digital file

57–59 *Gravity of Light*, 2004–05, curated by Jan Åman, Färgfabriken Kunsthalle, Stockholm, Sweden

60 *Leonardo's St. John or this is my middle finger* and *Ganjin* installation views, *Gravity of Light*, 2004–05, Färgfabriken Kunsthalle, Stockholm, Sweden

61 *Leonardo's St. John or this is my middle finger* (detail), 2004, steel, carbon, electronic components, Färgfabriken Kunsthalle, Stockholm, Sweden

62–63 *Gravity of Light*, 2004–05, curated by Jan Åman, Färgfabriken Kunsthalle, Stockholm, Sweden

64 *Leonardo's St. John or this is my middle finger* (detail view of plasma jet) 2004, Studio view, Brooklyn, New York

81 *Leonardo's St. John or this is my middle finger* (detail view of plasma jet) 2004, installation view, Doug + Mike Starn studio, Brooklyn, New York

82–85 *Gravity of Light*, 2008, curated by Murray Horne for the Wood Street Galleries, the Pipe Building, Pittsburgh, Pennsylvania

IMAGE INDEX

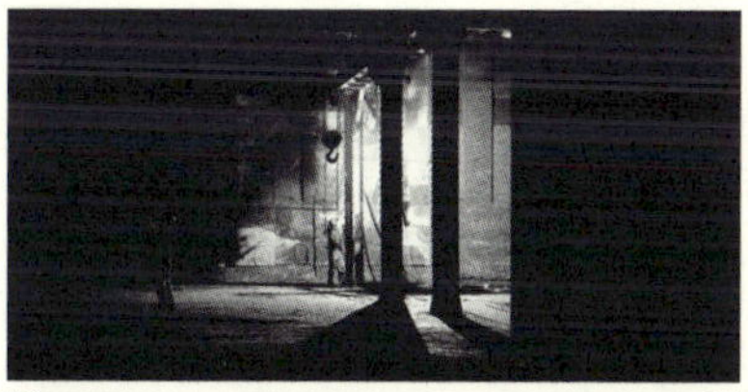

86 87

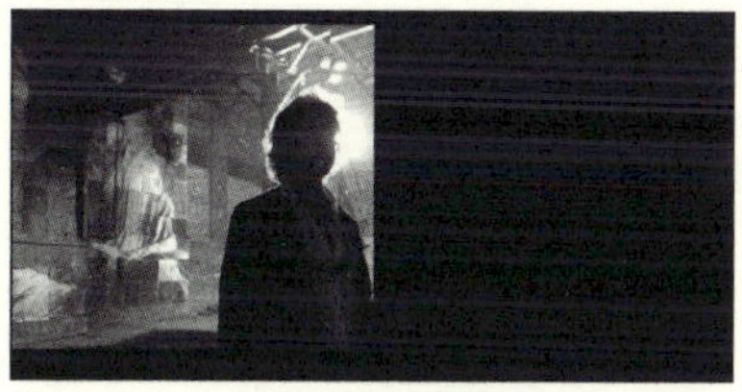

88 89

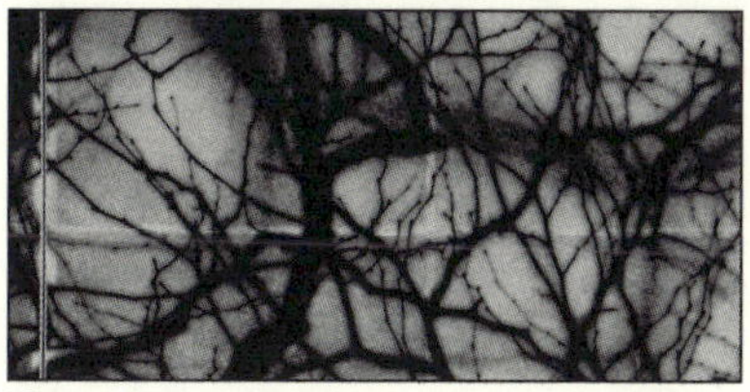

90 91

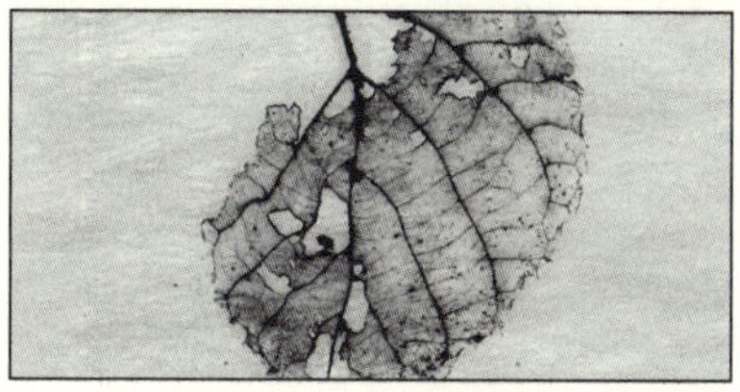

92 93

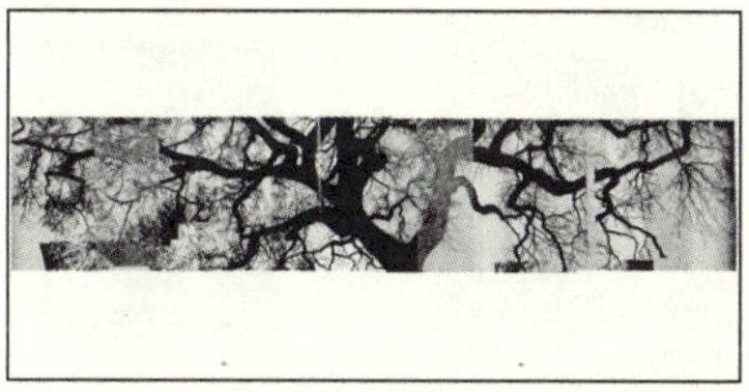

94 95

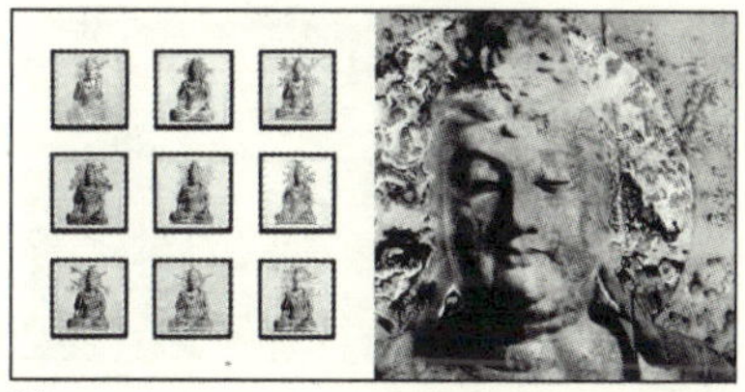

96 97

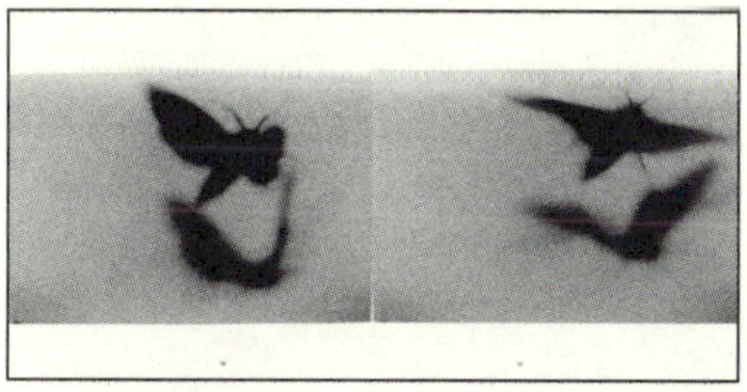

98 99

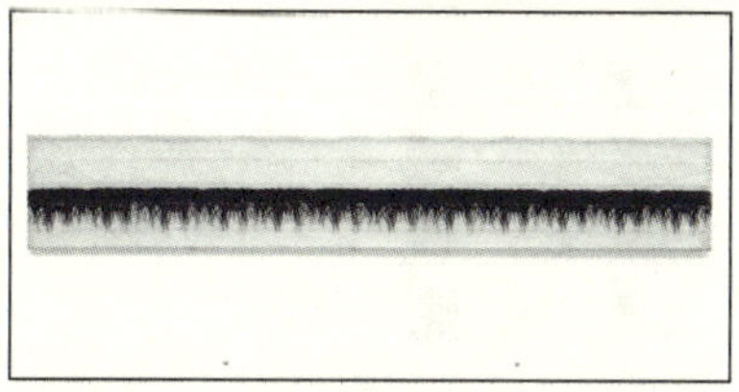

100 101

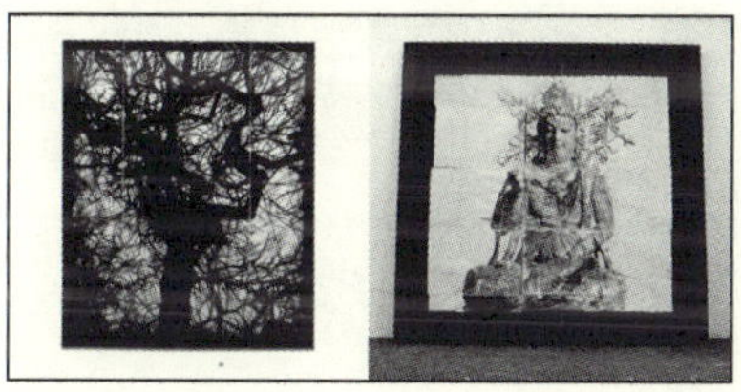

102 103

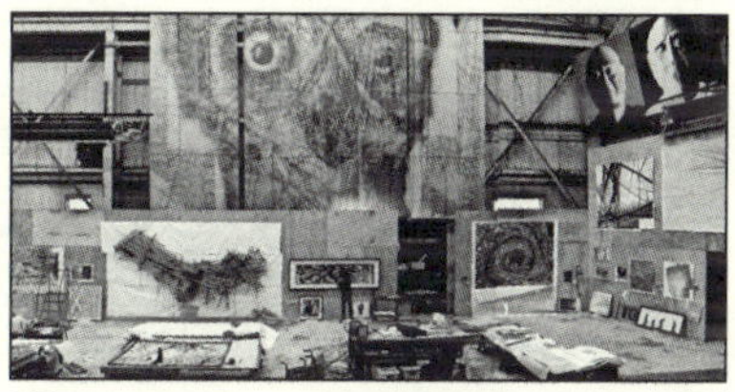

104 105

86–88 *Gravity of Light*, 2008, curated by Murray Horne for the Wood Street Galleries, the Pipe Building, Pittsburgh, Pennsylvania

90–91 *Bipdem*, 2001–10, ink-jet prints on Gampi paper with varnish and Scotch tape, 30.75 x 110.88 in.

92–93 *Black Pulse 6* (detail), 2000, MIS ink on Gampi paper with albumen and encaustic

94–95 *Structure of Thought 5* (detail), 2001–03, MIS and Lysonic ink-jet print on Thai mulberry, Gampi, and tissue papers with beeswax, encaustic, and varnish

96 From an intended installation of ninety-nine unique pieces 2005–07, color carbon print (watercolor pigments and gelatin) on Zerkall paper with 16k gold and palladium leaf water gilding and 24k illumination, each 20 x 20 in.

97 *and you wanna repent* (detail), 2005–09, unique color carbon print (watercolor pigments and gelatin) on Zerkall paper with 16k gold and palladium leaf water gilding and 24k illumination

98–99 *ATL Film Still 8* (detail), 1996–2003, digital file

100–101 *Structure of Thought 16*, 2001–05, MIS and Lysonic ink-jet print on Thai mulberry, Gampi, and tissue papers with beeswax, encaustic, and varnish, 27 x 104 in.

102 *Structure of Thought 6*, 2001–02, MIS and Lysonic ink-jet print on Thai mulberry, Gampi, and tissue papers with beeswax, encaustic, and varnish, 72 x 60 in.

103 *Mr. Motherfucker*, 2005–07, unique color carbon print (watercolor pigments and gelatin) on Zerkall paper with 16k gold and palladium leaf water gilding and 24k illumination, 94 x 94 in.

104–105 Studio view, 2012, Beacon, New York

IMAGE INDEX

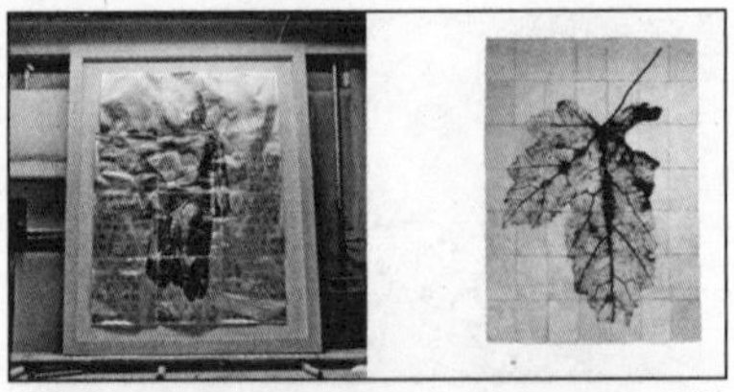

106 107

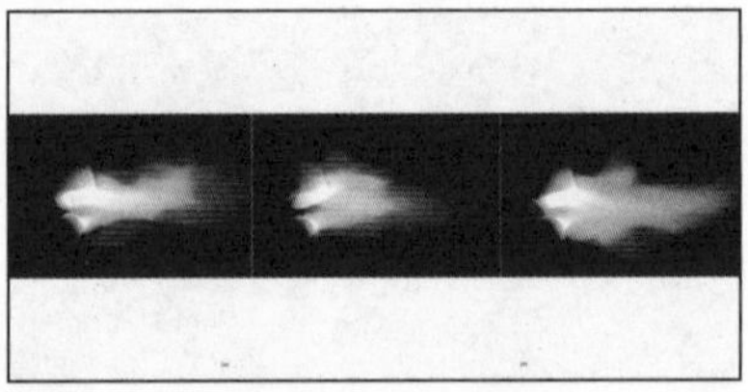

108 109

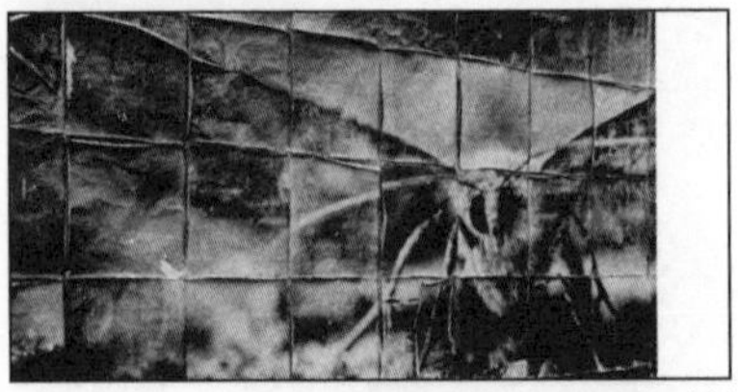

110 111

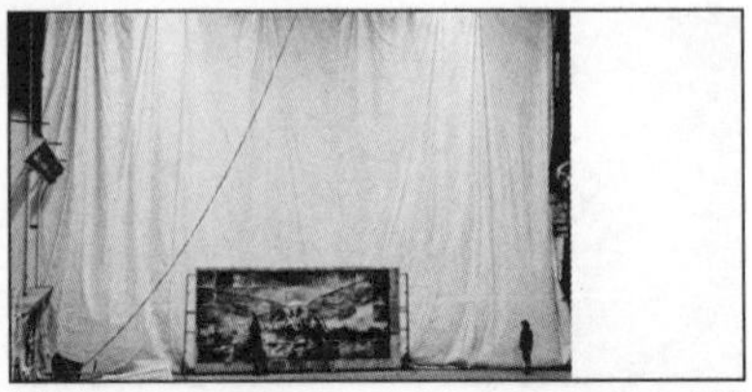

112 113

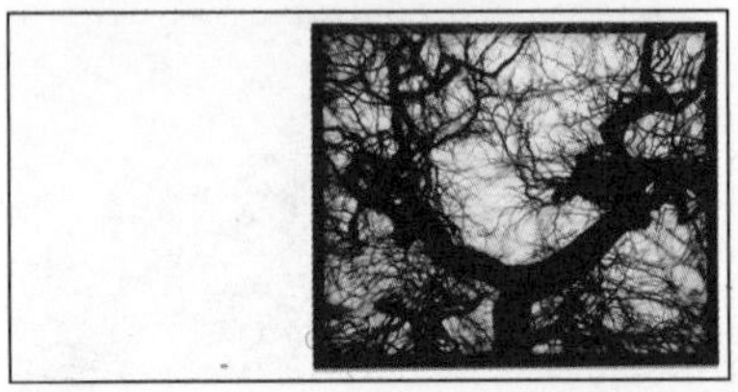

114 115

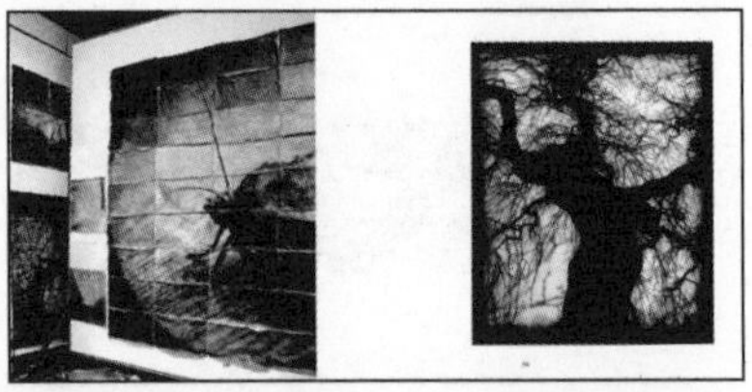

116 117

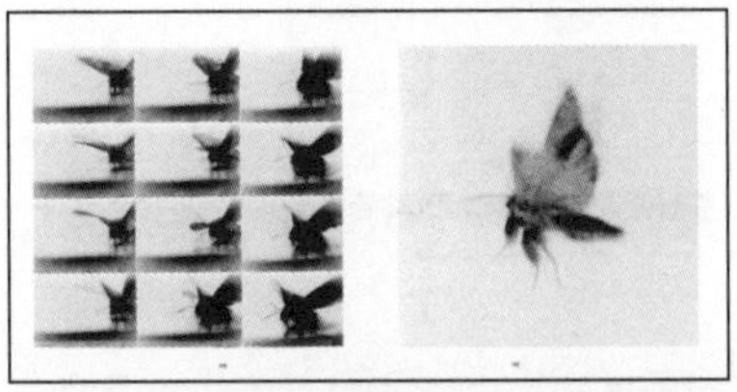

118 119

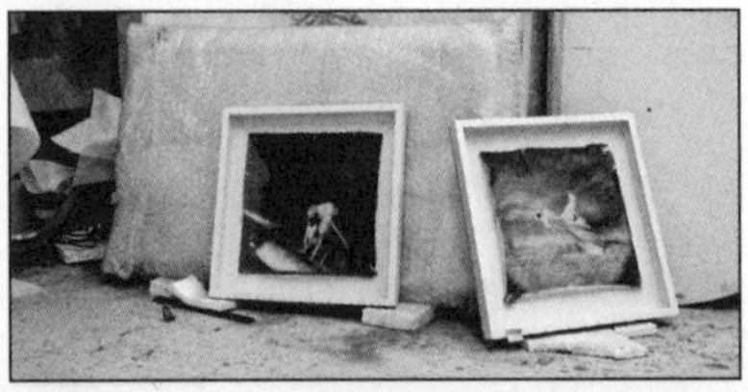

120 121

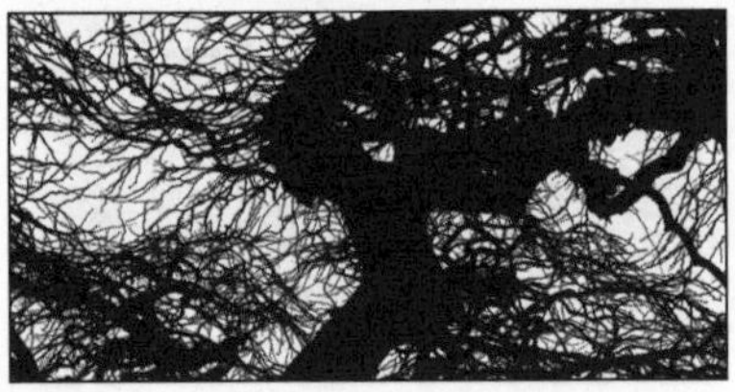

122 123

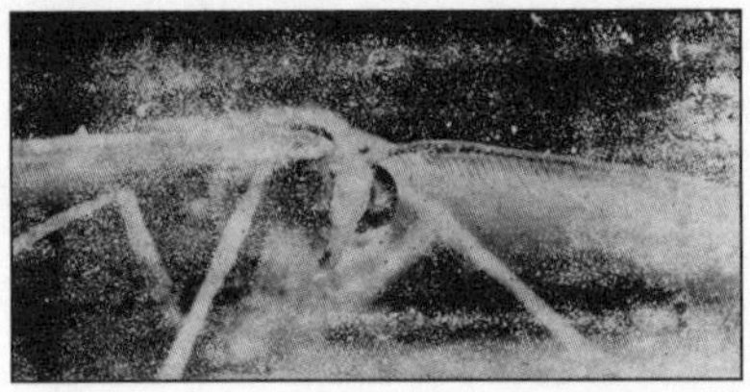

124 125

106 *Manjushri*, 2005–08, unique color carbon print (watercolor pigments and gelatin) on Zerkall paper with 16k gold and palladium leaf water gilding, 84 x 66 in.

107 *Black Pulse 3*, 2000–01, MIS ink jet print on Gampi paper with albumen and encaustic, 112 x 154 in.

108–109 *Leonardo's St. John or this is my middle finger*, 2004, lampkeeper's monitor view of plasma jet

110–111 *Attracted to Light 1* (detail), 1996–2003, sulfur toned hand-coated silver emulsion on tea-stained Thai mulberry paper with Scotch tape

112–113 Studio view, 2012, Beacon, New York

115 *Structure of Thought 5*, 2001–03, MIS and Lysonic ink-jet print on Thai mulberry and Gampi papers with varnish, 132 x 162 ft.

116 Studio view, 2003, Brooklyn, New York

117 *Structure of Thought 21*, 2003–09, MIS and Lysonic ink-jet print on Thai mulberry, Gampi, and tissue papers with beeswax, encaustic, and varnish, 120 x 108 ft.

118 *ATL Film Still 16*, 1996–2003, digital file

119 *ATL Film Still 1*, 1996–2003, digital file

120–121 Studio view, 2012, Beacon, New York

122–123 *Structure of Thought 14* (detail), 2003, digital file of Gampi layer

124–125 *ATL 19 Ephemera* (detail), 1996–2005, ink-jet print on cotton rag paper

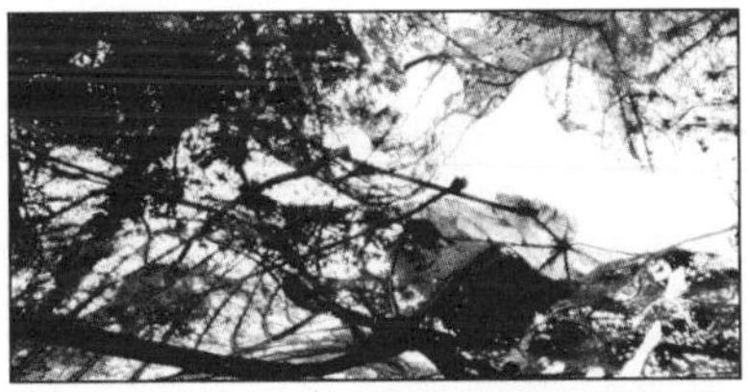

126 127

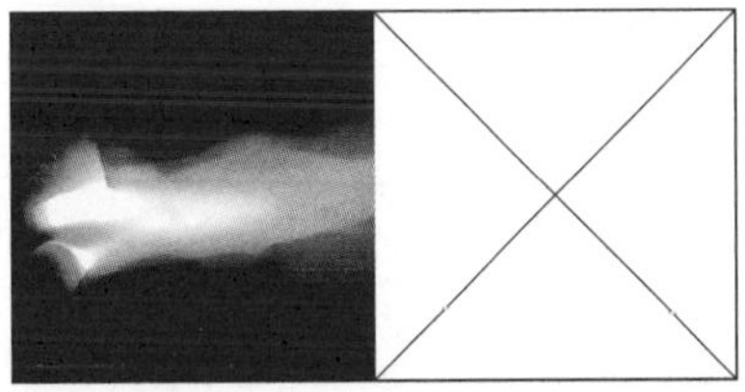

128

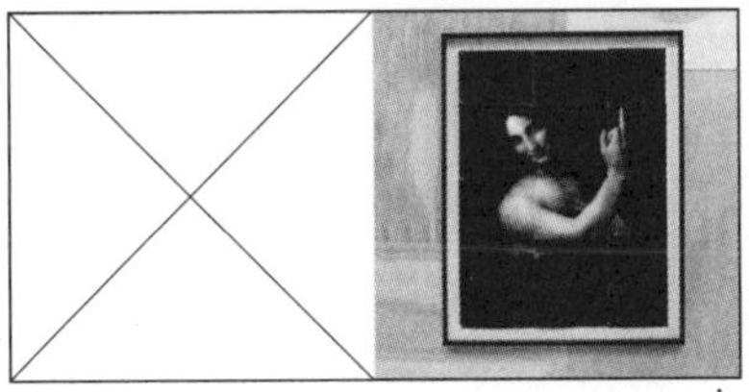

iv

v vi

126–127 *Daruma's P.O.V.* (detail), 2000–08, digital file

128 *Leonardo's St. John or this is my middle finger*, 2004, lampkeeper's monitor view of plasma jet

iv *And God rides high up in the ordinary sky*, 2004–10, Epson K3 Ultrachrome ink-jet print on gelatin-coated Zerkall paper, 77.5 x 55.125 in.

v *Gravity of Light*, 2008, curated by Murray Horne for the Wood Street Galleries, the Pipe Building, Pittsburgh, Pennsylvania

ACKNOWLEDGMENTS

We want to express our very special thanks to Jan Åman, who had the vision to commission *Gravity of Light* for Färgfabriken; and Murray Horne with the Wood Street Galleries in Pittsburgh offered its premiere in the U.S. Our deepest appreciation goes to James Crump, who with the Cincinnati Art Museum and with the remarkable support and engagement of Thomas R. Schiff and FotoFocus, Cincinnati, is bringing new extraordinary dimensions to the installations and perennity with Skira Rizzoli Publications, Inc., where Charles Miers, Margaret Chace, Jessica Fuller, and Kaija Markoe made this accompanying monograph possible. Thank you Garrick Gott for your wonderful design; it was real pleasure to work with you.

Over the years, many people have been involved with this exhibition and the artworks it features. We thank you all for your work, contributions, and enthusiasm at large.

AT THE STUDIO

Gaudéricq Robiliard
Fabio Cutró
Heather Love
Charles E. Reutter
Rebecca Schlossberg
Katrina Boemig
Ruthie Stringer
Lisa Elmaleh
Larra Nebel
John Morgan
Adrienne Trager
Aaron Anderson
Jordan Sullivan
Nathan George
Szymon Weglarski
Tammy Schoenfeld
Joe Infurnari
Vittoria Caproni
Sarah P. Hanson
Lorenzo Triburgo
Susan Schwartz
Francesco Cenicola
Tom Legnon
Dave Vegeto

The arc lamp was an incredibly difficult and complex beast to fabricate, we would like to thank Justin Downs and Erik Messerschmidt in our studio for their endless hours and dedication. And further thanks go to the following consultants for their contributions:

Douglas Irving Repetto
Henry Gifford
Dennis Pfister
Charles Byrd
Ron Bunker
Steven D. Smith
Bernadino Santistevan
John Philips from Philips Brothers Electrical Contracting

AT FÄRGFABRIKEN

Daniel Daboczy
Matti Molin

AT WOOD STREET GALLERIES

Marc Burgess
Curt Riegelnegg
Kate Little
Kevin McMahon, President of the Pittsburgh Cultural Trust

AT CINCINNATI ART MUSEUM

Aaron Betsky
Chris Williams
Susan Hudson
Harry Geimeier
FotoFocus Cincinnati
Neal Quinn and Mick Voynovich of Towne Properties

OUR FAMILIES

Anne Pasternak, Paris Starn
Nancy Bressler, Jules and Gemma Starn
and our parents, Bob and Cee Starn

and some of our friends who along the way brought guidance and tips:

Karin Greenfield-Sanders, Barbara Castelli, Martin Barnes, Harley Baldwin (in memoriam) and Richard Edwards, Sascha Hackel and Marcus Bury, Kate Stevens, Zara Horner, Björn Wetterling, Simone Schmid, Davide de Blasio and RoseAlba Impronta, Judith Miller, Frederik Kaufman, Melissa Harris, Demetrio Paparoni, Martin Weinstein, Hans Mayer, Adriaan van der Have (in memoria), Melanie Crean, and inspiration from Oliver Sacks

COPYRIGHT

Published by

Skira Rizzoli

Skira Rizzoli Publications, Inc.
300 Park Avenue South
New York, NY 10010
www.rizzoliusa.com

2012 2013 2014 2015 2016 / 10 9 8 7 6 5 4 3 2 1

Design: Garrick Gott
Skira Editor: Jessica Fuller

Printed in China

ISBN-13: 978-0-8478-3897-4
Library of Congress Catalog Control Number: 2011946049